Rereading the Spanish American Essay

THE TEXAS PAN AMERICAN SERIES

EDITED BY DORIS MEYER

Rereading the Spanish American Essay

Translations of 19th and 20th Century Women's Essays

University of Texas Press

Austin

First edition, 1995

Requests for permission to reproduce material from this work should
be sent to Permissions, University of Texas Press, Box 7819, Austin, TX
78713-7819.

∞ The paper used in this publication meets the minimum requirements of
American National Standard for Information Sciences—Permanence of
Paper for Printed Library Materials, ANSI z39.48-1984.

Library of Congress Cataloging-in-Publication Data
Rereading the Spanish American essay : translations of 19th & 20th
century women's essays / edited by Doris Meyer. — 1st ed.
        p.   cm. — (The Texas Pan American series)
    Second vol. of a project, of which the 1st vol. has title:
Reinterpreting the Spanish American essay.
        ISBN 0-292-75179-6 (alk. paper). — ISBN 0-292-75182-6 (pbk. : alk. paper)
        1. Spanish American essays—Women authors—Translations into En-
glish.   2. Spanish American essays—19th century—Translations into
English.   3. Spanish American essays—20th century—Translations into
English.   I. Meyer, Doris.   II. Series.
PQ7087.E5R38   1995
864.008'09287'098—dc20   95-3564

Contents

Preface

by Doris Meyer

This book is the second volume of a project intended to add a new interpretive dimension to the history of the essay in Spanish-speaking Latin America. Traditionally considered a male domain, the essay genre in Latin America since the era of Independence has been associated with an ongoing search for cultural and national identity. Essays written by women, however, were excluded from the canon and were marginalized and devalued along with other literature by women that did not conform to gender expectations. Ample evidence of this can be found in anthologies of Latin American essays, published in Spanish and English over the past half century, in which women's contributions to the genre have been virtually ignored.

   In the first volume of this project, entitled *Reinterpreting the Spanish American Essay: Women Writers of the 19th and 20th Centuries*, twenty-two scholars joined me in an effort to facilitate a revision of Latin American intellectual history, which is largely founded on essayistic writing. As their analyses show, essays by women authors have remained invisible because the dominant discourse ratified and reflected only the vision of a patriarchal society.[1] Critical studies, however, are not enough to rectify this oversight if women's essays remain virtually unknown. Even for those who can read the original texts in Spanish and, in a few cases, French, these essays are frequently inaccessible. Many earlier ones were published in little-known magazines or out-of-print books only found in their country of origin. I hope, with this volume, to bring them to light for a larger community of readers both within and beyond academia.

Although the two volumes can be read separately, my belief is that the authorial "I" and the critical eye will be mutually enlightening for the interested reader. This second volume includes essays by most of the authors studied in the earlier volume along with several other authors not found there. Together, they will help remap the literary terrain of the essay in Latin America to include the unexplored landscapes of women's intellectual discourse.

It is time to reread and reinterpret the essays produced so abundantly over the past two centuries in Latin America. However, our rereading should not be limited to works by women. When the male essay is reread as part of a larger essay tradition—part of an integrated intellectual discourse that includes women's perspective—it too will assume different meaning and proportions. Certainly, the question of Latin American identity will have to be defined anew.

All the essays in this book are translated here for the first time, many by the same scholars who wrote the studies for the first volume. Not only did this afford me the benefit of their advice in selecting the essays to be included, but it also assures the reader that the translations themselves are done by knowledgeable scholars sensitive to the nuances of gendered expression found in the original Spanish.

The order of translations is determined primarily by the date in which the works appeared rather than by the authors' birth dates. Whenever possible, I have selected several examples of an author's writing, but I have also had to balance the urge to add more essays with the desire to include a significant number of writers in the collection. My other major concerns were to represent the various historical periods and the myriad perspectives of female authors from different countries, social backgrounds, and intellectual orientations. Still, these bold, articulate women inevitably represent a privileged minority among the great masses of Latin American women who have been silenced over the centuries by virtue of their sex, race, class, or economic condition.

Many of the essays translated here are already considered classics by scholars familiar with the evolution of women's intellectual history in Latin America. They form part of a reiterated claim to autonomous female expression that can be traced back at least as far as Sor Juana Inés de la Cruz in Mexico in the late 1600s. Among notable examples of what Mary Louise Pratt calls the "gender identity essay," one could point to Gertrudis Gómez de Avellaneda's "Women," Soledad Acosta de Samper's "The Mission of the Woman Writer in Spanish America," Clorinda

Matto de Turner's "The Woman Worker and the Woman," Victoria
Ocampo's "Woman and Her Expression," Magda Portal's "Toward the
New Woman," Teresa de la Parra's "The Influence of Women in the
Formation of the American Soul," Rosario Castellanos' "Mexican Customs," Rosario Ferré's "Woman's Authenticity in Art," and Julieta Kirkwood's "Feminists and Political Women." But the volume also contains
many essays that are less well known and that bring to light fascinating
examples of women's lives and their efforts to make some provisional
sense of their time and place in the world. These include, among others,
the Countess of Merlin's "The Women of Havana," Eduarda Mansilla de
García's "Life on the Pampas," Alfonsina Storni's "The Immigrant Girl,"
Amanda Labarca Hubertson's "Personal Pages," Gabriela Mistral's "Similarities and Differences between the Americas," Carmen Naranjo's "Cultural Crisis in Costa Rica," Cristina Peri Rossi's "The Fantasy of the
Passive Object: Inflatable Dolls," and Elena Poniatowska's "The Last
Turkey." The reader will frequently discover issues and concerns that go
beyond the experience of gender but that are nevertheless seen from a
woman's viewpoint and thus refocus the cultural picture we have been
shown in most male-authored essays.

Some women's essays are intentionally transgressive in their questioning of received truths and their plea for new configurations of human
coexistence. Others intimately describe the private domestic spaces that
only Latin American women knew and in which they found mutual
sustenance. Still others reveal panoramas of the female imagination un-
bound by the frontiers of a vast continent or its varied cultures. From the
scrutiny of women's role in the Conquest to that of the blue whales that
swim through the texts of Western literature, these essays offer us alternative approaches to understanding the experience of living and writing
in Latin America.

In the interest of conserving space and enhancing readability, notes
have been kept to a minimum; those not followed by [Trans.] are the
author's notes. In a very few instances, passages have been cut in long
essays to avoid unnecessary repetitions or digressions; they are indicated
by [. . .]. Throughout, my concern as editor has been to ensure that the
translations are both faithful to the original texts and rendered well in
English; the reader will notice that each writer has a style of her own,
and that descriptive or persuasive prose of the nineteenth century can
be quite different from its counterpart in the twentieth. The voices and
personalities of these Latin American women writers, unique among

themselves as individuals, come to us across chronological, geographical, cultural, and linguistic boundaries that literature in translation does its best to negotiate.

To prepare the reader for these differences, each author is briefly introduced in a few pages prior to the translation of her works. Since these introductions were written by various scholars, they vary somewhat in length and content, but they all shed light on the importance of the translated essays to follow. For the reader who wishes to know more about a given author, I recommend the first volume of critical studies, each with helpful bibliographies; a table of contents is included at the end of this volume. An alternate and very useful reference for general information on women writers in Spanish America are the bio-bibliographic volumes edited by Diane Marting.

I am well aware of notable women authors whose essays do not appear in these pages. Limitations of space, in addition to the concerns expressed above, influenced the final selections. As a reader, I confess that personal preferences also figured in the equation. As an editor, my wish list had to be balanced by practical considerations, including the availability of willing and able translators. Ultimately, I am responsible for the contents and shape of this project, but it could not have been accomplished without the dedication and cooperation of the valued colleagues who have contributed to it so generously. I thank them all for their enthusiastic response, collaborative spirit, and the wealth of understanding they brought to this enterprise. The dialogic community of Latin American women writers and contemporary scholars is richly represented in these pages.

Finally, I would like to express my appreciation to two important sources of support for this project: the R. F. Johnson Faculty Development Fund of Connecticut College for two grant awards, and my husband, Richard Hertz, for the encouragement he gives me and the pleasure he takes in sharing my enthusiasm for Latin America and its cultures.

Essex, Connecticut
November 1993

NOTE

1. See my introduction to the first volume for an overview of women's essays in Spanish America and their importance in the history of the genre. For a detailed discussion of canons as self-confirming "*structures of exclusion*" and "*structures of value*" in Latin America, see Mary Louise Pratt's study, " 'Don't Interrupt Me': The Gender Essay as Conversation and Countercanon," also in the first volume.

Flora Tristan

Peru, 1803–1844

Flora Tristan is a truly international figure, a rare ac-
complishment for a woman of the early nineteenth century. She is recognized in several nations as a traveler,
researcher, writer, social critic, utopian socialist, and
spokesperson for the workers of the world. Born of a
French mother and a Peruvian father, she first traveled
to Peru in 1833, twelve years after the country's independence. Her best-known book, *Peregrinations of a
Pariah* (1837), which recounts her experiences in a cross
between autobiography and travel-writing, is dedicated
to her "fellow-Peruvians" though it is written in
French, her mother tongue. Tristan remains an important figure in Peru; she is esteemed as a strong, politically active woman, and her major works, *Peregrinations*,
London Journal (1840), and *Worker's Union* (1843), have
all been translated into Spanish. A Peruvian women's
magazine bears her name, *Flora*, as does Lima's women's
center, "Centro de la Mujer Peruana Flora Tristán"—
both concrete testimonies to her continuing significance
in her *patria*. Tristan's own bicultural position anticipates
the internationalist stance she takes in her political writings while her position as woman, and often as foreigner, forms the basis for much of her most perceptive
social analysis.

Tristan was born in France in 1803. Her parents met in
Spain where her mother, Thérèse Laisnay, was escaping

the violence of the French Revolution when she encountered Don Mariano Tristán de Moscoso, member
of an aristocratic Peruvian family; he was a colonel in
the Spanish army. When Tristan was five, her father
died and left her mother with no French marriage
certificate and no legal recognition; thus Don Mariano's
death introduced Tristan to a new life of economic privation. At eighteen Tristan married André Chazal, an
engraver, but she left the marriage because of her husband's violence. With two children to support and no
possibility of divorce, Tristan's economic desperation intensified, leading to her voyage to Peru to claim the
support she felt her father's family owed her. After this
claim was denied, Tristan returned to Paris and began
writing, publishing *Peregrinations* and a pamphlet on
women travelers. As her literary production increased,
so did her marital problems, culminating in Chazal's
1838 attempt on her life. Tristan's personal experience
of injustice and oppression and the financial and social
restraints on her independence clearly stimulated her
broader social consciousness.

The following selection, a public letter written in
1837 to the French Chamber of Deputies urging them
to reinstate divorce, in many ways mirrors Tristan's own
situation, but in spite of the close ties to her own life
Tristan claims that it is not personal interest that moves
her here but her solidarity with 300,000 married people
living separately in France. She characteristically crosses
the line between public and private realms in her zealous argument: she invokes the universalist sentiments of
the French Revolution and promotes divine laws over
man-made ones, reinterpreting Christ's admonition
against divorce to read: "Don't *join* what God has separated." Her attention to women's plight in this "despotic" relationship is typical, as is her use of political
terminology to characterize unhappy marriages. Tristan's
support of divorce is an indirect entreaty to reform the
traditional family, a concept she will extend to the reform of the working class as part of an international
"family." Tristan calls for unity and recognition of

mutual interests, concepts that will lead to her later class analysis and corresponding attention to the position of women and their need for autonomy in every nation (evidenced in *Worker's Union* and in her *London Journals*). This early piece on divorce is an important autobiographical document, but it is also a preface to the ideas and rhetorical strategies that become more explicit in Flora Tristan's later essays.

JILL KUHNHEIM

Flora Tristan

On Divorce

Gentlemen:

I would like you to consider more than my individual case in the petition that I have the honor of addressing to you for the reestablishment of divorce. The evils that the indissolubility of marriage produces are so striking that they escape no one's notice. God has given continuity to very few of our affections, and we would wish to impose immutability on the most fickle of them all! This institution is contrary to nature, and domestic happiness and public morality vanish before it. It is superfluous to point out that concord between spouses, as in all kinds of association, can only result from relations of equality; that the hideous union of despotism and servitude perverts master and slave; and that our nature is such that there is no affection that dependency does not destroy. These moral truths must be familiar to you, Gentlemen, for if any one of you were not infused by them, what claim would he have to the vote of his fellow citizens?

Gentlemen, our glorious revolution had as its goal the emancipation of thought, and it was greeted by the peoples' acclamations. All the governmental forms this emancipation established were intended to guarantee its duration and to favor the development of that divine liberty that contains all others. It continues the work of Christ; recognized as a natural consequence of the freedom of thought, the independence of affections also gave it legal existence, leaving the Pharisees' yoke to those who still consented

Translated by Kim Starr-Reid

to bear it. Divorce by mutual consent or by the will of one of the parties was instituted; and since physical separation was followed by legal separation, the legislator was no longer forced by dogma into the absurdity of recognizing a fictive paternity. This fiction, inseparable from the indissolubility of marriage, aptly shows that legislation is powerless to prevent the disorders that arise from exercising violence upon the liberty of the affections, disorders that manifest themselves more every day in the increasing number of illegitimate births.

Despotism needs only obedience. Napoleon would have wished to make divorce a royal privilege. Not daring to abolish it, he imposed on it conditions that were outrageous to families' sense of decency and often impossible to fulfill. He made it almost exclusively the right of the husband and determined its effects in a manner as immoral as it was arbitrary. The *Chambre introuvable*[1] arrived, whose chorus-leaders complained that the law was *atheistic*. Doubtless it is atheistic in those of its provisions that substitute a man's will for the voice of the people; but in these gentlemen's eyes the law's atheism lay in its isolation from Catholic dogma. They had to make it re-adhere to it, and so these elect of the retrograde party abrogated divorce, thus removing from the code the sole remedy for the extreme evils that result from the clauses of servitude it contains. They threw themselves headlong onto this path with blind temerity. By making the duration of marriages existing at that time perpetual, though it had been optional, they gave their law a retroactive effect and placed themselves in opposition to the principle of freedom of religion inscribed in the Charter.

Who would have thought in July 1830 that this barbarous monument of the gothic assembly would still exist in 1837? Twice the Chamber of Deputies defeated it by their vote; twice the peers of Charles X sustained it with theirs. With their feet in the grave these old courtesans still defend the morals of their time.

The antisocial law bore its fruits: there exist in France more than 300,000 separated marriages, and the annual record of illegitimate births testifies to the progressive growth in the number of persons who elude a bond that nothing can break. It equally enchains in perpetuity the young man whom love or ambition has seduced and the girl whose parents have compelled her to marry; it punishes a momentary error with lifelong torment and filial obedience with endless slavery. The morals that result from this state of affairs cannot agree with the solemn customs of the century and the advancement of progress in our generation. You will recognize,

Gentlemen, with all the journalists, that without divorce, religion and morality are powerless to give birth to steady morals, and that attached to this steadiness are public prosperity and domestic happiness; that the union of spouses would incontestably have more durability with the right to separate than it could have by the punitive clauses of the law and the power with which it has armed the husband. Protestant countries have permitted divorce. Are their morals any less pure than in those countries where the reign of indissolubility maintains the civil effects of marriage while the spouses are separated?

I have, Gentlemen, made a rough test of the misfortunes that the indissolubility of marriage entails. Forced to separate from my husband without material resources and while still very young, I had to provide for myself and my children's needs by working. It is rare that such a burden does not exceed the strength of women. Few receive the education appropriate for a profession, and when, without resources, they are deserted by their husbands or obliged to separate from them, one can only blame the law for the illicit unions they form, since that law does not permit them to contract legal unions, which would ensure their children a father's protection.

Gentlemen, in a work I recently published [*Peregrinations of a Pariah*] and which I had the honor of presenting to the Chamber, I provided a glimpse of some of the evils to which women in my position are exposed. Personal interest is not the motive for my initiative toward you: I have been brought to it out of love for others like me, convinced as I am by my own experience that there can be no happiness in families except under a reign of freedom. Christ said, "Do not separate what God has joined together." Could one not complete the precept by adding, "Do not join together what God has separated"?

In consequence of the foregoing, I respectfully request the Chamber to reestablish divorce and to institute it on the principle of reciprocity and by the will of one of the two persons joined, just as it had been under the laws previous to the code of Napoleon.

Yours faithfully, Gentlemen,
FLORA TRISTÁN
100a rue du Bac.

Letter 39 in *Flora Tristan: Lettres réunies*, ed. Stéphane Michaud. Paris: Seuil, 1980, pp. 73–76.

NOTE

1. Louis XVIII gave this name to the Chamber elected in 1814, mostly made up of younger men with little political experience, no family reputation, and strong ultra-royalist leanings. Historians of the period disagree as to its translation; it could be a label of scorn, thus "Chamber of Nobodies," but it could also be said that Louis called them this from sheer joy—he could not have assembled a chamber so disposed to his political desires had he gone out looking for members himself—and hence a possible translation as "Unfindable Chamber." [Trans.]

The Countess of Merlin

Cuba, 1789–1852

María de la Merced Beltrán de Santa Cruz y Montalvo, better known as the Countess of Merlin, was born into one of the most aristocratic families of Havana, Cuba, in 1789. Left by her parents in the care of her maternal grandmother just a few weeks after her birth, Mercedes had to wait until the age of nine to see her father again and until the age of twelve to be reunited with her mother and two siblings in Spain. Eight years later, in Madrid, the strikingly beautiful and gifted Mercedes married the French General Merlin. In 1812 they left for Paris, where she would reside until her death in 1852.

Around 1831, encouraged by her friends, she published *Mes douze premières années* (My First Twelve Years), an intimate volume she translated into Spanish in 1838. The four volumes that comprised her *Souvenirs et Mémoires de la Comtesse Merlin, publiés par elle-même* (Remembrances and Memoirs of the Countess of Merlin, Published by Herself) were enthusiastically received in 1836 by the public and the press.

Parisian life suited the talented Countess. She held a well-attended literary salon and gave recitals, benefit galas, and balls. During these decades (1820–1840) her reputation as a gifted singer with a sharp intellect and literary talent was solidified. Her apartments on the Rue de Bondy became the customary meeting place for a number of artists, including Balzac, George Sand, Alfred de Musset, Strauss, Rossini, Martínez de la Rosa, and Mérimée.

From 1836 until her death Mercedes Merlin poured herself into her writing. Some of her biographers have explained her literary endeavors as the result of financial uncertainty after the death of her husband in 1839. However, the desire to write apparently dated from childhood, according to her autobiographical works.

In 1840 Merlin traveled to Cuba for a very brief visit related to matters of inheritance. Residents of Havana paid homage to this famous and exotic daughter of their city. In June 1841, a few months after her return to Paris, the Countess published an essay, "Observations de Madame la Comtesse de Merlin sur l'etat des esclaves dans les colonies espagnoles" (Observations of the Countess of Merlin about the Condition of Slaves in the Spanish Colonies); a Spanish translation appeared in Madrid in February 1842. This essay would create considerable controversy and later would be part of Letter 20 in her work *La Havane* (Havana).

La Havane (1844), from which "The Women of Havana" is a selection, is unquestionably the Countess' most ambitious and important work. In three tomes she created an encyclopedic collection of essays disguised as epistolary texts. Her vivid childhood memories, her political and cultural perspectives, and her dual European/ Creole upbringing offered European readers a critical perspective from which to judge the Cuban situation. A shorter, sanitized version of this work, with a preface by her Cuban compatriot Gertrudis Gómez de Avellaneda, was published in Spain the same year.

On 21 September 1843, more than a year before the publication of the three volumes of *La Havane*, the Cuban newspaper *Faro Industrial de la Habana* printed a translation of the Countess' letter to George Sand on the mores and habits of the women of Havana. Excerpts from her work were also published in several other newspapers, occasioning a heated polemic over the merits and accuracy of her observations. Mercedes Merlin's writings about Cuba were, in fact, motivated by a complex array of factors: literary aspirations, intellectual curiosity, philosophical convictions, political gain, and monetary compensation. For Europeans, Merlin painted a reassuring image of colonial life in Cuba, but she also seemed to warn them that, if meddled with, this "island paradise" would collapse in anarchy. At the time white Cubans lived in constant fear of slave rebellions and were actively trying to recruit European immigrants to modify the racial composition of the island. The Countess, aware of this, could not paint a bleak picture of racial, political, and socioeconomic realities.

This letter to Sand, like many others in *La Havane,* points to a subtext. Merlin's nostalgic and hyperbolic memories represent a desperate attempt to bridge two worlds and two languages. Merlin tries to validate Havana by comparing it to Paris and, in many instances, by judging it superior in spite of its colonial status. Not only is the Countess reaffirming her voice within an American literary tradition; she is also consciously disseminating a falsely embellished image of her native land, an image that to some extent has prevailed in the mythologies with which Europeans try to make sense of the Americas.

CLAIRE EMILIE MARTIN

The Women of Havana

Summary

Their physical constitution—Nature's luxurious poetry—No corset at all—The *butaca*[1]—The *volante*—Passion for dancing—The orchestra—Music from the region—Particularities of its rhythm—The *Strauss* of Havana—His attire—Poor women—Houses at broad daylight—*Adiós, hasta cada momento* (Farewell, until soon)—*Esta casa es suya* (Make yourself at home)—Modesty and nudity—Marriage selection—Women from slave countries—Young Negress—Children's beauty—Luxury among the people of Havana—The young mother—Pepillo—Grandmother.

TO GEORGE SAND   Cuba, 1 July

Who could be better suited to read my observations on the women from my country, their way of life and their sensibility, than yourself, who understands our gender so well, and whose eloquent pen so often has moved the kindhearted about the sufferings of women in civilized societies? Do not expect either pathetic and steamy tales, colored by the tropical heat, or tragic stories whose interests lie in irate jealousy and bloodied daggers. This chaste woman from Havana, in spite of her fiery soul and her passionate nature, does not know the fancy refinements of these affairs of the heart, or about their torments and fictional voluptuousness; or of the fruits ripened in hothouses possessing neither perfume nor taste; or of imaginary passions, those parasitic plants that dry out the greenish vigor from the young sap.

Translated by Claire Emilie Martin

This woman from Havana is generally of medium height and slim; but, however slender she may be, her shapeliness is always remarkable. She has the tiny and delicate limbs of a child. Her feet, small and plump, don, or better yet, are delicately surrounded by white satin, for her shoes barely have soles and have never stepped on street pavement. The foot of this woman from Havana is not merely a foot but nature's poetic luxury. Her neck, handsomely planted, gently moves her voluptuous head. Her naturally thin waist has never been restricted by a corset, and it is in harmony with the rest of her body; her beauty has never asked for an extravagant disproportion that art and nature would surely rebuff. Because of the freedom she has enjoyed from childhood and the constant and sweet warmth of the air, her limbs maintain the same original freshness and flexibility and give a velvetlike softness to her skin, which is often a pale shade of white; but underneath one can perceive a warm and golden luminescence as if the sun had suffused it with its rays. Her movements, marked by a languorous voluptuousness, her deliberate and indolent walk, and her soft and rhythmic speech sometimes contrast with her vivacious physiognomy and with the fiery blaze that escapes from her large black eyes, whose gaze proves incomparable. She never exposes herself to the sun except when she travels. She only goes out at dusk, and never on foot. Aside from the inconvenience of the heat outside her house, her aristocratic pride does not allow her to mingle with the street crowds. Industrious by nature, one can find her working from early morning with her own hands on the clothes of her Negroes or on her son's *canastilla* (layette). However, as soon as the sun's rays weigh heavily in the air, she is incapable of any activity whatsoever. She hardly walks, and spends a good portion of the day bathing or eating fruit; the rest of the day she spends rocking in a *butaca* (easy-chair). As the sun sets, the gracious sylph, all dressed in white and with flowers in her hair, comes alive; she gets into the *volante* (Cuban open carriage) and goes to different shops; she never gets out since she makes the whole shop come to the footboard of her carriage; later, she goes out for some fresh air. If it is a question of traveling out to the countryside, she effortlessly goes from her chair to the carriage defying the most burning sun in her white dress, her head uncovered and without the benefit of a parasol. One could compare her to a hero defying cannons from the trenches.

In an easily understandable contradiction, the women of Havana love to dance; they spend whole nights moving their feet, excitedly turning round and round until they collapse from exhaustion.

The traditional dance of Havana is executed with the whole body rather than with the feet; it is a mix of a waltz of gliding steps and swings of such soft and undeniable voluptuousness that it lasts until the fatigue felt by the dancers comes to the rescue of the musicians in the orchestra. The latter are very amusing in their extravagant attires. This traditional music, as well as the steps of the dance, expresses the Creole character, a mixture of lethargy and passion. The song's phrase, always syncopated, usually pauses before ending the rhythm, and later it suddenly starts anew, as if it had fallen back to keep the beat and was hurriedly trying to catch up with it. These local musical compositions are in general in a minor key, as are almost all primitive melodies; the musicians' inspirations are largely the work of intuition rather than art; they have plenty of strange and innocent harmonies whose charm is at once a sense of melancholy and deliriousness. The orchestra conductor is always the elegant Negro "Plácido," the Strauss of Havana,[2] who invents the dance's melodies. As original as his compositions is his attire, completely drawn from the French 1798 fashion. He wears a double-tail dress coat, and his yellow trousers are tied at the knee by ribbons that fall midway down his leg. His socks are made of silken damask; he wears fine suede leather shoes with a rosette the color of pansies; and to complete the costume he wears a vest and lace cuffs.

In this land, women born to the higher classes appreciate the advantages of their condition; they preserve their ways but remain humble and of a sweet disposition; they do not try to convince others of their own importance by being impertinent and disdainful. There is something endearing about their flattering countenance and the humble greatness they display in front of their inferiors. I admire the angelic generosity my aunt shows for the dispossessed, when I see poor women enter the most intimate rooms of the house and, even before asking for alms, sit down without permission and prolong their stay unsuspecting of their annoying presence.

One of the local habits, to which Europeans rarely adapt, is to see people come and go freely everywhere inside the house. All doors are open, starting with the main entrance, which is open at all times and for everyone. You are surrounded by a hundred Negroes, and not one of them will spare you an inconvenience. Women receive guests at all hours. At first this habit of living in full broad light due to the climate may seem tiresome to northerners used to enjoying their isolation and the meditation that accompanies it; however, this situation can offer some advantages. If one has company at all hours, one does not have to fuss about them as much: this habit results in friendships, with affection replacing the rigidity of ceremonious etiquette. The persons you accept become members of your family and share your moments of pleasure and your suffering. And regarding those inevitably inopportune people, one need not worry; men leave and women continue eating fruit and rocking gently, and if at times they have too much company, they will surely never be lonely. Your women in France do have more control over their time, and manage their social engagements in a manner that suits them: so they have their days and hours reserved for receiving company, thus avoiding unpleasant visits; however, in protecting their privacy they pay with selfishness. For, once the visitors' minimum of courteous behavior is finished, these women see their guests disappear sometimes for months or years, unless their presence is requested at a party or some such diversion. Let us admit that in spite of the inconveniences occasioned by Creole affability, to women it is a sweet refuge, since by instinct they need to be sustained by affection, as in the words of a friend saying "Adiós, hasta cada momento" (Farewell, until soon). They are adorable both for their manners and their hospitality with strangers. From the very first visit they receive them as friends of the household, and when they state "Make yourself at home," it's not just a mere formality but a heartfelt offering: you can be assured that you will find a place set at the table for you every day, and your bed ready in the country home.

Nothing rivals the naive charm, the caressing words of our women, and the harmony that exists among the musicality of their voices, the original turn of phrase, and their seductive gestures. Yet, there is no malice in their innocence nor anything untrue in their gaiety.

The intimate nature of family life could create inconveniences if certain habits did not ward off dangers. This familiarity runs parallel with their in-nocence. The relentless public aspect of private family life, the constant presence of Negroes who remain nude until the age of eight, only destroy in our young women one sort of modesty: that of the sight, which does not offend the purity of their thoughts and the honesty that they always preserve. Their imaginations have never been soiled by depraved learning nor by perverse precepts; they do not become falsely agitated nor do they set out to scrutinize nature's secrets. Thus, this primitive innocence of our women from Havana, which is without perils for those of precocious and passionate temperament, in some European countries would become a source of scandal and chaos for certain pale, irritable, and ignorant women of the North, who meet love by ways of an unnatural culture and lose their virginity of heart before tasting passion.

In these parts the young woman, still a child, can marry the man she chooses as long as he is related to the family. Families rarely ally themselves to one another. The high aristocracy, however tolerant in everyday dealings, greatly fears the union with a family belonging to the inferior classes, or even to mix their blood with that of foreigners, even when the latter's is as pure as theirs. The marriages of children who grew up together are almost always happy ones. Mutual love, compounded with the tender affection of childhood friendships, similar to the fraternal love that ensues, does not allow in any case forgetfulness or evil conduct. In spite of the dangers arising from an ardent blood, the renunciation of a private life, and the sensual habits of women, these are moral creatures who possess a deep-rooted instinct of natural honesty. Their unadorned education and their fervent and exalted piety lead them to that which is good for love of God, not for fear.

There is a fact I consider worthy of note: in Havana, as in all countries where there is slavery, the female occupies a higher position than in other nations. Reigning as queen of an obsequious vassalage, surrounded by love and consideration, having much influence over her household, she is rarely moved to a wicked thought. Since ambitions, vanity, and sensual longings are never consulted in choosing a husband, the man she marries is always in accord with her age and tastes. She loves him, and does not arrive at the nuptial bed with her heart in turmoil, her imagination beguiled by other unions and other desires. She is not condemned to the most horrid of all torments, that of deception. Her life is more modest, her pleasures less glamorous than those of women of more refined civilizations; but she does not suffer the tortures of humbled vanity, nor the mortal anguish of a heart exhausted in a futile search, consumed by chimerical or fleeting emotions, bruised by jealousy and sorrow. She has not been punished by a lover on account of a husband, nor by a husband because of a lover. Severely judged by public opinion and by herself, sickened by everything, lonely inside, she does not seek compensation for her frustrated life by spilling the bitterness of her heart on people's lives. In conclusion, she has never had the infernal idea of looking for a strong sensation in somebody else's suffering by lovelessly stealing a friend's lover.

As soon as a little girl starts to babble, she is given a little Negro girl who becomes her playmate and later her chambermaid and who, after a few years, obtains her freedom. The wet nurse is a sort of matron who is given her freedom, if she is a slave, as soon as she stops nursing, but who stays in the house, where she is highly regarded. The affection these Negro women profess for the children they have raised is a kind of cult.

Utterly obsessed by these feelings, they remain almost indifferent to their own children.

Nothing compares to the beauty of Havana's children. They are flowers, at once strong and exquisite, blooming in the heat of this blazing sky. Neither ribbon nor strap has ever tightened their delicate flesh. Children's attire is reduced to a light, sleeveless linen shirt that barely covers the knees, with a low neckline and adorned with lace and with ribbons on the shoulders; their little heads are as naked as the rest of the body. Then they are placed on a mat. What a sight when their bodies are left in total freedom, and they grow round and strong, unabashedly looking forward to developing their strength and their life; and that elastic skin, full of life, keeps getting stronger in contact with the air, and delightful dimples appear in the folds of the skin with each movement and each gesture. No, Albane has never imagined anything more charming.

This light attire worn by children is extremely expensive. Each little shirt is embroidered in colored silk and is only worn once. One could certainly embroider it in wool and it would be much sturdier. But, in fact, that is exactly why one doesn't. Women's sense of luxury is greatly refined; it's not extravagant but sensual. To them it is a way of being and living, since their clothes are of the utmost simplicity. During the morning hours they wear an ample robe or a linen suit; at night, their dresses are also made of linen, but they have short sleeves and low necks, and on their neatly coiffed heads women wear natural flowers, placed without art or artifice. Hidden behind this simplicity lie exotic refinements. Their lingerie, changed twice a day, is of the most exquisite batiste adorned with lace. The embroidered linen suits are always worn new, and when washed they are given to the Negro women servants. Women from Havana use only new silk hose, and when they take them off they discard them. Their tiny shoes are soon abandoned, and like everything else they are passed on to the Negro women who, incidentally, do not lack originality in matters of fashion. It is very amusing to see these Negro women cross the enormous rooms lit by sunlight while singing or smoking. With their linen suits worn over shirts that hang barely over their knees, the whole hanging loose over their chests and backs, with their satin shoes that they wear as slippers showing the heels, and their black ebony legs, one would be tempted to compare them to bats flapping their translucent wings in daylight.

Women from Havana never wear their ball gowns twice, even though they are extremely luxurious and are brought from Paris at a great expense. However, a young lady would prefer not to attend a ball than to wear a previously worn gown. At theater performances, as well as at balls, women are always very well dressed, and they show off some of the vast number of diamonds from Paris that they own. Their sheets, like the rest of their linen and lingerie, are made of the finest batiste, and they are carefully starched; imagine my surprise when I was first presented with a starched and embroidered hand towel. Beds are made of iron with embroidered canopies and covered with damask cloth. Given my European upbringing, my aunt made the delicate gesture of offering me a little blue damask mattress the width of a sealing-wax bar. Pillows are of a similar material, covered with linen, embroidered with insertions of material, with wide strips of lace on the borders, and closed with blue ribbons. The bed's linen curtains are suspended and gathered with ribbons of the same color. The sheets are made of very fine batiste. The flat sheet, the only type of cover people use here, is always embroidered with lace. Just imagine the pathetic effect that my simple Dutch linen shirts and my poor Scottish thread hose had in comparison with this marvelous luxury! . . . What became a true scandal for everyone, however, were my crude Moroccan leather shoes discovered at the bottom of one of my trunks.— "*Jesús María!* (Sweet Jesus)," they exclaimed, "What is that? . . . Those shoes for your feet in Havana! Oh!" I felt thoroughly mortified, for they could not understand that my skin had hardened in Europe to the point that I had to bear the torture of wearing those shoes. And yet, I thought with bitterness, I have the same difficulty in walking as do all the women in Europe!

The extreme youth of mothers and the precocious development of children do a great disservice to their early upbringing. Children treat their mothers as companions from the very beginning, and the inherent Creole insouciance deprives mothers of the energy to scold them and to validate their rights as parents. Due to this maternal weakness, the male child becomes domineering and capricious. The damage is less in the daughter's education, for the sweet, loving, and malleable character of the little girl turns itself tenderly onto her parents. It is, then, the early education of boys that often fails. If you had been with me at a brief scene I witnessed a few days ago as an example of the upbringing in Havana, you would understand.

It was in the afternoon; I was in the company of some young women in the salon, facing the harbor; we were all sitting, or rather reclining, in comfortable Moroccan leather chairs. That day the heat was intense, and yet a strong breeze slammed doors and windows and played with our white, light robes. An enormous tray full of fruit placed in front of us soothed our insatiable thirst. More avid than the rest, I was about to taste these treasures that I had been so long deprived of; all of a sudden, amidst my delirious happiness, while I was tenderly greeting my former and dear acquaintances and was giving them unequivocal proof that I remembered them, I saw a little man enter the room whom I would have thought a midget had it not been for his beautiful eyes, so innocent and transparent, and the delicate skin of his face resembling that of a peach. He was probably around twelve years of age. He wore boots, a French-style suit, a shirt with frills, a hat on his head and a whip in his hand. . . . One could say he looked like Puss in Boots!

"Mother," he said upon entering, "my carriage is ready. I'm going to have supper with a friend; good-bye, until tonight."

"But Pepillo," said his mother in a languid and sweet voice. "Pepillo, what an idea to go out in this heat!"

"It's not hot, mother."

"But I don't want you to eat out; you spent the whole day yesterday with your friends."

"I will spend today with them also, mother."

"But you know you have to go to the ball tonight, and you will have to come back to dress and the whole thing will make you tired."

"I won't be tired, mother." With each answer he would bite on a piece of fruit.

"Well, Pepillo, I don't want you to go out . . . Do you hear me?"

"Good-bye, mother." And turning around, he left.

"What a boy!" said the mother in a half tender, half sad tone of voice, while following him with her eyes.

And nothing else was said.

"Tell me, China," I asked the mother, "is that the way you bring up your children?"

"What else can we do?"

"Force them to obey."

"And how?"

"With your will."

"And if he doesn't want to do what he's told?"

"You lock him up."

"*¿Y si le da la alferecía?* (And what if he suffers an epileptic attack?)"

These weak mothers do not hesitate for a minute when they have to send their children to be educated in Europe, and with heroic courage they set them at sea to search for new knowledge and useful learning.

Such is the nature of these women . . . pusillanimous about the little things, sublime about the important ones.

Poor mother, don't you know that your blind tenderness imposes upon your son the tremendous task of one day having to drown the bad seeds that your weakness has allowed to develop in him, and that often become impossible to eradicate? that your guilty indulgence makes him impetuous, selfish and cowardly when faced with work? that true maternal love resides not in a broken will but in the strength that guides? that filial love is tied to respect, and that the kindness that inspires trust is not incompatible with the inevitable firmness that justice demands? that there is nothing too frivolous nor too indifferent in childhood? lastly, that first impressions, like the roots of a tree, develop and nourish branches and leaves with their sap? . . . Dear compatriots, forgive me for this advice, born from the sisterly love that I feel for you!

In spite of the bad results engendered by these young mothers' weakness, filial love is more profound here, more exalted, than in other parts. The never-ending kindness of the maternal heart acts forcefully upon the fiery natures, predisposed to live only through affective bonds. All the tenderness of this independent existence, all this pervading love that surrounds the child, become one with the image of she who is the soul and the shelter of all the joys of the heart, of all feelings of gratitude.

It is touching to see how much respect people give mothers when they reach old age! A powerful source of numerous progeny, the grandmother is the center of everyone's attentions and veneration. Parties and wedding banquets are always held at her house. She presides at the table, dressed in all simplicity; her white hair is braided, never concealed by vanity. All compliments, all jokes are for her or come from her, and when the time comes to end this patriarchal life, it goes out softly without suffering and without regrets, as she has lived it.

One has to pity the worldly European woman when age strips her of youthful charms, for it is rare that such a woman would know how to grow old. Much common sense and preparation is needed, and perhaps her whole life before, to be ready for that serious stage of life. But what shall she do if all her time has been devoted to the concerns brought on by vanity and gallantry, if her life has been dedicated wholly to the fictitious pleasures she now sees being taken away one by one by the youth that surrounds her? Then, she looks around for the first time and realizes that if she has not nurtured abnegation and has lived only for herself, nobody feels obligated to attend to her. Isolated and bitter, she tries to make friends with those in the political sphere or with those whose lives are tied to intrigues, and she dies the same way she lived, searching for happiness amidst sterile and impotent emotions.

Letter 25 from *La Havane,* vol. 2. Paris: Librairie D'Amyot, 1844.

NOTES

1. The words in *italics* throughout the text indicate that the original text also used Spanish. [Trans.]

2. Poet-musician Gabriel de la Concepción Valdés, known as Plácido, would be at the center of the infamous Conspiracy of La Escalera in 1844, and would be executed for his alleged leadership. For a lively and well-documented study on Cuban slavery and this particular event, see Robert L. Paquette's *Sugar Is Made with Blood: The Conspiracy of La Escalera and the Conflict between Empires over Slavery in Cuba* (Middletown, Conn.: Wesleyan University Press, 1988). [Trans.]

Gertrudis Gómez de Avellaneda
Cuba, 1814–1873

Gertrudis Gómez de Avellaneda was born in central
Cuba to an aristocratic Creole mother and a Spanish father, a member of the colonial administration of the island. After her father's early death, the mother married
another Spanish official who decided to leave Cuba because he feared a slave uprising. Avellaneda thus had to
leave Cuba for Spain when she was in her mid-twenties;
she chose to live in Seville, and began to make a name
for herself as a poet and playwright.

Avellaneda soon moved to Madrid, the literary center, and continued writing both poetry and drama. She
was well received, and her plays proved so popular that
she was able to support herself financially. Both in her
writing and in her personal life Avellaneda dared to
break the rules. In 1841 she published her controversial
novel *Sab*, which told of the love of a Cuban mulatto
slave for a white woman, a topic so taboo at the time
that the book was officially banned in Cuba. The following year Avellaneda wrote *Dos mujeres* (Two Women),
whose heroine was an adulteress, and a sympathetic
one at that. This novel was also banned in her home
country.

Like her French contemporary George Sand, Avellaneda espoused sexual independence. She had a number of open liaisons, one of which resulted in the birth
of a daughter who died in infancy. She married twice

but had no further children. In 1853 she attempted to storm the bastions of one of the most hallowed institutions: the Spanish Royal Academy of Letters. Many of its male members supported her candidacy, as she was by then a famous author, but gender inequalities being what they were, Avellaneda was turned down. Long-festering resentment connected with this issue would surface in her essay on "La Mujer" (Women).

Avellaneda wrote this essay late in her life, in 1860, when she was back in Cuba with her second husband. Madrid might have denied her the literary pinnacle she craved; Cuba did not. She was lionized and honored in Havana, where she founded and published the women's journal *El Album Cubano de lo Bueno y lo Bello* (The Cuban Album of the Good and the Beautiful). Avellaneda not only used her journal as a forum for her militantly feminist essay, but she proved very astute at surrounding it with other contributions that would alternately soften and enhance its message. Although the young Cuban firebrand had gradually changed into an increasingly conservative and pious matron, her essay on "Women" proved that there was life in the old girl yet.

NINA M. SCOTT

Women

I

Much has been written about women and much still needs to be said, as was rightfully observed by an elegant Spanish writer (Don Severo Catalina) who has recently enriched the history of the fair sex with a beautiful volume, dedicated exclusively to the study thereof. Nevertheless, the idea does not enter our minds to accompany him in the vast field of his philosophic exploration, nor to offer him new and unknown facts to broaden and support his theories. For the present, we shall mainly take a brief look at women's precursors in the realm of the emotions, beginning with religious feelings—that is, with the roles women have been able to play in the high drama of God's relations with fallen and redeemed humanity.

* * *

We concede without the slightest reluctance that, given the duality that characterizes our species, Nature endowed man with superior physical strength, and we will not even dispute that he has greater intellectual prowess, which he appropriates for himself with little modesty. What suffices for us, and we say this sincerely, is the conviction that no one in good faith can deny our sex supremacy when it comes to feelings, or the title of sovereignty in the immense sphere of the emotions.

"Great souls," a poet said, "aspire to lower themselves, not because of laxness, but because of an instinct for true exaltation, which consists of sacrifice." That is precisely what a woman's character is: she possesses the

Translated by Nina M. Scott

intuition of true greatness, the instinct of supreme heroism that takes pleasure in *lowering itself,* an instinct that becomes glorified through suffering,
and that consecrates her heart as a secret altar of continuous sacrifices. But
do not fear that this great heart—in which is housed the boundless affection of a daughter, a wife, a mother, exacting a threefold tribute of unnoticed sacrifices—might weaken or break because it was unable to contain
these feelings. It is true that these emotions overflow and pour themselves
out everywhere, but they do this in order to soothe the ulcers that eat
away at the heart; they also do so in order to create the beneficent organizations that have all had a woman as founder or guardian. Ah! She is
not a mother only in the concrete sense of the word: her soul's maternal
drive encompasses the universe. Providence itself willed it so, when the
Divine Representative of the redeemed world was born from Mary's virginal womb.

* * *

Painful motherhood, atonement in the case of Eve, triumph in the case
of Mary (who was, nevertheless, the greatest martyr among all mothers),
encircles woman's brow, be she penitent or saint, with the noble halo of
sacrifice; she is invested with the highest form of priesthood—because it
demands the greatest self-sacrifice—the priesthood of love. Ah, yes! Eve
weeps for the enslavement of her children, thrust into the world with the
pain of her womb, while Mary redeems them with tears as well, and by
the burnt offering of her soul opens to them the gates of Heaven. We
might say that these two women incorporate the whole history of their
sex. Ever the sacrifice, until the hour of triumph! In this way woman rises
by *divine right* to be queen over the vast dominions of emotion; she reigns
supreme in the suffering of atonement, she reigns supreme as well in the
glorious suffering of battle and of victory.

Take good note of this, those of you who ceaselessly recall the first
mother's weakness, judging it an indelible stigma on the countenance of
this sex; take note that Mary was hailed as *full of grace* by the heavenly messenger before grace had become enfleshed as man. Take note that Adam
sinned along with Eve, and along with her produced corrupt progeny, but
Mary *triumphed alone* and—without the intervention of any Adam—produced a divine descendant. Mary's glory expunged Eve's shame and covered it with eternal splendor. Adam's defeat needed a Man-God to make
amends for it.

* * *

In spite of the base notions that emanate from its heart in detraction of
the feminine sex, the world has not been able to refuse this sex the desig-

nation of *beautiful, tender, pious*, even though it denigrates this praise by also calling it *weak*. Nevertheless, were we to demand that they prove the justice of this last assessment, people would find themselves hard pressed when they look at the way in which the female sex figures in the bloody pages of religious heroism. And this even though women are not taught to be strong nor to scorn life!

It would also be very hard to find in the history of nations a people or a century that could not provide admirable examples of generous women glorified by extraordinary deeds of patriotism that have made them worthy of the astonishment and approbation of posterity. And this even though women are not permitted to take part in public affairs, nor have ever had access to the halls of government!

But that is not where we now propose to seek them, nor where the most beautiful examples of women's glory are.

Go back, go back to those days in which occurred the greatest of all the events the world has ever seen, the days in which the light so long awaited shone, casting its splendor even on *those who lay in the shadow of death*.

* * *

The Redeemer travels through Judah, giving voice to the dumb, movement to the paralyzed, sight to the blind and, according to His own words, *preaching the Gospel to the poor*.

The doctors of the law persecute Him, accusing Him of disrupting public order.

Ignorant women follow Him, blessing the womb in which He was conceived.

The Pharisee who boasts of being a just man and who receives Him in his house, fails to offer Him water for the customary washing.

The sinful woman comes to wash His feet with her tears and to dry them with her hair.

Pilate, powerless before the elders and the priests who demand innocent blood of him, makes it flow under the blows of the lash, and abandons the Messiah to the taunting of his soldiers.

The Roman governor's wife leaps from her bed, troubled by mysterious presentiments, and sends messengers fervently to entreat her husband not to permit the just man's blood to be shed.

But Pilate, the doctors, the priests, the elders, and the people all condemn the Son of God, all send Him to his execution bearing His cross.

The daughters of Jerusalem follow Him, wailing and shedding their tears on the Divine Martyr's last steps.

* * *

Oh! Behold the cross erected between Heaven and Earth, which He unites with his bloodied arms. The holy Victim, nailed to the tree (which on contact with Him changes from an instrument of death to a symbol of life), casts his dying glances on his hard bed of pain. . . . What has become of the disciples He honored with His love and instructed with His doctrine? Where are the privileged men He chose for the high ministry, invested by Him with power against Hell? Only one is there! Only one! But on the other hand *there are three women*. None of them was present at the glory of Tabor; all come to share in the ignominy of Golgotha.[1]

Later, when night casts its dismal mantle over the deicidal city, who are the ones who keep watch in the midst of the silence, preparing perfumes with their pious hands to anoint the holy remains? Behold: women again. This is why they deserve to have one of their number hear before all others the solemn message of joy to all humankind: "Woman, He whom you seek is not here; He is risen, just as He said."

And this is not all: another joy, another grace was set apart for us. A woman—who was the first to receive the news of the victory—was also the first who cast her eyes on the *Firstborn among the dead*.

It was just: for she had accompanied Him in suffering and sought Him out in the tomb.

* * *

Earlier we looked at Eve and Mary—the sinful mother and the Most Blessed Mother—who equally offered up to Heaven abundant tribute of their maternal suffering. Let us now look at Mary and at Magdalene—the spotless Virgin and the repentant courtesan—equally offering up sublime examples of love's steadfastness for the world to admire.

We see them at the foot of the cross, and one there, the other beside the tomb, hear the word "Woman!" from divine angelic lips, a word that in both cases has a glorious meaning.

"Woman! Behold your son," the Redeemer says to Mary, symbolizing all mankind in his disciple Saint John. Note that He does not call her His mother, because here the Queen of Martyrs does not represent the venerable Mother of the Messiah: she represents *woman* . . . restored woman, sanctified woman, co-redeeming woman, whose great heart can embrace the motherhood of the universe.

"Woman!" the angel also says to Magdalene, "The one you seek is not here; He is risen, as He said."

The penitent lover is not called by her name either; the term uttered by the celestial messenger is the same the Redeemer uses to direct His last words to Mary: "Woman!", because the sinner, who was absolved because *she loved greatly*, and the spotless Virgin personify their entire sex . . . the sex that accompanied Jesus to Calvary, that blessed Him when men cursed Him, that sought Him in the tomb when He was forgotten by an entire people whom He had showered with blessings, a sex that—having won for itself once and for all the designation of *pious and loving*—deserved the joy of being the first to know that love had conquered death and had opened the eternal gates of glory.

In the divine Christian epic Mary and Magdalene, purity and penitence, both wear the spotless crown of feeling, in that way representing their sex, which has always been great because of its heart.

Read the sacred pages of the Gospel and in them you will find *woman's* entire history; through them you will understand how noble, how beautiful, how majestic has been the role that woman has been asked to play in the history of humankind.

Mary, full of grace, Magdalene, full of love; Mary, mother and model for all redeemed generations, Magdalene, sister and example to all penitent souls; both of them loving, both suffering, both at the foot of the cross, they equally symbolize the magnanimous sex to whom the Eternal granted sovereignty in all feelings, and—by the merits gained by all their sacrifices—the first fruits of all victories.

II

In the preceding article we wanted to look at man's helpmeet only under the aspect that most distinguishes her—that is, in the domain of feeling, which constitutes her most legitimate legacy. Seen in this way, and limiting ourselves as we did to a quick examination of the role she—because of her unquestionable supremacy—was assigned to play in the sacred chronicles of religion, we felt at that juncture a kind of proud complacency in showing disdain for any glory but that one, leaving the so-called "stronger sex" in tranquil possession of all the exclusive gifts it attributes to itself. Today, however, it occurs to us to take another brief look at the history of our "weaker sex," perhaps for no other reason than to look for the origins of this categorization we have accepted for so many centuries. Yes, we confess that it piques us somewhat to determine if the greater delicacy of our physical frame is an insurmountable obstacle that Nature placed in opposition to intellectual and moral vigor, and whether, though enriched by treasures of the heart, our universal Father on the other hand cut us off from inheriting the great faculties of intelligence and character.

At first glance it seems to us that as soon as we examine this question, far from having our superiority in sentiment exclude other admirable qualities, the most powerful stimuli for all the soul's resources derive therefrom, and—when we recall so many marvels wrought by ardent zeal—we are not only ready to declare with Pascal that *great thoughts are born of the heart*, but the idea occurs to us that the most glorious deeds recorded in the annals of humankind have always been products of sentiment, and that the mightiest heroes have always been those with the richest hearts.

Great intelligence paired with meager affective power—should this even exist—is a monstrosity. We sometimes encounter geniuses who have become depraved or been led astray by violent passions, but it is extremely rare, if not impossible, to find great intellectual power in unfortunate beings deprived of passionate sensitivity. In the same way a vigorous temperament, one capable of initiating great deeds and seeing them through, one that dares to assume enormous responsibility, is not usually a trait exhibited by arid, cold men in whom action has no impetus but unfeeling calculation.

The power of the heart, therefore, is the origin and center of many other faculties, and although at times this power may cause character and intelligence to adopt a mistaken initiative, or, when it is badly trained and directed—as it often is in a woman—this same power might be employed in an unworthy or pitiful manner, yet none of this will allow us to diminish its incomparable importance. Quite the contrary: along with Lacordaire we should say, *He who wishes to strip away man's passion because of the evils of which he has sometimes been the instrument would be like the fool who smashes Homer's lyre because it has been used to sing of false gods.*

* * *

As affective power is the source and impetus of other drives, and since woman possesses this power in a privileged way, the conspicuous result is that instead of being incapable of exercising any influence that does not spring exclusively from love, she owes to and finds in this power a surprising strength, whose sphere of action may be very risky to determine.

Shall we look for facts to justify this theory? The difficulty we encounter consists in having to limit ourselves to selecting only a few from the innumerable examples that tradition and history offer us.

Nothing seems so removed from a tender feminine heart, nothing so incompatible with the label *weaker* that characterizes us, as extraordinary deeds of rash bravery and invincible steadfastness. Nevertheless, look at Deborah declaring war on the Canaanites while seated under the palm tree that serves as her canopied throne as she administers justice to the sons of Israel, and leading them herself into a battle in which they defeat the proud enemy. Look at Jahel, who with a firm hand drives the hammer that pierces Sisara's temples; at Judith, who enters Holofernes' tent in order to leave it with the invader's bloody head; at the mother of the Maccabees, heroically witnessing the sacrifice of her sons, victims of patriotic love.

And if we raise our eyes from this sacred book—the oldest and most authentic in the world—we will see the Spartan women, who, when Pyrrhus approaches to finish the destruction of their city, resist being sent to the island of Crete—where the Senate had determined to send them to protect their lives—and, appearing before this body while brandishing swords in their white hands, declare that they will never obey a decree that dishonors them, for all are determined to vanquish or die with their fellow citizens. We see the daughters of the Theban Antipides, who do not hesitate to immolate themselves when the oracle declares that Thebes will only triumph when noble blood is sacrificed in a burnt offering to the gods. We see Boadicea avenging the enslavement of her people with the death of seventy thousand Romans; the Argive women defending the city that is being attacked by the Lacedemonian king, and repelling him with enormous losses; a Sarmatian princess—installed at the head of her government in the flower of her age—not only administering righteous justice but surprising and dethroning an ambitious monarch who had dared to threaten her kingdom by mocking the weakness of her sex. We see Artemisia—as an aide to Xerxes—battling in Salamis, after having enlightened him with such sage advice that, when the Persian followed it, Greece counted one laurel less in its crown of glory. We see the good wife of Germanicus arise from the bed on which she had just become a mother, to cry encouragement to the encamped troops and, in her husband's absence, take over as general. We see the dissolute Antonina, always ready to wash the sheets of her nuptial bed with the enemy blood her sword spilled on the battlefield, [where she fought] at the side of her husband Belisarius. We see the matrons of Székesfehérvár—in Hungary—heroically defend the fortress the Turks were besieging, when their discouraged men wanted to surrender it. I do not need to remind you of particulars in the marvelous story of Joan of Arc. We see the illustrious Greek woman Bobolina who defied the might of the Turks, the oppressors of her country, who armed ships, commanded them, and with the insignia *liberty or death* succeeded in having her banner, which was triumphant on the seas, sow fear within the walls of Constantinople. Then there is the famous Polish woman Kazanowska who appeared before her husband, the governor of a besieged fortress, with two daggers in her hand, telling him resolutely, *one will pierce your breast and the other mine if you are weak enough to surrender.* Then there is a most noteworthy figure of the French Revolution, whose name is Mme. de Roland, and the no less extraordinary woman, Charlotte Corday, who stained her delicate right hand with Marat's filthy blood. . . . But why sift through the annals of the world, picking out heroines from among their pages?

It suffices for us to open our own national pages for a moment. They show us the illustrious widow Padilla, her husband's rival for glory; María Pita, brandishing the steel let fall by the dead defenders of La Coruña, and throwing herself into the breach the English had already taken; the unfortunate Pineda, victim of love and liberty, who went to her execution with tranquil mien; the unforgettable Agustina de Aragón, who snatched the fuse from the dying hands of the last gunner to defend the Portillo Gate, under attack by the French in the first siege of Zaragoza, and fired the cannon that sowed terror in the enemy ranks.

Can these examples, and many others we could cite (not even mentioning the uncounted religious martyrs), leave us with any doubt as to the solution we should assert with respect to the problem we are examining? Will we be accused of capriciousness or partiality if we maintain that when it comes to courage and energy the *stronger sex* cannot present us with any title that the *weaker one* cannot rival with unquestionable right?

Oh, and don't forget that in no country the world over are women trained to undergo hardships, face dangers, protect the public interest, or garner civic laurels.

* * *

However, we do admit that it is possible that the ardor that so fills passionate hearts may, under certain circumstances, lend women momentary courage, which is all the more exalted and startling because it is alien to her nature. If we follow that way of thinking, the most amazing acts of boldness and enterprise are not enough to prove that the sex that is principally endowed with beauty and feeling has also been given great attributes of character.

Opposites are related—you might tell us—weakness can often exhibit flashes of reckless daring: thus, without denying that a woman may be capable of remarkable deeds in a rush of passion, we will not yet concede to you that she is as qualified as a man to carry out long-term, difficult projects. In a word, before accepting a woman's capacity to be a man's equal in all aspects, we need something more than these extraordinary deeds, which only convince us that you were right in saying that zeal can be the author of great marvels.

Well, then, sister readers, rightly keeping the above in mind, let us take another brief look at the record of our sex with respect to intelligence and character, beginning with what is most arduous, transcendental, and sublime.

Nothing requires greater amounts of skill, firmness, and constancy, nothing is invested with more gravity and greatness than the government of nations. To rule men is the most difficult task there is, and to rule them well is the greatest glory of all.

Can a woman aspire to this glory? Only one example thereof would be enough to show that her physical makeup is not incompatible with the most powerful intellectual faculties, but—why hide it?—we royally disdain to limit ourselves to only one or two examples, as convincing as they might be. And thus—with no prior selection but all jumbled together, just as they come to mind—by citing some of the infinite reminders the world cherishes of women who were famous in the administration of important public interests, we will attempt to prove not so much the equality of the sexes as the *superiority of ours* in carrying out this high calling, the most difficult Heaven saw fit to entrust to humankind.

III

Although we are indebted to Christianity for the solemn proclamation of a woman's dignity, whose rights as man's companion and co-inheritor of Heaven were forever established, in spite of this—in deplorable proof of the resistance that dark human reason set up against the radiant spirit of the Gospel—it is true that there were still laughable debates on the singular question of whether or not our sex was to be considered an integral part of the rational species.[2] It is no less evident a fact that ever since long ago—and in spite of all the egotistic theories of the dominant sex—the latter in practice surrendered to the powerful influence of those subjugated, even instinctively recognizing in women a kind of greatness that the male sex could not explain other than by the attribution of divine inspiration. The history of the Franks, the Celts, and the Germanic peoples constantly show us the veneration those nations manifested toward women, in whose hands—in moments of crisis—they would deposit all civil and political authority. The Franks could freely criticize the conduct of their judges, but it was not permitted to question the wisdom of the female councils because they were held to be heavenly oracles.

In Gallic territories a tribunal of noble women was established that for many years was that nation's most distinguished and respectable body: the high opinion in which it was held, even among foreigners, shines forth in the fact that when Hannibal signed a peace treaty with the Gauls, he solemnly stipulated that if any of the latter affronted a Carthaginian, the Gaul would be subject to the decision of the women's senate, and to no other body.

An important fact! When women's influence in Gaul waned, and the administration of the country was left exclusively in the hands of the Druids, it did not take long for that nation, which until then had been independent and victorious, to become Rome's tributary.[3]

* * *

Notwithstanding her past degradation, there has never been a time when a woman has not sometimes taken up the scepter of power, and—another important fact!—she has almost always wielded it with glory.

Tomyris, besides being queen, was a legislator of the Scythians. Dido founded the nation that in time became the feared rival of the ruler of the world. Semiramis shines among the Chaldean monarchs with a splendor that has pierced the shadows of time and reached our own days. Deborah, whom we already cited as a warlike heroine, was just as outstanding in her administration of justice. The two Artemisias deserve to have their names live on. Zenobia did not prove to the Romans that she was a great captain until after her subjects venerated her as a great queen, and thus her friends gave her the glorious title of *Augusta*.

If we stop going back to such remote ages and look for a moment in Christian times, we have a throng of examples: Amalasunta, who conquers for herself the title of the *Solomon of her sex*; Alix of Champagne, who rules turbulent France with singular skill as regent for her young son Philip Augustus; Margaret of Valdemar, on whose head rests the crown of Norway, Denmark, and Sweden, and who was acclaimed the *Semiramis of the North*; Sancha of León, who earned the name of *lioness heroine*; Berenguela of Castile, whom History has called *the Great*; the mother of Saint Louis [Blanca of Castile], who deserved this title as well as that of sister to the great Berenguela; Maria Theresa, whose historical figure has no rivals among the Austrian monarchs; Elizabeth of England, mistress of political knowledge; María de Molina, who takes the helm of the ship of state in difficult times and becomes famous for her prudence . . . Turn your eyes as well to the illustrious Russian princesses [the empresses Elizabeth and Catherine the Great], preservers of the astonishing revolution begun by Peter the Great, who during their female reign are seen to stamp out torture, promote reforms, cultivate art and science, carry out colossal undertakings that increase the borders and power of their state, as both the Mediterranean and the Ocean become crowded with ships built on the shores of the Baltic and the Black Sea.

Then, in conclusion (because surely you men will not ask us for more examples), take a few minutes to look with justified national pride at the magnificent figure of Isabella the Catholic. See her receive a nation on the brink of ruin from the hands of an impotent king, and with a strong hand take up the scepter that for so long had been the plaything of political factions. Then, silencing the complaints of a husband who judges himself affronted because she will not give him exclusive power over the reins of government, we see her tirelessly making long series of wise decisions by means of which she puts a stop to blind factionalism; suppresses the mad ambitions of an unruly oligarchy; annuls the anarchic power of the military orders, whose high offices are taken over by the throne; overthrows former privileges; reforms the clergy; sets up organizations that purge the nation of criminals; reestablishes and guarantees peace in towns and villages; and—by furthering commerce, shipping, industry, agriculture, and the sciences—opens the way to honor and riches for hardworking men of creative talent. . . . With the help of the legislature see her rescue the treasury from the profound ruin to which previous incompetent administrations had reduced it, set down the initial strokes in the gigantic task of establishing a harmonious legislature that would be the same in all her dominions. See her finally establish her monarchy on firm foundations and—when she has revived it by infusing it with a new spirit—call her country to arms, put on the warrior's helmet, take up Pelayo's sword, and, under the banner of the cross, lead it to expel the Ishmaelites, whose presence was still staining the beautiful soil of Granada, and send them away to the desert sands of Africa.

The Europe of that age hails such exalted feminine glory with surprise—a triumph that already foretells Spain's future victories in Roussillon and Italy—and Providence opens a New World to Spain, one where she triumphantly extends her territories to build that glorious empire of which men said that the sun never set upon it.

After this, who would dare to question a woman's privileged ability to take on the arduous duties of government? Take good note of the fact that I said *privileged*, because the members of our sex who have governed nations are in a tiny minority compared with those of the masculine sex, yet taking this difference into account, there are more royal feminine names consecrated by History than masculine ones.

We can throw down the gauntlet to the stronger sex and force it into this decisive contest: we women steadfastly maintain that of any ten queens we can point to at least five who are deserving of respectful memory; dare men show us fifty out of any hundred kings who deserve the same honor?

IV

If we still needed new proofs that a woman's moral and intellectual force at the very least equals that of a man, we need only to cast the most cursory of glances at the vast field of literature and the arts in order to find them. We cannot claim the same in the sciences, because as science is based solely on factual knowledge, a knowledge that even the greatest geniuses cannot possess by intuition, it would be absurd to try to find a great number of eminent scientists in our half of the rational species, to whom all the gates of serious institutions are closed, and the aspirations of whose souls to profounder studies are even considered to be ridiculous. The capacity of women to study science is not even put to the test by those who authoritatively decide to deny them this opportunity, yet—given all this—it is astonishing that there is no lack of glorious examples of persevering female talents who every now and then have forced entry into the sanctuary to snatch some of the mysterious deity's secrets. Let us hear from Aretha (the daughter of Aristippus), the author of forty scientific books, teacher of 150 distinguished philosophers, who (according to what the Athenians said) inherited Socrates' soul and Homer's fecundity. Let Aspasia speak—from whom Pericles and Alcibiades learned rhetoric, and to whom Athens owed a school of eloquence; and Laura Bassi, as celebrated by her contemporaries as she was learned in physics, algebra, and geometry and inspired in poetry; and the princess of Piombino, theologian and philosopher; and Madame Chatelet, renowned as an astronomer, etc.

If—in spite of these and other brilliant proofs of her scientific ability—a woman is still excluded from the temple of serious knowledge, don't think for a moment that her acceptance in literature and the arts has been a fact of many centuries' duration: oh, no! here, too, the field has been disputed inch by inch by blind masculine adherence to one idea. Even today she is regarded there as an intruder and a usurper and is consequently treated with certain animosity and distrust, which is most visible in the distance at which she is kept from the *bearded* academies. Let this adjective pass, dear sister readers, because it flowed naturally from our pen on mentioning those illustrious associations of literary types whose primary and most important attribute is *having a beard*. As unfortunately the greatest intellectual prowess in the world is not enough to cause that animal abundance of hair that requires a razor's edge to sprout on the lower half of a human face, this has come to be the only and insurmountable distinction of male literati, who—as they are daily dispossessed of other prerogatives they claimed were exclusively theirs—cling to this distinction with all the strength of the *stronger sex*, prudently making it the *sine qua non* of academic glories.

But admire the audacity and the astuteness of the *weaker sex*! There are *those* who, I know not how, suddenly appear in doctoral regalia.[4] There are others who, hiding their beardless faces behind masculine masks, without more ado penetrate so far into the temple of fame that when it is discovered that *they lack a beard* and that therefore they cannot be admitted to the academic societies, there is no real way to deny that they have the rightful qualifications to figure eternally among European luminaries.[5]

* * *

There is an even greater number—tremble and quake, gentlemen!—yes, an even greater number of bare-faced, fearless women who have managed to get themselves inscribed *sans façon* in the intellect's glorious annals. And why cite examples, when the facts are so obvious and well known?

From remotest antiquity on down we see women showing evidence that they were born with the gift of artistic instinct, and this was finally to overcome all the obstacles put in their path. The mythological muses probably were the apotheosis of famous women of those early times, the founders of the arts, but without needing to rely on hypotheses, and basing ourselves on respectable sources, we know that the invention of painting was the work of a woman, and another laid the foundations for the first society of fine arts, establishing the first poetry competitions for troubadors.[6] . . . And who does not know that Sappho was famous among the most illustrious Greek poets of her age, that Corinna defeated Pindar, and that Thessalida with the magic tones of her lyre infused the young hearts of the Argive maidens with warlike heroism?

We will not even attempt to cover modern times: Europe alone would overwhelm us with the enormous number of female triumphs, and America—that very young world in which I was born—America itself would shower us with a multitude of names of illustrious women, who [on this continent] sustain intellectual pursuits that are threatened with extinction, in some places because of the preponderance of material interests, in others because of civil strife.

And why should it not be so, when Columbus, on discovering a part of these virgin lands, noted with surprise that the incipient civilization and poetic genius of those peoples were incarnate in the body of a beautiful woman? Anacaona was the inspired sibyl of one of our rich tropical isles.

At the sound of her voice, resonating among forest harmonies, the customs of those barbarous tribes were tempered, the sovereignty of intelligence was revealed to their minds, and they obeyed as a queen one whom they revered as an oracle.

* * *

With respect to the capabilities of contemporary women, we will only add in conclusion that two works have just been published in France that are noteworthy for more than one reason. The first, from the pen of Mlle. Marchet, bears the title *Women, Their Past, Present and Future.* The other, whose author is the already famous Countess Dora d'Istria, has as its epigraph *Women in the Orient.* We have not had the pleasure of reading either one of the aforementioned works, but, judging by the opinions of the Paris press, both are most interesting in content and beautiful in style. All the scattered documents pertaining to the great cause of half of the human race, i.e., all that proves something in favor of the emancipation of women, appears to have been collected and catalogued by the former of the authors here cited, and this topic of important social interest is supported by arguments of irrefutable logic. According to a reputable newspaper, Countess Dora d'Istria's book forcefully confirms Mlle. Girard's text, saying "that it adds the testimony of another part of the world, based on living archives such as travellers, historians, customs and daily life."

"Women," the paper in question also says, "at last appear decided to take their own interests into their hands, and—apart from the strength that the arguments contained in those books might have—it must be stated that the books themselves are two irrefutable arguments in favor of the intellectual equality of the sexes."

Far be it from the humble person who signs her name to these articles, dear readers, to aspire to present herself to you as the worthy champion of our common desire, but—as she is filled with pride at the achievements of our sex—allow her at the conclusion of these brief observations to point out to you one evident fact, which perhaps proves more than all other arguments.

In nations where women are honored and where their influence holds sway in society, there you will surely find civilization, progress, public life.

In countries in which women are degraded, there is nothing great: those countries are condemned to an inevitable destiny of servitude, barbarism, and moral decay.

Album Cubano de lo Bueno y lo Bello, Havana, 1860.

NOTES

1. Saint John was the only disciple to witness the Crucifixion. Tabor is the mountain where Jesus underwent the Transfiguration. Golgotha is the site of the Crucifixion. [Trans.]

2. This question was seriously discussed in a council (not an ecumenical one), in which the affirmative was stated only after great difficulties. See *The History of Gregory of Tours*, book 8, and Saint Foix's *Essays*.

3. *History of Gaul*, by the Benedictine D. Martin, volume 1.

4. Let us recall, among others, the famous Doña María de Guzmán, also known as the Doctora of Alcalá.

5. We are content to cite George Sand, captain of all the masked no-beards. The masculine name she distinguished by her writing would have figured among the most illustrious of the French Academy, but oh, woe! It was discovered prematurely that that great, true talent's beard was a false one, and here we have it that all the glory of the French Byron can never compensate for the lack of that precious appendage.

6. Clemence Isaure, whose beautiful portrait we have had the pleasure of seeing exhibited with great veneration in the halls of the Academy of Arts and Sciences in Toulouse, France.

Eduarda Mansilla de García

Argentina, 1834–1892

Eduarda Mansilla de García, one of Argentina's most
prominent women of the nineteenth century, brings to
the scene of writing a striking combination of talents.
Novelist, essayist, playwright, translator, and musical
composer, she entered the Argentine cultural world
with the privilege of education and lineage and with a
clear sense of belonging among the nation's elites. Niece
of Juan Manuel de Rosas and daughter of General Lucio
Mansilla, one of the heroes of the wars for independence from Spain, Eduarda was welcomed among international circles of nineteenth-century gentlemen of culture. Just as her brother, Lucio, was to gain prominence
among members of the Argentine generation of 1880
for his charming memoirs and narrative about criollo
encounters with Ranquel Indians, Eduarda's place in
national literary history was secured through the un-
rivaled eloquence of her writings and the celebrated
reception of her work both in Argentina and abroad.
These siblings thus set the style for cultured writing in
the late nineteenth century by insisting that refinement,
elegance, and measured taste be the *sine qua non* for Argentine letters. In a gesture not uncharacteristic of her
social position and training, Mansilla wrote in both
French and Spanish and saw her works translated into
other languages such as German and English. As part of
an international ambassadorial class, she traveled

through Europe and the United States in the company of her husband, Manuel Rafael García, a diplomat of unitarian heritage who was similarly endowed with the exquisite education and training belonging to members of high society. Nevertheless, a conflict ensued between the Mansilla family's federalist alliances and the Garcías' unitarian values. This conflict is reflected in many of her works in which she rejected the formal programs of political parties in favor of an individualized and humanitarian treatment of all citizens in the Argentine nation.

Mansilla de García's texts repeatedly insist on this ethical and didactic mission, combined with a careful formal elegance unequaled by other writers of her times. This is seen in her first novel, *El médico de San Luis* (1860; The Doctor of San Luis), considered a classic of nineteenth-century Argentine literature; in her indictment of the Conquest as read in the novel *Lucía Miranda* (1861, 1882); and in her numerous volumes of short stories designed to illuminate the crisis of values besetting the modern nation (e.g., *Creaciones*, 1883; *Cuentos*, 1881). As the first Argentine woman to write a travel memoir, *Recuerdos de viaje* (1882; Travel Memories), she observed customs in the United States in order to speculate about democracy and morals. Her dramaturgy and literature for children continued these investigations insofar as she always emphasized the ethical dilemmas facing characters in moments of crisis. Mansilla de García was also an active contributor to *La Nación, El Nacional,* and *La Tribuna,* the principal Argentine newspapers of her time, in which she wrote about public affairs and the choices facing citizens in the late nineteenth century.

The following translation, rendered from the French, is excerpted from Eduarda Mansilla's *Pablo ou la vie dans les pampas* (1869; Paul, or Life on the Pampas). A hybrid text combining elements of fiction and essay, this work is a reflection on the state of affairs in modern Argentina as seen from the perspective of one who travels from Buenos Aires to the backlands. A book that rivals Sarmiento's *Facundo* (1845) for its repositioning of the

conflicts between "civilization and barbarism," *Pablo,*
for its reflection on the gauchos and indigenous masses,
also anticipates to some degree her brother Lucio's
study, *Una excursión a los indios ranqueles* (1870; An Excursion to the Ranquel Indians). Progress, religion,
and the white man's conquest of the wilderness are all
brought under ethical scrutiny by Eduarda Mansilla de
García as she indicts the European project of backwoods
expansion yet laments the incorrigible heathenism that
she sees among the gauchos.

FRANCINE MASIELLO

Life on the Pampas

(Selection)

Micaela, like all women of the pampa, had her own religion. In that vast wilderness women very rarely have the opportunity to busy themselves with official religion: there are many among them who have never seen a priest. Most of the time the gauchos *live to-gether,* as they say, with the intention of having their union blessed later on; they wait for the opportunity to come to them, and it is understood that the matter is of but mediocre importance.

To understand this state of affairs in that part of the New World (so different from the Old), one must take into account a host of local circumstances.

At the mouth of the great river La Plata, whose waters blend with the Atlantic Ocean, lies a vast and beautiful city: Buenos Aires.

Upon arrival in this city the European finds all the resources that the most ancient cities of the civilized world offer the foreigner in Europe, whether a center for work or material pleasures.

It is there that numerous vessels come to us, laden with the surplus population that Europe incessantly shoves off from the Old World to the New, this artery that God, at a given moment, opened one day to the human spirit.

It is there that the law that rules the worlds works the miracle of modern times every day, "law imposing itself by force"; it is there that, despite and because of the material obstacles that man finds he must constantly

Translated by Kim Starr-Reid

overcome simply to survive, his spark of life seems to maintain itself in all its strength, in all its primordial purity.

His personality finds there its free flight, and each one learns to sense himself alive in himself, absolute master of his actions as of his thought.

Individualism creates some great difficulties there, it is true, but at least it develops there at all hours what the human creature judges to be most precious on this earth, the sense of his rights still abiding after the greatest storms.

Man is obliged nonetheless to find a powerful, terrible enemy in this new world: the immensity, the excess of land—that unlimited solitude that seems to absorb him and reduce him to nothing.

Just as the thinking being—finding himself alone, isolated—has been in some sense closer to God, the man of the pampa also has a highly developed sense of the Divinity. Never does he speak of God without expressing himself in a language that proves to what extent he is penetrated with His greatness and His strength. But all that pertains to form of worship, to dogma, is for him unknown or insignificant. It is remarkable that the gaucho has an unshakable faith in the goodness of God, and it is precisely this that often causes him to entrust himself too much. God is good, he says, He always pardons His children.

Who knows? Perhaps this way of imagining Providence is not completely at odds with the spirit of the Gospel.

The gaucho has unlimited confidence in God's goodness; it is his whole religion, and this religion is transmitted from father to son, without commentary as without practice.

In the Argentine republic, religious ideas never had the fanatical character they have had in Peru and Chile; and very often I have wondered what the reason is for this phenomenon, since they were the same Spanish people who populated Peru, Chile, and the rest of Spanish America.

Was it because to our country—a land whose surface is as flat and poor as its interior is lacking in that gold that attracted ruined nobles from the court of Charles and of Philip—came only poor devils indifferent to everything except to their sufferings accrued by the spirit of intolerance and by the haughtiness of the arrogant? Was it because frequent contact with the English heretics, whom love of smuggling attracted toward these regions, had sufficiently prepared their spirits for religious tolerance, making them envisage different religious groups under a new day? Or was it simply because certain seeds do not grow so well in a new land?

Whether it be for this reason or another, or perhaps indeed for all these reasons together, the fact is that the day when the spirit of the eighteenth century penetrated into the young republic of the south with the writings of Rousseau and the encyclopedists, it found no opposition from any class. And, more astonishing still, even the priests fancied themselves at the head of social reform, with an ardor that had the character of the apostolate.

Catholicism continued, but it gained a foundation of tolerance and kindness that it has maintained down to our own times.

At the birth of this nation, which revealed itself to the world imbued with all the great ideals of the French Revolution, the clergy, composed of illumined men, managed to reconcile their duties as Catholic priests with the love of liberty, and they have almost always aided liberty with all their power. They have shown, down there, that such a thing is possible.

This handful of individuals, who found themselves lost out there in that immense space, flowed naturally toward the center, where they always expected to see the dawning of the light.

Europe—Spain—had always been the focal point for everyone in the colony. The ship that brought news from the Peninsula was the great event. The day when all eyes turned toward France, the anticipation must have been even stronger. France of '89 sent over its great, sublime truths, its gigantic aspirations, its acute errors; but the influence from so far away was limited to that. People of the young republic remained faithful to the French Revolution, and for them there was no Ninth of Thermidor.[1]

The population always flocked toward the sea. Each day the differences between the inhabitants of the coast and those of the interior were more perceptible.

On the one hand, one saw civilization—with all its refinements, all its aspirations, all its requirements—grow in creative power and expand its new horizons; while on the other hand, the mute and implacable wilderness—with its terrible force of inertia—opposed the civilizing current.

And thus we see how, in a country where class differences never needed to exist, nor social distinctions of any kind; where the democratic sentiment, having taken root the first day, had abolished every trace of privilege; there the terrible enemy arose that, from birth, would divide the Republic for a long time into two parties: the man of the city and the man of the country, the civilized man and the gaucho. How many struggles between these two elements, so opposed to each other and yet so necessary, were in store for the future! . . . The city dweller, the man who read, who studied, who dreamed of progress, wanted to attain immediately the political and social ideal to which he had aspired from the day the word "liberty" had for the first time in the New World made hearts pound in the subjects of the King of Spain.

The representative system, with all its hazards and intoxications, was implanted instantly and without struggle in the young republic, and for the first time these lofty dreamers tasted the bittersweet fruit of uncontrolled liberty. They thought about everything. In that solemn moment, slavery was abolished by a stroke of the pen; religious tolerance and the most liberal laws were voted in unanimously. They were splendid with sham confidence and holy aspirations, these American patriots who, following the example of their sublime masters from overseas, believed that a few men of good will would be sufficient to make the passage from chaos to enlightenment. The French revolutionaries did not count on the heritage of the centuries; the patriots of La Plata, too, forgot about the Uncivilized Element.

The new man committed two errors: the first was making light of that unpolished element, that keeper of beasts who made him live and whom he should have regarded as his strength. (Oh, but who does not know the sublime madness of saying to oneself, "I am the smartest" or "I am the strongest"?) The second fault, graver still, was wanting to impose what they could not quickly attain. Freedom was often imposed by strokes of the sword, and the love of justice was almost always used to oppress.

That terrible struggle between the element of life and crude stationary force, the struggle that, when people in Europe speak of our country, causes the first words from their mouths to be, "Is it true that they always fight in your country?"

Alas! Europeans judge us too severely. For them we will always be wild primitives. It is time for them to learn to judge us otherwise.

There is fighting among us, it is true; in Europe there is fighting too, and here as there one always sees the two currents that agitate the world coming to grips with each other . . . Light and shadow. . . .

Give it one name in backward America and another in civilized Europe; progress and immobility will always be found to be the same, here as there, whether they fight in the pampas or divide the most civilized portion of the known world into two camps, the future and the past. Consequently, in a country where men were so few in number and the number of priests was proportionate to the population, since profit was so easy there and even exaggerated in other professions, never did the idea of exploiting the Church occur to anyone. Now, everywhere, very few individuals follow the ecclesiastical career as a real vocation. There were barely enough priests for the cities; consider whether there were enough of them to spread throughout the countryside. The missionary, that character who had given such strange fruits in Paraguay, did not exist among us, and I believe the idea of converting our Indians by any means other than the sword and the carbine never occurred to anyone.

There you have our gauchos, given over to their own devices in matters of religion. Forced to journey sixty or eighty leagues on horseback each time they need to fulfill their religious duties, or—more terrible for them—to find themselves in the necessity of entering a city, a condition nonetheless indispensable when it is a question of blessing their marriages or baptizing their children. Besides the excessive expense, especially for those who almost never hold legal tender, the laziness inherent to inhabitants of the pampas renders these excursions hateful to them. Furthermore, as I said above, the gaucho, who does not suffer in the least by lying in the pampa under the stars, finds himself in exile[2] once he has entered a city.

"One of these days," he says upon the birth of his child, and meanwhile time flies rapidly by, as it always does for those whose existence is but a constant monotony, and the hour of his death arrives without his having found the opportunity to fulfill his religious obligations, either for himself or for his family.

Are we to believe that God therefore turns His eyes away from him in wrath at the moment of his last breath? His wife and mother are not of that opinion: they always continue to call *Our Father who art in heaven* the one who sees all and understands all. Thus prayer *par excellence* continues to be transmitted from mother to daughter, world without end. . . .

The towns grow, the desert loses some of its extent every day, temples multiply, even schools begin to be more numerous. Does the spirit of religion gain much in this? I doubt it.

Micaela prayed fervently that night; she lifted her maternal heart toward that Father who is in heaven and, for the first time since her misfortune, she believed she saw a glint of hope. As the day of her departure for the town approached, it seemed to her that the difficulties were less, the dangers imaginary.

"Once there," she said to herself, "I'll go find the governor; he will give me back my Pablo. He is the one who took him from me, it would only be right." And the mother hoped and rejoiced in advance.

Pablo ou la vie dans las pampas. Paris: E. Lachaud, 1869, pp. 185–195.

NOTES

1. 27 July 1794, the fall of Robespierre, who was executed with his followers. [Trans.]

2. Or *out of his element.* [Trans.]

Juana Manuela Gorriti

Argentina, 1818–1892

Juana Manuela Gorriti was one of South America's most successful and prolific nineteenth-century writers. Best known for her many stories and novels, she also wrote extensive memoirs, biographies, and travel accounts, most of which have been included in the major collections of Gorriti's prose published during her lifetime. Among these works are *Sueños y realidades* (1865; Dreams and Realities), *Panoramas de la vida* (1876; Panoramas of Life), *Misceláneas* (1878), and *El mundo de los recuerdos* (1886; The World of Memories). Many of the essays Gorriti wrote for magazines were published in collections as well, and several separate volumes include some of her short biographies (*Perfiles*, 1892; Profiles), travel memoirs (*La tierra natal*, 1889; Native Land), and favorite reminiscences (*Lo íntimo*, 1893; Intimate Things).

Gorriti was born in 1818 in northern Argentina to a family dedicated to patriotic militarism. In 1831 the family had to seek political asylum just across the Bolivian border, and in 1833 the fourteen-year-old Gorriti married a Bolivian army officer, Manuel Isidoro Belzu, who would later become president of Bolivia. Gorriti eventually left her husband and established herself in Lima with her two small daughters, where she ran a school for girls; she began to publish fiction there in 1845. During the next several decades, she moved back and forth between Lima and Buenos Aires, becoming a

well-known literary figure in both capitals. She founded
schools and literary journals and won prizes and awards.
Her literary gatherings and her loyal and enduring friendships added to her fame. When she died in 1892, after
publishing nearly seventy works of fiction, her funeral
was a major public event in Buenos Aires.

"Juana Azurduy" draws upon Gorriti's fond childhood memory of a visit from the brave Bolivian woman
who dressed in a scarlet tunic to increase her visibility
to the men and women soldiers she led in battles against
the Spanish during the revolutionary wars in Alto Perú
(Bolivia). "Emma Verdier" is also a memoir of a distinc-
tive woman, but a fictional one, invented first by one of
Gorriti's good friends, who slipped poems by this imaginary poet into real anthologies of the 1870s. It offers
a glimpse of their friendship, and of Gorriti's whole-
hearted delight in words and stories. "Chincha" is another memoir of an affectionate friendship, in this case
with the Peruvian novelist Mercedes Cabello de Carbonera. Gorriti rejoices in her recollections of a vaca-
tion she and her son Julio Sandoval spent with Mercedes Cabello and her husband. The essay is shadowed
by the Chilean invasion of Lima, by ill health, and by
awareness of subsequent griefs, yet it celebrates life as a
constant banquet of fascinating events and people and,
above all, of the tales that can be told.

MARY G. BERG

Juana Azurduy de Padilla

In this present age, when the ease and affluence of our society have devalued woman's strength of character, making her a slave of luxury with no greater purpose in life than the indulgence of her personal vanity, and with no more important passion than the cultivation of her own beauty, it is both useful and beneficial to remember exceptional women of the past. Yes, it is both important and inspiring to commemorate those women who, guided by the precepts of the Church and by the dictates of their hearts, accompanied their husbands everywhere, whether they crossed vast plains or scaled mountain peaks. Uncomplaining, they traversed steep slopes and precipices, motivated only by loyalty and patriotism.

One of these heroines was Juana Azurduy, born in 1781 in Chuquisaca.[1]

A beautiful woman of proud bearing, she married at the age of twenty-four and on her wedding night itself she abandoned her nuptial bed in order to accompany her husband, Manuel Asensio Padilla, in the momentous war waged by the patriots against the battle-skilled Spanish troops of Alto Perú.

While her husband, as leader of the patriot forces, was making himself feared for his courage and audacity, all the way from the Río Grande to the Pilcomayo, Juana Azurduy was making herself loved for her virtues and kindness. Everyone who met her esteemed her, and she inspired great loyalty in her followers, who regarded her as an affectionate mother.

Translated by Mary G. Berg

II

Her husband entrusted her with holding the town of El Villar when Padilla's troops had been forced to retreat after their surprise attack on Chuquisaca, which was occupied by Colonel de la Hera. During that attack she cheered on her men amidst heavy crossfire, and she capably fended off the Royalist troops that attacked her, putting them to flight. She personally took possession of the battle flag of the *Centro* Battalion, grabbing it from the hands of the standard-bearer as he fell.

III

Only a few days later, on 14 September 1816, while they were in the middle of combat, Juana Azurduy's husband fell as they were fighting side by side, and he was killed. Far from admitting defeat in the face of this great loss, instead of giving up, she locked away her tears of grief in the depths of her heart, summoned up new energy, and, grabbing the blue banner of her regiment, raised high this symbol of freedom and guided her husband's troops in one of their most heroic battles. When she and her troops were trapped and besieged by the enemy in an arid mountainous region, she endured the horrors of hunger and thirst for a month, providing her troops with an example of the most stoic selflessness and courage.

Some of the *caudillos*, leaders who, like Padilla's widow, were engaging enemy troops in combat, were envious of this glorious woman, and their hostility toward her disheartened her. She eventually chose a new leader for her troops, and then she retired to the United Provinces of the River Plate where my father, who was in command in Salta, received her with the honors due true heroes.

It was there, when I was still a small child, that I had the honor of meeting her. The fame of her accomplishments floated in my eyes like a cloud of incense all around that extraordinary woman, encircling her head like a halo. The memory of her is still vivid in my mind as though I could see her now, dressed in her long mourning dress, with her serene and thoughtful face.

Padilla was one of the great leaders in that most important war. At that time there were no official ranks, and our bravest warriors, like Padilla, were simply called heroes. Only later was our country able to award those who survived those deadly encounters in combat with the title of General or Marshal.

IV

In 1824, when the Battle of Ayacucho brought liberty to America, Juana Azurduy left Salta to return to her own country.

What happened to her then?

She disappeared from public view like those stars that illuminate space and are then lost in its immensity.[2]

Perfiles. Buenos Aires: Félix Lajouane, 1892, pp. 5–9.

NOTES

1. Chuquisaca is now Sucre, Bolivia. [Trans.]

2. Juana Azurduy lived quietly in Sucre until her death in 1862. [Trans.]

Emma Verdier

With this name, two dreamers invented a toy for their own playful amusement. But without their ever intending it or putting any effort into it at all, this toy turned into an illusion that took on a life of its own, as you will hear in the following tale:

I

One day, around the time of my first journey to Buenos Aires, I was alone in my room at La Universal, on San Martín Street, when a visit from Mr. D was announced.

"Madam, please permit me the honor of paying my respects."

"Sir," I said to the gentleman, after the various introductory ceremonies, "I beseech you to provide me with information about that most interesting poetess whose verses and biography you contributed to Domingo Cortés' book."[1]

"Emma Verdier, madam? . . . Ah . . . I don't know if I should. . . . Well . . . since you are the one asking, I am obliged to say that you may find her very nearby."

"In this neighborhood? What a delight!"

"Right beside you, madam."

"Do you mean in the house to the left? Because the Stock Exchange is to the right."

"Right in front of you, madam. And begging your forgiveness for having hidden his age and his sex behind the disguise of a pretty name."

Translated by Mary G. Berg

I was totally astonished, and stared at my companion.

"What!" I exclaimed, "those verses of youthful freshness where the sweet young girl runs laughing through the flowering groves, where the virgin dreams in the glimmering twilight of the ideal being who will fulfill her soul. You mean that whole sweet idyll was only . . . ?"

"The fruit of the leisure hours of a poetic wallflower," answered Mr. D, with the embarrassment of a child caught in a naughty prank. "All my life it has given me great pleasure to write idyllic verses, which would be considered a serious character flaw in the legal profession. It has been a failing I have kept hidden well out of sight, in the back of my bottom desk drawer, under the dossiers of human litigation, alongside my other attempts at elaborate rhyme schemes, full of lofty moral assertions."

"But, ah!, what writer can say he never aspired, not even once, to see his fanciful hoax in print on the pages of a book. I felt that irresistible yearning, and so Emma Verdier came into existence. For everyone else, my heroine flourishes in the lush countryside of Entre Ríos, that hotbed of poets. You are the only one who knows my secret."

"Oh, this pleases me immensely!" I exclaimed, immediately enchanted with that fantasy which reminded me of the laughing ghost of one of my childhood pranks so long ago.

"So," I went on, "let me ask you, would you allow me to endow this graceful poetess with real life?"

"Real life? . . . I don't understand. . . ."

"I'll show you what I mean."

And leaving Mr. D in a state of expectant curiosity, I flipped through the pages of an album of beautiful Lima socialites that my nephew Federico Puch treasured; for him it was an album of nostalgic memories. I robbed him of the portrait of the prettiest of them all, Isabel Bergman, a lovely young woman who had succumbed to the shadows of death in the early dawn of her existence.

I hid the name and caption under a garland of forget-me-nots, encircled by a romantic inscription written in gothic lettering: "When I have been uprooted from the soil of my native land, then may you weep for my death." A ridiculous jeremiad in this cosmopolitan era, but a moving lament for such a pure soul: a lament that stirred up indignation and protests and that softened many a strong heart.

I arranged the portrait between two crystal panes, in a pretty ebony frame, and set it upon a pedestal decorated with flowers and lace, between two lamps on the main table in the parlor.

Then I turned back to Mr. D, who was gazing at me, baffled.

"Here you have Emma Verdier," I told him. "Much better to have the picture be of her than of one who has faded into the shadows of the past."

"Oh, I understand, I see what you're doing. What an enchanting creature! That white tunic, the classic drapery of beauty throughout the ages, covering her body without hiding any of its features; that jet black hair falling in curls over her shoulders and back; that pose of utter relaxation and absorption as she leans over a balcony railing, her magnificent eyes focused on an infinite distance, in search of the ideal you were speaking of just now; that mouth with its sighing lips that seem to offer themselves to the kisses of a long-yearned-for love. . . ."

And Mr. D, that capable functionary of legalistic complexities, was suddenly transformed into a twenty-year-old troubadour.

"Celestial woman!" he exclaimed, "wherever you draw breath, be it within the highest or the most humble ranks of life, you are worthy to preside over a throne or altar. And you, all of you who pay tribute to beauty idealized by sentiment, come, draw near and prostrate yourselves in adoration!"

II

As though conjured up by this entreaty, four dear friends, four Argentine celebrities, burst into my parlor.

They were Colonel G——, the lawyer P——, Señora de Sagasta y Urbino, and Rafael de Urbino, winner of the First Prize of Rome for his poems, and worthy of the glorious pseudonym I had given him.

Possessed by the same enthusiastic admiration as Mr. D——, they crowded around the little altar, asking to know the name of that beautiful woman.

And, in the solemn manner of a royal presentation, I said, "She is the daughter of the muses. The sweet poetess of Entre Ríos, Emma Verdier."

"My compatriot!" exclaimed lovely Josefina, kissing the portrait with such profound devotion that I would have felt pangs of guilt had I not seen the total joy that shone in her eyes.

And surprising in Urbino a gaze of ecstatic passion, I was startled by the dangerous turn that the innocent joke was taking.

I thought I had better explain a little, and I began by saying, "Well, here you are. That is Emma Verdier. Her father, a wealthy Frenchman who intends to return to his native land, has sold his holdings and reduced his considerable fortune to a handful of bank drafts, and is passing through Buenos Aires on his way to Europe.

"Emma's heart has leapt with joy at the sight of the handsome metropolis where she had yearned to live, love, and be loved. But these sweet dreams have been shattered by the inflexible will of her father, who is returning to France to establish himself in Rouen, his native city, where he will give Emma in marriage to a wealthy relative who occupies a high position in the French Republic.

"Emma, in mute protest, locks herself in. A fruitless protest, because the tyrant, fearing that some sweet emotion will germinate in the soul of his daughter, has, upon their arrival in Buenos Aires, sequestered her in a suburban mansion where she is surrounded by his loyal servants, and where no one sees her except for Mr. D——, who is her agent in the world of finances.

"But I have been extremely interested in Emma, ever since I read her verses and her biography there on the shores of the Rímac River. Happily, I have been able to prevail upon the gallant kindness of Mr. D——, and he has managed, on my behalf, to speak so eloquently in my favor, that, to my great joy, he has managed to arrange an exception to the usual prohibition, thus allowing me to visit Emma.

"Introduced by my protector, a tender friendship now unites me to the poetess of Entre Ríos. Emma weeps in my arms, lamenting the destiny that imprisons her far from the poetic rivers, far from the beloved forests of her native land, far from Buenos Aires, the ideal city of her dreams. And why? Because her father wants to bestow her upon a relative, a stranger to her, who will not know how to understand her ideas, her feelings, and to whom, nevertheless, she will have to give up her life."

"Never!" exclaimed Urbino.

"Better to die!" added Dr. P——.

"Thus entrusted with the most intimate emotions of that beautiful creature, I am pained by her sufferings and I have offered to do all I can to alleviate her anguish.

"'Ah,'" she sighs to me, 'what can we do against the inexorable? You, my friend, pity me. As for me, alas, I can only struggle, suffer, die. . . .'"

III

Carefully avoiding each other, the Colonel, the lawyer, and the poet visited me frequently, eagerly seeking news of the ideal being whose atmosphere they perceived in my rooms. They became more impassioned with each passing day.

Even I myself was so caught up in this beautiful fiction that it began to obsess me. But the songs sung in her honor and for love of her were short-lived. . . . My collaborator's sheer laziness killed off Emma Verdier, who would still be alive if I had not absented myself from Buenos Aires just at that time. And if it is true that illusion is happiness, then that most beautiful creation would have meant joy for many. . . .

How many illusions, like that one, have simply vanished into thin air? I would give some years of my life, even now that I must ration them with great care; yes, I would give up some of my own years if I could breathe life into that graceful creature we two old people invented so innocently, if I could see beautiful Emma Verdier smile and dance about in the real world.

Lo íntimo. Buenos Aires: Ramón Espasa, 1893, pp. 165–169.

NOTE

1. A poem by "Ema A. Berdier (Arjentina)" is included in the 1875 anthology of *Poetisas americanas: Ramillete poético del bello sexo hispano-americano,* compiled by José Domingo Cortés (Paris and Mexico: Librería de A. Bouret e hijo, pp. 179–184), an elegant blue and gold album that includes poems by many well-known women poets of Spanish America. In the poem, Ema Berdier says that she is submitting these verses at the request and insistence of her friend Bernabé Demaria. In the unsettled orthography of the era, it is not unusual that *Ema* and *Emma* are interchanged, or that *b* and *v* are substituted for one another. [Trans.]

Juana Manuela Gorriti

Chincha

To Mariano A. Pelliza

I was ill at that time, and suffering much discomfort, but far more tormenting than any physical pain was the revulsion occasioned by the offensive presence of the enemy, who was grinding my beloved Lima under his filthy boots.[1] I felt obliged to leave the city in order to be able to breathe, and I prepared to seek refuge in the verdant countryside some distance from town.

Nevertheless, I found myself most reluctant to leave the suffering city. I imagined that I could hear the voice of a dying friend, reproaching me for abandoning her to her executioners. I even wished I could separate myself from this group of companions with whom I was making a pact of voluntary exile. I had decided that I had to leave, but at the same time I yearned to stay on there, clinging to those sacred walls, awaiting pillage, demolition, and death.

I felt overwhelmed by this contradictory grief, and yet, amidst all the horrors of Lima, once we were actually in the carriage that would take us away, we were impatient to be off. The presence of the invaders made us eager for the moment when we could put space between ourselves and them.

Finally, we arrived at the port and, although we were still surrounded on all sides by those loathsome soldiers, we were able to embark. Flanking their fleet, which was anchored in the bay, we went aboard the steamship that would take us to Tambo de Mora, on the coast just a league from Chincha.

We departed.

Translated by Mary G. Berg

"Thank God!" chorused feminine voices, "we won't see any more of the enemy."

But, alas, just when we thought we were finally free of them, we looked up and what did we see, flying from the top of the main mast, but the repugnant banner in the name of which so many horrors had just been perpetrated.

When we saw that flag, the ladies' indignation was such that we all felt seasick. When he was informed of this, the captain, a brave and capable man who wished to please us, ordered the solitary star of Chile lowered and the friendly leopard of England displayed in its place. The passengers all applauded loudly.

II

When we awakened the next morning, we found ourselves at anchor just offshore the settlement of Tambo de Mora. Mercedes Cabello de Carbonera, my beloved traveling companion, came to find me in my cabin, and together we went up on deck to receive the captain of that strange port, which has no pier or wharf.

The personage who came to meet us was plump and ruddy-faced, and he eventually informed us, after elaborate flattery and ceremonious remarks, that he had orders from Mercedes' husband, a Chincha resident, to help us disembark and find transport to that town. This port captain seemed to take these instructions so seriously that he did not wish to permit my son to make any arrangements for us at all. He ordered his sailboat to tie up alongside the ladder of the steamship. Then he had all of our luggage shifted to it, and he asked Julio to precede us in disembarking, because—he said—it was his duty, and his alone, to conduct us to shore.

When all this had been done—in full view of all the passengers, of course, who were lined up along the railing, leaning over to watch this performance—the port captain gave a proud look around, climbed quickly down the ladder, and leaped into the sailboat with a flourish.

"What," asked Julio, "have you done with the ladies?"

"Oh, what a mind I have!" exclaimed the poor man. "Would you believe I forgot them completely?"

And in the midst of general laughter, he clambered up the rungs again, taking them four at a time; but this time he was followed by Julio, who feared he was either insane or drunk.

On this last point he was right: we realized it when he came over to us. He said a thousand polite things; he begged us to excuse his fit of distraction, ascribing it to an attack of the vertigo from which he occasionally suffered. He carried off Mercedes, got her into the sailboat, and made her sit by his side at the helm. Julio helped me to climb down the ladder.

The port captain immediately gave the order to cast off, and we started off toward the shore in a very rough sea, with the boat rocking from side to side. With my arms around my son, I felt safe. But my poor Mercedes trembled at the side of that odd gentleman who, insisting that he had been given his orders by her husband, refused to permit anyone else to come near her.

Suddenly an immense wave, crowned by a white crest of foam, roared down upon us and crashed into the sailboat, which began to rock like a nutshell and fill with water. Mercedes, perhaps out of fear (but I think it was to punish the captain for his drunkenness), grabbed hold of his necktie and hung onto it until he nearly drowned. Fortunately for the poor devil, that wave also managed to run the sailboat aground on the sandy beach.

We were safe at last.

Mercedes let go of her captive, and four black beach hands picked us up in their arms and deposited us at the door of the Customhouse.

III

The road from Tambo de Mora to the heights of Chincha follows a delicious succession of vineyards and orchards, set with half-hidden picturesque cottages inhabited by people who seemed so happy that Mercedes and I found it impossible to resist the temptation to imagine them as characters in a series of amorous idylls we made up. We were totally absorbed in this amusement until we arrived at the first streets of the town.

Chincha Alta is a large town where Mercedes' husband, a resident there for reasons of health, had his house and a prosperous pharmaceutical establishment. Dr. Carbonera, a distinguished physician, was considered the neighborhood oracle, and because of this very high regard in which he was held, his neighbors greeted us with great friendliness.

Dr. Carbonera had rented a precious furnished cottage for me, which seduced Mercedes as soon as she set eyes on it. It inspired her to desert her conjugal roof in order to come over and live with me; she was so charming about it that she managed to displace Julio, who went over to keep the abandoned husband company.

We sweetened the terms of this forced arrangement: we promised our two gentlemen the delights of an exquisite table, whose menu, selected alternately by the two ladies of the house, would leave nothing to be desired.

And we fulfilled our promise to everyone's great content. To keep too many cooks from spoiling the broth, and to avoid argument, we took turns being in charge each for a week at a time. And you can just imagine the great care that each of us took to keep up with the other, both in the order and spotlessness of the house and, above all, in culinary masterpieces.

Not wanting to limit ourselves to the resources of the local market, we rode our horses, followed by the manservant, equipped with big panniers on both sides of his steed's haunches. And so off we went to seek and buy, in the gardens and hamlets of the countryside, the best fruit, barnyard fowl, baby lambs, and choice vegetables, which, when transformed into exquisite dishes of modern cuisine, were much savored by our guests and helped Carbonera and Julio to forget that they were widower and orphan.

When Saturday came—the final day of each turn—after dinner had been served and we had had our coffee, we gathered around the table, while the retiring cook read her message and passed on the chair to her successor.

When we drew lots to see who would go first, I won, so the first week was mine, and at the end of it, I inaugurated the successive reign with the following

Message.

GENTLEMEN:

As the period dedicated to your service comes to an end, I have the honor of setting forth for your consideration the following summary of tasks executed during the course of this past week, and an indication of the extensive duties that will be attended to during this second week, when my honorable colleague will preside.

As the week began, I aspired to total perfection in all matters relating to our housekeeping venture, deeming this essential as a foundation for our culinary enterprise. This turned out to require a good deal of effort, since we are living in such a dusty place.

I soon noticed that, in order to save fuel, the Son of the Celestial Empire[2] was skimping on cooking time when he prepared foods. I have managed to take advantage of the moments when this exotic being has absented himself from the kitchen to fire up the stove again and thus serve up meals that are both piping hot and fully cooked.

In search of ways to modify recipes so that they would please all our tastes, my innovations have been to substitute parsley sauce for that disagreeable cheese, to dissolve bread crumbs in the custard cream—which imparted a delicious flavor—and in that same recipe, as well as in sunflower custard, to use aromatic orange juice instead of that indigestible vinegar.

I have changed the use of chopped vegetables in the standard stew recipe, replacing them with a selection of aromatic herbs that, when cooked with the meat, have given both the meat and the broth a wonderful flavor.

In my desire to extend the repertoire of our house specialties, I have tried to remember and recreate some of the better culinary experiences of my nomadic life. From the various different countries that offered me their hospitality in the past, I have selected the dishes I deemed most worthy of our discerning palates; and I have served you a very special stew made with six kinds of meat, squash blossom salad, cakes and biscuits baked on heated stones, and the famous beef dish of the native Pampa that is cooked in its own hide.

My mind is full of the most delicious recipes, which I have not yet had an opportunity to serve you because of the deplorable state of my health. For this same reason, I beg you to also forgive the lapses in the proper level of service, since I have not been able to supervise it properly.

My beautiful colleague, since you are young and enjoy the precious gift of good health, it is up to you to complete my work, and thus I now place in your lovely hands this symbol of life, the dining room key.[3] I am delighted by the happy prospect of your succession.

And here I conclude.

IV

What agreeable hours I spent in that quiet town, at the side of that woman endowed with all the virtues of heart and soul:

Mercedes Cabello de Carbonera.

As I have already mentioned, she is the daughter of a distinguished family, originally from Moquegua. She is one of the most remarkable and eminent women of Peru, distinguished for her beauty, intelligence, and erudition. Very early on in her life, she dedicated herself to her writing, and in this field she has shone, producing works of substantial merit that more than once, in literary competitions, have caused her beautiful brow to be adorned with the laurel wreath of success. Her articles appear regularly in many European periodicals, and just recently the newspaper *El Correo de Ultramar* adorned its columns with a fine novel of hers, *Hortensia's Love*.

Her writing combines feminine delicacy with such virile strength that once, when he heard her read, the poet Palma exclaimed, in the words of Gallegos, "This woman is quite a man!"

After a terrible interruption in her literary work—the death of her husband—Mercedes has now returned to her writing, endowing her new pages with yet one more attribute: the heart of a grieving widow!

At the time I am reminiscing about, she was happy; and we were so fully content with our joyfully shared lives that, like the disciples of the Transfiguration, we would have liked to set up our tents and live forever in that green paradise of Tabor.

But, alas, *tout passe, tout casse,* as the proverb says; and those radiant days slipped by quickly, as happens, on this earth, with all that is beautiful and good. . . .

El mundo de los recuerdos. Buenos Aires: Félix Lajouane, 1886, pp. 311–322.

NOTES

1. During the War of the Pacific, over twenty-two thousand Chilean soldiers landed in Peru in early 1881 to assure the conquest of Lima. The city was devastated, and during the Chilean occupation a great many of Lima's inhabitants fled. [Trans.]

2. I am referring to the Chinese cook by this name so that, if he is present, he will not be able to guess that I am speaking of him.

3. A huge corroded key, which I found in an old strongbox.

Soledad Acosta de Samper

Colombia, 1833–1913

The only child of a Scottish mother and a Colombian father who was a high-level Colombian statesman, Soledad Acosta de Samper had a childhood that included year-long stays in Quito and Washington, travels in eastern Canada, and a decade of schooling in France. She was born in 1833, and her early years coincided with what she here calls the "childhood" of the new republics of Spanish America. From the mid-nineteenth century on, she was a prominent participant in the struggles to claim a more equal place for women in the secular, postcolonial societies of the Americas, and particularly in her native Colombia. During her long literary career, Acosta wrote in every genre that existed in her time, from textbooks to newspaper reporting to drama. In a climate of prejudice against women writers, she became one of the first generation of Spanish American women to make a profession of writing. Her husband, the statesman and man of letters José Samper, publicly supported her literary career.

Much of Acosta's fictional writing is collected in *Novelas y cuadros de la vida sur-americana* (Novels and Sketches of South American Life), first published in Belgium in 1869. *Dolores, Teresa la limeña* (Teresa of Lima), and *El corazón de la mujer* (The Heart of Woman), all from this collection, are read today as particularly memorable explorations of women's struggles for self in unequal societies. Journalistic activity was a very important aspect of Acosta's life, and at times a lifesaving source of income. In Colombia, she wrote and published widely in newspapers and periodicals, founding and editing *La Mujer* (Woman, 1878–1881), a magazine produced exclusively by women. Later she founded periodicals titled *La Familia* (The Family) and *Lecturas para el Hogar* (Readings for the Home).

The essay translated in this volume appears in Acosta's book *La mujer en la sociedad moderna* (Woman in Modern Society), which was published in 1895 in Paris by Garnier. With a perspective that is deliberately encyclopedic and transnational, Acosta directs the work to teachers and parents of Spanish American girls, "whose education has been so neglected." The four-hundred-page volume documents the achievements of dozens of women of Europe and the Americas since the French Revolution, grouped under six categories: Social Benefactors, Missionaries, Moral Activists, Scientists, Politicians and Artists, and Women of Letters. This broad picture, she says, should enable young women to choose the career and life path that best suit them.

Interestingly enough, in her introduction to the volume Acosta adopts some stances rather different from those she takes in the essay translated here. While "Misión de la escritora en Hispano-América" (The Mission of the Woman Writer in Spanish America) stresses the gains that have been made for Spanish American women, the introduction declares women "still far from fulfilling the mission Providence intends for them." More striking is Acosta's passionate critique of marriage. While in this essay Acosta praises women writers for having been mistresses of their households while "scribbling in their idle hours," in her introduction she declares that one of her main aims is to show young women that marriage is not their "only mission in life" and "is not essential to women's happiness." In terms that resonate with contemporary feminist theory, Acosta argues that making marriage truly optional for women will invariably reform society because men will have to change their behavior to win respect, and wives.

Acosta's essay exemplifies many aspects of nineteenth-century middle-class feminism in the Americas. Like most American thinkers of the period, she subscribes optimistically to the paradigm of progress and to the notion that society in the New World is young and fresh in comparison with a decadent Europe. Like many of her contemporaries, she sees the United States as a model of material progress and social enlightenment. This attitude, shared with many Independence-era thinkers, was to change dramatically at the end of the century when the United States began asserting itself as an imperial power in Latin America. Like many nineteenth-century feminists, Acosta sees women's social mission, and their social power, as based in the sphere of morality, in the promotion of constructive values and conduct. Education lies at the center of her feminist concerns, while other issues such as economic justice or sexual liberation are absent. This educational focus is usually linked to a bourgeois perspective on gender that seeks greater equality but does not question the socio-economic order, and that maintains a repressive silence toward women's sensuality. By the end of the nineteenth century more radical feminist movements, notably the Argentine anarchists, were breaking these silences.

On the other hand, unlike more conservative feminists of her time, Acosta does not see women's role as centered on maternity and domesticity. In this essay she specifically proposes that women take up the very public task of founding a new Spanish American literature born out of the synthesis of truth, goodness, and beauty. By entwining the moral function of literature with the "moralizing" (one of her favorite words) powers of women, Acosta imagines, and demands, a central and public role for women in the drama of nation building that she is witnessing.

MARY LOUISE PRATT

The Mission of the Woman Writer in Spanish America

T he question that I propose—I will not say to elucidate, for I lack the strength to do so—but to touch in passing, is first of all this: what is the mission of woman in the world? Undoubtedly, to moderate customs, to promote morality and Christianity in societies—that is, to give them a civilization adequate to the needs of the time and, in the process, to prepare humanity for the future. But now let us ask another question: What is the mission of the woman writer in the New World?

Let us first examine what Mr. Varigny says in his volume on *Women in the United States*. "Every race," he writes,

> has formed its own ideal of what woman should be.
> Ideas, like languages, vary; let me explain my own
> thinking. For the *French*, woman personifies and incar-
> nates all the delicate and exquisite perfections of civi-
> lization; for the *Spaniard*, she is a virgin in a church; for
> the *Italian*, a flower in a garden; for the *Turk,* a device
> for pleasure [*mueble de dicha*]. Let us not forget the art-
> less complaint of the young Arab woman: "Before he
> was my husband he kissed the ground I walked on, and
> now he hitches me up with his ass to his plow and makes
> me work." The *Englishman*, precursor of the American,
> sees in woman above all the mother of his children
> and the mistress of his house. On leaving England, the
> women who went to live in North America did not

Translated by Mary Louise Pratt

leave their customs and traditions in Europe. All emigrants, rich or poor, carry a world with them, an invisible world of ideas, the result of their early upbringing,
the legacy of previous generations, things they never
leave behind even when they are leaving behind everything, things they reverently conserve.

Thus for North Americans the ideal is the same as for the English, though
in North America the woman is even more mistress of her house than in
England.

The Spanish American, more advanced in these matters than his Spanish ancestors, sees in woman something more than "a virgin in a church."
It has been observed that in all the republics formed after independence,
efforts have been made from the outset to give women a better education
and a broader role in social life. Governments have made great efforts to
redeem us from the lower status—let us say lowest rather than lower—to
which colonial customs condemned us daughters of the Spaniards.

In Colombia, for example, young women receive a fairly progressive
education at the normal school and afterward become primary school
teachers for both sexes. It has been observed that in primary education
they are greatly superior to male teachers in their level of learning, orderliness, conduct, and so on. In Bogota there is a Music Academy for girls
that has produced first-class teachers; in the past there was an Academy of
Drawing and Painting in which the female students achieved equally with
the young men. The School of Telegraphy, directed by a lady dedicated to
teaching this subject, has produced very talented employees who serve the
government in many national offices. The School of Medicine in Bogota
has admitted young women who attend classes and are highly respected
by the male students. A broader horizon is thus opening up for women's
aspirations in Colombia and in other Spanish American nations, as we
have seen elsewhere in this book. Soon it will come to pass in these republics as in North America that women's influence will be considered essential to the successful functioning of society.

Once woman has conquered the important position she now occupies
in Spanish American society, she must reflect on that position and recognize what is expected of the influence she will exercise in these new
countries, which now seem to be leaving behind the period of political
turbulence and conspiracy that obscured the social horizon of the new republics for more than eighty years. She must dedicate herself to work, to

a judicious unfolding of progress. We must reflect with maturity on the role women will play in the new order of things that is emerging.

These governments have concluded the period of ferment that, according to the laws of nature, is essential to produce *a nation* out of heterogeneous, distinct, and arbitrary elements. "I would compare," said Carnot (the father of the man who became president of France), "a revolutionary country to our great wine harvest barrels: in the vat of the passions everything stirs around from top to bottom, from the most generous of wines to the most disgusting sediments; but the fermentation purifies and ennobles the liquor."

From this time forward we will doubtless witness public upheavals, changes of government and perhaps of entire political systems, but our nations will be safe in the arms of civilization, whose laws will prevent them from falling behind on the paths of progress they now so knowingly traverse, and the governments will quickly reconstruct themselves on solid and respectable footing.

The United States, whose prosperity so astounds, should provide Spanish America with wholesome examples in this regard. And in that country, which finds itself ahead of all others in material advances, woman enjoys an immense and acknowledged influence. Why is this? Because she is respected by all. And why is she respected? Because her actions, her character, her moral courage make her respectable; because, besides fulfilling her duties as wife and mother, she is genuinely and positively the companion of man. She is not a flower, a dream, a toy, a decoration, a servant. She is the equal of her husband and her brother, through the soundness of her education, her noble strength of character, her spiritual gifts. Hence all careers are open to her, except one, the least desirable—that of politics. In North America, not only do women work as public employees, lawyers, doctors, farmers, bankers, and so on, but they also compete with men in these positions as equals. They are given nothing as a favor. They are praised only when they deserve it; they are given awards and positions of honor only because they are more entitled to hold them than any man. This is true justice, and we should aspire to it as well if we wish to exercise a genuinely positive influence on our fellow citizens. But to deserve this justice we must work seriously, renounce special treatment, demand strict justice and nothing more.

Among the nations of the Spanish race, women are still regarded as inferior beings, as children, and whenever they raise themselves slightly above mediocrity they are praised with embarrassing exaggeration. Nevertheless, we should reject certain kinds of adulation almost as an offense, for they confirm that so little was expected of us that anything we do involving learning or talent is alien to our sex and must be applauded as an uncommon rarity. Let us not pride ourselves, then, with passing praise that is soon gone with the wind, for it has no weight. Let us attend to the mission that we ourselves must undertake.

The moral redemption [*moralización*] of Spanish American societies, soured by a long series of revolutions, disorders, and bad governments, is undoubtedly in the hands of women whose influence, as mothers of the future generations, as teachers of the young in their early years, and as writers disseminating good ideas, will save society and set it forth on the right path.

But, it will be said, though there are women writers in Spanish America, in fact they are so few; and they rely so little on their intellectual faculties that they could not possibly have even the smallest influence on the workings of society. So it seems in fact, and yet there would be more women writers if they were less timid, if they convinced themselves that they have a beneficent mission to carry out—women of character always want to be useful, and they forget obstacles if they are convinced they have a chance to do good.

In Colombia at least, women are highly respected, and I trust that other South American republics will not, please God!, repeat the situation in Spain where, in the words of the renowned writer and diplomat Don Juan Valera, "any woman who tries to be a writer must be more courageous than the nun Alferez or even Pentesilea herself. . . . Every dandy she happens to meet," he adds, "will be an Achilles against her, more to kill her than to weep for her beauty after death. Leaving mythologies aside, I mean that in literature, women writers are looked upon like those odd older bachelors, somehow abnormal, disorderly, and improper, posing problems for the prospects of a good marriage, etc., etc."

No, among us in Spanish America, it is not like this, and a woman who writes for the press is not looked down upon in society. On the contrary, she is listened to and respected (unless she is being undermined out of envy). This respect must arise from the fact that our women poets have all been mistresses of their households as well. They have not neglected this role merely because in their idle hours they scribble on paper. Thus they have readily been permitted, and even encouraged, to write verse and prose, and they are praised highly by the press—too highly, as we said earlier, because such praise deludes the novices.

Once the career of writer is open and women can embrace it freely, all who feel called to it should focus on one thing: the good they can do with their pens. If God has given them intellectual capacities, let them use those abilities to push the cart of civilization in their own particular way. Let us not imitate the fashion today in foreign literatures, especially the French; let us depict not the vices of others but rather the virtues of our own homeland. Providence did not endow America with the riches of the most beautiful nature in the world in order for us to recoil from describing it; God has not put us in these new countries struggling to form themselves so that we will neglect their history and customs and the teachings to be distilled from them.

While the masculine side of society deals with politics, remakes laws, attends to material progress, and orders social life, would it not be truly great for the feminine side to undertake the creation of a new literature? A *sui generis* American literature, American in its descriptions, in its inclinations, doctrinaire, civilizing, artistic, beneficial to the soul; a literature so beautiful and so pure that its works could appear in all the salons of the countries where the language of Cervantes is spoken; a literature that could be placed in the hands of our daughters, that would elevate the ideas of whoever read it, that would instruct and at the same time display the newness and originality of the countries in which it was born. In this literature of our dreams would be found no descriptions of crimes or scenes depicting the wicked ways imported to our societies from the corrupt civilization of Europe. For whatever the modern writers might say, the novel should not simply be the exact description of what happens in real life among degenerate people; the novel can be interesting *despite* being moral. It should graphically depict human existence and at the same time the ideal, what should be, what men and women could be if they conducted themselves well.

What greater mission for a woman than conveying gratifying and heartwarming lessons to society? Take note that all the works that still hang from the branch of great literature not only possess moral grounding but also use an elegant, polished language that awakens only pure and beautiful images. The exceptions to this rule are few, and they confirm it.

Our countries are beginning to take shape. Like the sapling that can grow straight or crooked, we must see to it that our ways of life develop straight and well formed, and that we the women writers of the new South American world can present ourselves with the same distinction, the same healthy and altruistic vitality as our counterparts in North America.

In societies that have not only reached maturity but have begun to slide down the slope of decay, writers can stop along the way to pick the poisonous flowers, point out the swamps, describe the cesspools of vice they

encounter. There, one finds readers of all classes, and many whose intelligence, perverted by the excesses of civilization, requires a dish spiced with
descriptions ever more violently exaggerated and pictures that move their
sensibilities dulled by a refinement bordering on corruption. The ripest
fruit has already begun to rot. But our societies have not reached this
point. They are growing up, and they require an intellectual sustenance
that is healthy and hygienic. What a glory it would be for American women
if they could offer our incipient societies the literature they need to live
with their souls, after using their faculties to work for the material side of
our social and political institutions!

We do not believe that one morally educates readers by putting in front
of their eyes pictures of vice and corruption, even when afterwards one
intends to point out the drawbacks of those vices. Readers devour the
descriptions, their attention so absorbed they often forget the moral of
the story—but not the scenes of disorder and the bad examples—and care
little about the punishment of vice.

There exists a concern that the virtue and sacrifice of noble souls, the
adventures and happenstance of good people cannot make an interesting
plot, that only the arrows of love attract attention, provided they are sinful, that readers will enjoy only farfetched intrigues that offend modesty
and should not be read by girls. But this is a concern and nothing more.
The unified *truth* of an agreeable style will always be popular and last
longer than any narrative that addresses those false, inconstant, frivolous
passions that pass without a trace like fashions and are forgotten like the
cut of last year's dress. No. The women writers of America must dedicate
themselves seriously to making a lasting name for themselves, doing good
with literary works written to fulfill the mission that I believe they have in
the new Spanish American literature that is dawning.

La mujer en la sociedad moderna. Paris: Garnier, 1895, pp. 381–390.

Clorinda Matto de Turner

Peru, 1852–1909

Clorinda Matto was born and educated in Cusco, Peru.
As a schoolgirl, she wrote plays, poems, and essays, and
after her marriage to an English businessman, Joseph
Turner, who encouraged her literary efforts, her work
began to appear frequently in newspapers and magazines. In February 1876 she began to publish a weekly
magazine, *El Recreo*; the first issue included Matto's
short biography of Francisca Zubiaga de Gamarra,
which follows. It was reprinted immediately in a Lima
magazine, and Matto chose to include it in several collections of her essays. It is the first of over one hundred
biographies of varied lengths in which Matto examined
the attributes and circumstances that make some individual lives memorable. Matto was particularly fascinated by women's lives, and was a lifelong outspoken
advocate for women's rights and women's education.

The aspects of Francisca Zubiaga's life that most interest Matto are her subject's extraordinary capability
for leadership and her combination of masculine and
feminine qualities. Zubiaga is that rare person who not
only possesses both sets of attributes but is able to develop and exercise them both, thus becoming, in Matto's
view, a truly superior being.

Matto held that, while the historian's obligation is to
present an objective account of lives and events, the biographer's task is to select from these materials those

qualities and incidents that portray the person as exemplary, worthy of our attention and admiration. She is much more interested in the beginning and end of Zubiaga's life than she is in its middle part, when Zubiaga was the conspicuous wife of a controversial president of Peru. Matto's analysis thus focuses on how her subject developed into a woman of power, and in her final ability to confront mortality with grace and courage.

During the 1880s and 1890s, Matto became prominent in many capacities: as editor of newspapers and magazines; as author of three novels, including her best known, *Aves sin nido* (1889; *Birds without a Nest*, 1904); as author of many collections of historical sketches, biographies, and essays; as a playwright; and as an increasingly controversial champion of rights for women and Indians, anticlericalism, and the exposure of institutionalized corruption. In 1895 Matto was excommunicated from the Catholic Church; burned in effigy; compelled to resign as editor of the journal *El Perú Ilustrado*; and forced to leave Peru after her feminist printing shop was smashed by mobs.

She settled in Buenos Aires, where she became involved in women's education, both as a teacher and as a prolific essayist. There she founded the bimonthly review *El Búcaro Americano* and was frequently invited to address groups interested in progress for women. One of these occasions was her 1904 lecture to the National Council of Women of the Argentine Republic, "The Woman Worker and the Woman," on the subject of labor unions, the rights and duties of women workers, and how the upper-class city ladies (to whom Matto's remarks are addressed) might relate themselves to their working sisters. Matto approved of protective laws for women and believed in the existence of profound physical, intellectual, and moral differences between men and women, yet she came out vehemently in favor of equal pay for equal work. Matto urged all women to fight for better lives but to be insistent in productive and peaceful ways rather than be seduced by a facile rhetoric of violence. Underlying her whole optimistic speech about the marvels of progress is a conviction that the future well-being of America should and must be entrusted to the competent hands (and minds and hearts) of women, for only thus will equality, justice, and harmony prevail.

In her lifelong crusade for the betterment of women's lives, Matto saw no reason why women should not have it all: the best of both male and female attributes (as in her example of Francisca Zubiaga), the best of both liberal and conservative reform endeavors, and ultimately both domestic harmony and political power.

MARY G. BERG

Francisca Zubiaga de Gamarra

To my second mother, Mrs. Juana Manuela Gorriti

Illustrious women are attracted to each other; hence I set forth
your glorious name at the head of this essay, which, despite its
imperfections, is meaningful to you and to your adoptive daughter.

C. M. DE T.

I

Since one of the goals of journalism is to immortalize the names
of those worthy of celebrity, I have chosen to dedicate my first efforts, however imperfect, to the memory of Mrs. Francisca Zubiaga
de Gamarra. In this I am motivated by the desire that the name and life
story of this illustrious Cusco resident should not be lost in the dark mists
of time.

I fear that my pen is not skilled enough to do justice to this singular and
most admirable woman, especially given this publication's restrictions on
column length that limit the ample discussion I would desire. The biographical narrative of my subject's life is thus a task far beyond my abilities, and I will leave this endeavor to another's more able pen, limiting
myself here to the honor of providing a mere introduction. I will just try
to set down a few historical details that may eventually serve for Mrs. Zubiaga's biography, a work long desired by Cusco residents but unfortunately not yet undertaken by anyone.

If the facts I present here are not chronologically precise, it is because
they have fallen prey to the all-obliterating sweep of time, and there are
no longer very many people still alive who can speak definitively of the
wife of Don Augusto Gamarra, Generalísimo of the Sea and of the Earth.

Translated by Mary G. Berg and Elena C. Berg

Our heroine owed her existence to the honorable gentleman Don Antonio Zubiaga, a native of Güipuzcoa, in the Basque country of Spain, who was employed by the royal government in the area of finance, and to his wife, Doña Antonia Bernales de Zubiaga, a native of Cusco and a descendent of a family long established in that monumental city.

Mr. Zubiaga and his wife were undertaking a journey when she unexpectedly felt the first symptoms of labor just as they had arrived at the place called Huacaray or Anchibamba, in the San Salvador district of Oropeza, some five leagues from the city of Cusco. Thus it happened that it was right there, sometime in 1802 or 1803, that Doña Antonia gave birth to a beautiful girl who was baptized in Oropeza with the name of Francisca. Her godfather was Don Juan Pascual Laza, one of Mr. Zubiaga's compatriots, a man Doña Francisca always esteemed and considered as a father.

Doña Francisca's first years were spent in the city of Cusco, but when her father's government job caused him to be transferred to Lima, his family accompanied him. Doña Francisca and her sisters received an excellent education in Lima, the best that was available to women in those days. Right from the very beginning, she demonstrated a sharp and vigorous intelligence and an aggressively courageous personality: she always preferred boys' sports and games.

Her alabaster complexion, her deep brown eyes, her lively and penetrating gaze, her slightly turned-up nose, her small mouth, her abundant silky hair, blonde enough to show that it had been golden when she was a child, her height and the extreme gracefulness of her speech and gestures made Doña Francisca an unusually intriguing and beautiful woman. Her face was round, her figure robust and vigorous yet slim, and she possessed a deep voice and masculine mannerisms. She rode a horse with elegance and consummate skill; she was a good shot with a pistol and an admirable swimmer. She found the companionship of other women generally irritating and always preferred the company of men, but when she did meet a woman she deemed worthy of her friendship, she was a most devoted and true friend. She had a very pronounced Lima accent, and one of her favorite entertainments was cock fighting; in Cusco she liked to go to the cock fights and bet heavily.

Colonel Agustín Gamarra met Francisca Zubiaga after the death of his first wife, Doña Juana Manuela Alvarado, who came from Jujuy. Gamarra was much impressed with Francisca Zubiaga's beauty, and especially with her virile personality and obvious intelligence. Their betrothal took place in Lima, shortly before the battle of Ayacucho.

After this famous clash of arms that permanently sundered the oppressive chains that held us in bondage to the Spanish Crown, General Gamarra was the first patriot leader to occupy the capital city of Cusco, which welcomed him with a sumptuous reception. Immediately upon being named prefect of this regional department, he notified Doña Francisca, who had been living in Lima, and she set out on the journey overland. Eager for news of her progress, he set out to meet her, traveling down to the Apurímac River. In the town of Zurite (in the province of Anta), Don Agustín and Doña Francisca spoke their marriage vows and received the nuptial benediction. The entire city of Cusco celebrated the union of these illustrious Cusco citizens and manifested great joy at such a splendid match.

The town of Urubamba (now a city) invited the new prefect and his wife to spend a few days of leisure in that delicious province that can well be called the garden of Cusco. Among the many celebrations the inhabitants organized were some bullfights that made great show of the town's wealth.

Because the regular army garrison there was small, the national guardsmen of Urubamba were called upon to participate in a spritely demonstration drill as part of the festivities. At the end of their performance, they used gold and silver coins in place of the traditional flowers, evoking cheers and applause for the liveliness of their performance.

When the bullfight was over, Mrs. Zubiaga summoned the captain who had been in charge of the brilliant demonstration, and she was delighted to discover that he was a young officer who would distinguish himself in the military for his gallant bearing, intelligence, and understanding of all military matters. The young man's name was Mariano La Torre and, despite the objections of his aged father, he was named a lieutenant in Colonel Frías' regiment. He would later become famous as the brave cavalry leader Colonel Mariano La Torre, victim of those who prevailed at Yanacocha, shot by Cerdeña in the town of San Sebastián despite being a prisoner of war.[1]

This example shows that Mrs. Zubiaga possessed the perceptiveness and discernment to single out the men of genuine merit, just as she was endowed with an extraordinary ability to explain her opinions concisely.

When the visit of the Liberator Don Simón Bolívar was announced in Cusco, everyone was excited and enthusiastic, particularly the women of the town, who prepared a diamond-studded crown to offer as homage to this most valiant soldier. Doña Francisca was named to preside over a committee composed of beautiful young women charged with greeting Bolívar and presenting him with the valuable gift from these Daughters of the Sun.

At the entrance to Cusco they constructed triumphal arches and a platform where Bolívar would receive the greatest possible ovations from a town that knew how to reward noble feats and esteem the valor of those who so courageously fought for the sainted cause of liberty.

Mrs. Zubiaga greeted Bolívar with a patriotic speech and placed the crown upon his head. It slipped down onto his shoulders, since, not knowing Don Simón's head size, they had asked the goldsmith to make it large. This fortunate warrior, who pulled a large part of South America out from under the yoke of Spain, accepted the gift with gracious acknowledgments of gratitude. After thanking the patriotic society of the ancient capital of the Incas, he took off the crown in order to present it to the most beautiful of the Cusco ladies present, who was indisputably Doña Francisca.

As a mother, Mrs. Zubiaga was a true woman, for she always showed affection and concern for her children although they all died in infancy. As a wife she must have been both dutiful and loving, since she was constantly present and accompanied her husband on various military missions, managing on the campaign trail like any other soldier and sharing equally in all the fatigue and privation of military life.

The occasion when Mrs. Zubiaga completely revealed both her warrior's personality and the noble and exceptional attributes of her woman's heart was in the campaign in Alto Perú (Bolivia) in 1828. She accompanied her husband and traversed that entire republic with the Peruvian army. She was separated from Gamarra only when she went to Argentina to look for her stepson Andrés, her husband's son from his first marriage. Doña Francisca loved this young man, who is today Colonel Gamarra, like a true mother, once again demonstrating the nobility and magnanimity of her heart.

Upon her return from Argentina, she took charge of a battalion, and with her escort squadron of twenty-five lancers led by a Captain Navarrete (alias El Colorado)[2] she personally captured the main plaza of Paria. With her advice and acute political skills, she was largely responsible for the defeat of the Bolivian army in its encounter with our own forces in Piquiza, after which victory her husband was proclaimed Grand Marshal by the Peruvian army.

When she returned to Peru, she stopped in Lima and went right on to Cusco because she was so eager to get back to the beloved country of her birth. This would be the last time her feet would touch her native soil.

While she was in Cusco, an infantry battalion rose up in revolt against her. In her impatience to know what was happening, she disguised herself as a man, asked for a saddled horse, and, wrapped up in a military cape, marched straight into the revolutionary barracks; once inside, she uncovered her face and called out to the soldiers: "Boys, are you against me?"[3] to which the rebels replied with a rousing "Long live our leader!" The revolt ended right then and there, and Zubiaga strode out, tossing the soldiers a few fistfuls of silver coins.

During the disagreement between Peru and Bolivia in 1833, Grand Marshal Gamarra was obliged to leave the Peruvian capital and station himself on the Bolivian border. Meanwhile Doña Francisca was informed that General La Fuente was revealing his opposition to Gamarra by refusing to supply the reinforcement troops he needed. As a wife who was vigilant of her husband's best interests, and as a remarkable patriot who was willing to sacrifice herself for the national good, she took it upon herself to arrest La Fuente and deprive him of all the authority he had assumed; she did this, and when she informed her husband, she received his approval and gratitude.

A short time later (on 3 January 1834), a revolt broke out against General Bermúdez, whom Gamarra had caused to be elected president.[4] Doña Francisca took command of the few loyal troops that remained, and left Lima on horseback, brandishing a pistol in her fist and opening a passageway through a mob stirred into rebellion and protest in favor of Orbegoso. Since Orbegoso had already taken over the fortresses of Callao and reinforced them, and since Zubiaga knew that she lacked sufficient troops to retake the fortresses by force, she ordered a countermarch along the road toward the mountains in the direction of Jauja, taking along a division composed of two battalions and a cavalry squadron. The battalions were commanded by Colonel Zubiaga, Doña Francisca's brother, and Colonel Guillén, who years later would be killed in a revolt in Ayacucho. Captain Manuel Ignacio Vivanco, who later became a general, commanded one of the infantry companies, and Navarrete led the cavalry escort guard. General Antonio Elizalde accompanied Mrs. Zubiaga in this retreat, which took place at midnight.

While Mrs. Zubiaga was occupied in preparations for the defense she planned to make, she received the news that Gamarra had returned from his expedition to the North. She ordered her troops to turn around (in accord with a plan discussed previously, no doubt), and together they re-occupied the capital, which put up no resistance to this modern Nino and Semiramis, if we may be allowed this comparison. They subsequently both headed toward the city of Cusco.

Later during this same year (1834), Mrs. Zubiaga was in Arequipa during an outbreak of political demonstrations led by Lobatón in favor of Orbegoso. After the battles fought by the San Román Division on 2 and 5 April in Miraflores and Cangallo, in which General Nieto was defeated, Gamarra left for Tacna in pursuit of the vanquished leader. The assembled mobs dispersed the "Pultunchara" battalion, which had been charged with keeping order in the city, and attacked the house of Mr. Gamio, where Mrs. Zubiaga was staying. Since she did not have any troops under her command that she could use to repel her enemies, she had to resort to flight. On this occasion, she made a great leap from the roof of the house down into the back courtyard of the adjoining house, where by the grace of Providence she found a hat and a clergyman's cape, put them on, and went out into the street against the advice and even supplications of the house owners. She sought asylum in the house across the street and from there she watched, with the greatest composure, while the house she had been in was attacked and the mob searched for her in order to put her to death. During the night she moved to the house of other friends, and just after that, disguised as a man, she proceeded toward the coast in order to reach a port. She eventually embarked in Islay on a ship sailing for Valparaiso.

Even this summary account should serve to adequately demonstrate the warrior's character and the depth of soul and profound intelligence with which Nature endowed Mrs. Francisca Zubiaga de Gamarra.

This extraordinary woman is most outstanding for the lively interest she took in the army, doing her utmost to procure the best possible provisions for them. She spent many nights keeping watch over the sick and wounded, caring for them with true Christian charity. Even on the battlefields themselves, she was always first to provide an example of courage and to fulfill the duties of the Daughters of Saint Vincent de Paul.

III

The marriage of Don Agustín Gamarra and Doña Francisca Zubiaga, which was so celebrated when it occurred and which was sustained for some happy years, was broken off completely in 1834 for reasons we do not wish to discuss, since we do not believe ourselves privileged to penetrate the sacred zone of private life and since when we speak of those who have already been judged by God, we should not disturb the gravestones beneath which they are buried. Such matters may perhaps be more appropriately discussed by her biographer.

The internal injuries sustained by Mrs. Zubiaga during her escape from Arequipa, when she leapt from the roof, brought an end to her precious existence at the early age of thirty-three or thirty-four.

Quillota, a city twelve leagues from Valparaiso, a place famous for its picturesque vegetation and much favored by convalescents because of its mild climate, was the location recommended by the doctors for the restoration of the illustrious invalid's health; but unfortunately the climate did not have its anticipated effect and she had to return to Valparaiso.

Grand Marshal La Fuente—according to Colonel Andrés Gamarra— assigned her a doctor from a battleship that had just anchored at that port. The doctor examined her with great care, and his opinion was that her life would soon come to an end. This is what transpired, and this admirable woman from Cusco died at dawn on 5 May 1835. Her final disposition of her property was as remarkable as her life.

IV

She called her doctor to her and said, "Doctor, I believe that my affliction is without remedy and that I am moving quickly toward my final moments of life. You, like all the other doctors, attempt to hide the truth from me, undoubtedly believing that you will distress me with the news of my impending end. But such an assumption is misguided; I have often come face to face with death during my passage through this world; I know that I was born mortal and that, like every other human creature, my turn will come to pay this tribute to Nature. So, with that said, Doctor, how many more days do you expect me to live? Please tell me frankly."

The doctor stammered a few excuses, but thus cornered, he was forced to tell her the truth, assuring her that she could only expect to live for a few more days.

The news did not in the least alarm Doña Francisca; on the contrary, she thanked the doctor. That same day she called two other medical specialists to her, and after serenely hearing their unanimous opinions, she begged that they say nothing to her servants, and she proceeded to make her spiritual preparations.

She made her confession, and said to her confessor, "Have the viaticum brought to me simply and without fanfare, for I am now a poor penitent and not the *presidenta* of Peru."

After receiving the Eucharist with exemplary devotion, she demonstrated the greatest possible tranquillity and even joy in front of her servants, in order to avoid those sad moments that precede the eternal separation. On the evening before her last day, she ordered that no one should enter her bedroom because she needed to rest by herself until the afternoon of the following day, without having anyone disturb her.

Those who attended her acquiesced uneasily with this willful order. Alone, Mrs. Zubiaga managed to change her clothing completely; she put on a pure white dress, combed and arranged her beautiful hair, perfumed her bedroom, and left a brief final testament upon her bedside table in which she declared that never—despite the prominence of her position, achieved by so few women, nor during the course of her extraordinary accomplishments—had she for a moment denied or deviated from the holy religion in which her parents had raised her. Among her other final stipulations was an order that her heart should be cut out and sent to Peru, to her husband, if he were still living; and that in case he had died, since she recognized that a life committed to military action was more precarious than that of other professions, her heart should be given to her uncle on her mother's side, Don Pedro P. Bernales, dean of the Cusco Cathedral. She requested that her few jewels be distributed among her servants, etc.

Having resolved all the matters she considered important, this illustrious daughter of Cusco, Doña Francisca Zubiaga de Gamarra, lay back gracefully upon her divan and entered into eternal rest, bequeathing to her country an honorable memory, and to posterity, an example worthy of the highest praise.

v

Mrs. Zubiaga's final legacies and wishes were carried out with religious punctiliousness. Her heart, which was surprisingly large, was preserved in alcohol, carried to Cusco by Major Luis La Puerta, today a general, and publicly exhibited in 1841 in the memorial pavilion constructed for the funeral ceremonies of the Generalísimo of the Sea and of the Earth, Don Agustín Gamarra.

After the death of the distinguished dean Dr. Bernales, Mrs. Zubiaga's heart was deposited in the Convent of Saint Teresa here in Cusco, but unfortunately this treasured relic may no longer be found there, for they did not know how to esteem it or preserve it.

El Recreo (Cusco) 1 (8 February 1876): 2–4.

NOTES

1. This leader was the father of Don Benigno La Torre and of Colonel José La Torre.

2. It is not certain that Navarrete was the captain, but this is generally believed to be so.

3. "Cholos ustedes contra mí": these words, as well as the response "¡Viva nuestra patrona!" are verified as authentic.

4. Gamarra was named president of Peru (with La Fuente as his vice-president) by Congress on 1 September 1829 for a four-year term, which he fulfilled. During these four years, Francisca Zubiaga's presence (some say despotism) was much felt. Many said she ruled the country as a monarch. At the end of Gamarra's term of office, General Luis de Orbegoso was elected to succeed him. Unwilling to relinquish power, the Gamarras insisted that their own candidate, General Pedro Pablo Bermúdez, be elected. A four-month civil war restored Orbegoso to power. Matto's omissions in the telling of this story are interesting. Abraham Valdelomar's 1914 biography of Doña Pancha (always referred to by Matto as Doña Francisca), *La Mariscala*, included in volume 2 of his *Obras* (Lima: Ediciones Edubanco, 1988, pp. 11–63), provides a more controversial portrait. [Trans.]

The Woman Worker
and the Woman

*To His Excellency the Minister of Justice and Public
Education, Doctor Joaquín V. González, author of
the Labor Law*

LADIES:

Since I have no wish to bore this intelligent audience, I will not embark here upon an extensive analysis of the many definitions of that
ominous word "strike," and of what this term has come to signify
within modern society. I would like instead to remark briefly upon a series of issues and to discuss some examples that will be familiar and vivid
to every woman who works for the cause of women under the slogan
"Not for Herself Alone but for Humanity," which the National Council
for Women of the Argentine Republic has engraved on the hearts of its
members just as it prints it on its propaganda flyers.

Many are the authoritative voices that have shared the wealth of their
wise thoughts through newspapers, magazines, lectures, and books intended to inform working women. They have investigated various topics,
sought ways to improve conditions, and proposed plans of action designed
to accelerate the improvement of present conditions through increases in
salaries and better hygiene in factories where women work. The women
who have spoken out include those who are about to give birth, those
who are breastfeeding the workers of tomorrow, those who are virgins
and in danger of premature moral deflowering, and those who are desti-
tute widows: almost all of these are women who have been bestialized by
ignorance and deprived of their ideals and hopes!

Translated by Mary G. Berg and Elena C. Berg

It is only honest to admit that these examples suggest a much darker picture than truth would demand, because the situation of the working woman in America, especially in Buenos Aires, is less grievous than in Europe. In fact, if our society were not so disgracefully obsessed with imitating Europe and were more intent on following its own common sense, and if the news that reaches us by telegraph were not so provocative, it is quite possible that we would not yet have witnessed the phenomenon of strikes here. Those who have actually visited the European centers in order to study the social structure of towns and workers' conditions can testify to us that salaries, housing, food, and general living conditions of European workers are inferior, far inferior, to those in America.

There, the worker receives a very low salary, can afford to eat meat on only two or three special days of the year, and lives in cramped quarters. If he is a farmer, he tills the land in order to give the landowner the best of the harvest, able to keep for himself only what is left over, and he dresses in the roughest of cloth. Hence those who come to hear something about this New World get so enthusiastic that they hurry to emigrate to this Promised Land where their hopes are fulfilled: from the moment they disembark at their port of entry here, they are welcomed as ladies and gentlemen, and they find that everything is set up for the beneficial transformation of their lives. If they want to work, work is available that is appropriate to their skills and abilities, and government assistance is readily available to them through the Department of Immigration. Farmers rejoice at the prospect of vast expanses of Argentine soil with all of its varied crops, where everything the farmers harvest or earn belongs to them, to them alone, and does not have to be shared with anyone else. Our fraternal republic offers them equality before the law, and the sublime energies of philanthropy, the soul of which is woman, open the doors of asylums to those who meet with misfortune.

Evidence of the well-being of honest workers who love order and hard work may be seen on every public sidewalk and in the public schools attended by their children; all the children are well cared for and if in some of the poorer neighborhoods we do see occasional ragged children, it is because there are problems there that are real exceptions to the general rule we are discussing: matters of dubious parentage, lazy people who are dissatisfied but do not choose to work, or that ridiculous type of men who live off women.

Very well then. If, as Spencer sustains, a society is an organism whose development and growth depend upon the components that constitute it, then our workers' society is very well established and so can generate other organisms or perfect those that are undeveloped or weak, like pale sapless plants that have sprouted in the dark and cannot be expected to contribute much to national progress. Only yesterday, ladies, it was said that all greatness distances itself from the common crowds: the eagle seeks heights and the thinker isolates himself in his garret; but today, in this age of new technology, when it is man himself who controls light through his understanding of electricity, the eagle flies from the peaks into the hands of men, and the thinker mingles with the populace, hearts draw nearer, and physical force and intellectual power, in intimate fusion, turn the great wheel of human progress. Strikes are perturbations that only momentarily interrupt the forward motion of that great wheel, without providing any positive benefit for anyone.

This disagreeable subject has been studied at length by men of such moral probity as Dr. Eduardo Dato, a former Spanish government minister and author of laws protecting workers; José Canalejas y Méndez, president of the Academy of Jurisprudence and Legislation; José Gascón y Marín; and others who are no less eminent. They describe grievous situations that have resulted from conflict of interest between owners and workers. However, these clashes, which embitter and intensify the struggle between capital and labor, are rare in this country, as rare as many of the social vices that are unknown in the homes of our pure young workers. The aforementioned Mr. Canalejas tells us of the many different factors that contribute to the gravity of these struggles. It will suffice to recall that once the worker has stopped being a *slave and servant* and has become a *free individual*, which represents undeniable progress, he continues to be a salaried proletarian. That is to say, he lives in conditions that are more conspicuously inferior than ever when he is aware of the contrast between his situation and that of the few men or groups of men who have been privileged by fortune and who have accumulated enormous wealth. This extreme inequality does not exist among us, for in Argentina we are all free in the most ample definition of the word "liberty." Our republican government consecrates equality as state law, and the precepts of Jesus Christ, teacher of true and pure socialism, are established as fundamental. Our basic law is that *All good that stems from evil is reprehensible.*

It is true as Mr. Dato affirms, with respect to Bilbao society, that the most popular movement, both here and in Spain, is a socialism that has been adulterated by subsequent theories, such as those of the evolutionists. Although utopian concepts such as total equality of social classes, work-sharing by everyone, and collective property would undoubtedly lead to general chaos if they were ever put into practice, these are still the dreams that seduce many workers. Without stopping to realize that differences between classes will always exist, without taking into account that social inequalities are as immutable as the laws of physics, imposed by God upon Humanity, and without noticing that we all have different abilities, that some of us are more virtuous or more beautiful than others, that we do not all share the same feelings, and that some of us are blonds while others are brunettes, these misguided workers give themselves up to unfulfillable promises and put themselves right into the hands of agitators who seek a political end or personal notoriety, often without any sense of civic responsibility.

In our view, the worker is the most respectable element of our society because it is he who carries the banner of progress and he who is the priest of the sublime religion of work in whose temple the joy of life is born.

A sharing of all labor! Who would direct it? Who would have to do the unhealthy and dangerous jobs? What difference would there be between intellectual and mechanical labor? Who would decide the salaries? How would we take into account the needs of each man, whether single or married, with or without a family? What would we do about the vagrant, the criminal, the dull-witted? The mind must ponder these profound and complex matters!

No! The honest worker, conscious of his acts, does not wish for collectivism. He will accept Christian socialism when it is likely to improve his condition and bring him happiness, but he knows perfectly well that a glowing utopian future is an illusion. When he recognizes liberty stemming from legal right, he must say to himself, "I have the freedom to decide whether to work or not, but I do not have the right to deprive others of their freedom to work." And following from this is the whole code of the perfectibility of relationships between all the men of the world. *Do unto others as you would have others do unto you.*

At the level of civilization we have reached, there is no reason to impose a sacrifice on anyone; it is more a question of insisting upon equality in decision-making procedures on the part of both owners and workers.

Does the owner wish that the worker not squander time or money? Well then, he should not cheat the worker. . . . Does he demand equality and justice for himself? Well then, he should want that same equality and justice for the laborers, without changing its terms. Those who became enemies in a time of egotism and inhumanity will become friends today and live together in the fraternal city of light, where there are no blizzards that paralyze the generous impulses of the spirit beneath the ice of positivism.

Until now, we have focused on the statements of others regarding strikes in general. Having established that the merit of man should be measured by the good he does to his fellow men, it is now time for us to move on to discuss the main topic of this speech, the woman worker. We could certainly say that she regards matters of social equality from a rather different point of view than do men, for her natural talents and observations have focused upon her sewing machine, and she dedicates her energies to the perfection of her assigned tasks, to the precise completion of the garments she sews. When they have been observed in large factories, women have proved extraordinarily capable of making the fine adjustments of bobbins and shuttles that produce perfect results.

Women, then, with their ability to make quick assessments and their perceptive feminine intuition stemming from their close attunement to domestic matters, understand the delicacy and importance of labor negotiations, and thus the woman worker, honest and thoughtful, does not go on strike.

For the same reasons, she will dissuade her husband and her children from participating, because she knows what a week without work means for her family, and she knows from experience not to place her trust in collective promises. She knows that strikes that influence the industrial world endanger the worker more than anyone else: the lost wages are never recovered, the vices her husband acquires during his days of being laid off stay with him, and when the strikers have triumphed, it usually means that the factories will close, thus reducing them to poverty. There will be less employment, fewer places to work, and . . . children who cry for bread!

Our sisters, the women who work, are mistrustful of the women who urge them along the path of disorder. Our working sisters are guided by their instinct for maintaining domestic harmony, a harmony that is the immediate result of uninterrupted labor. It is urgent that we who work with these women should draw closer to them in order to be able to convince them that to be both skilled and employed is to be happy. Our propaganda should have as its object, then, that the woman worker should love her work, orderliness, and domestic economy, without being ignorant that all living beings drag the same chains of suffering and march on toward the same unknown finality of death.

The doctrine of evolution, which is the synthesis of the Spencerian system I have just mentioned, must surely bring incalculable advantages to the cause of the *individual woman* [*la mujer persona*] without violating the boundaries of reason by suggesting a ridiculous absolute equality between men and women, for there are biological differences impossible to ignore.

To reduce this to its simplest terms: how can a man be a mother?

But we should remember, too, that both men and women are made up of spirit and physical matter, are one with infinite creation, and are nurtured by woman's milk.

This is the propitious moment, when those of us who have upheld the cause of protectionism for women must act. We must move on to further achievements and not allow ourselves to be intimidated by our egotistic detractors' derision of our cause. We must remember the initial struggles of all the great movements and all the great causes that have contributed to human progress, and this solidarity will uplift our spirits.

When Stephenson utilized Fulton's discovery of the uses of steam in order to make railroad engines run, what did the skeptics say? That it was surely the work of the devil, one of those heretical inventions that threatens the faith of simple folk. But those instigators of universal progress did not give up so easily, and within a half century, we saw that progress was taking hold, like Galileo's view of the earth, gradually establishing itself as irrefutable. The locomotive triumphant, the iron monster taking over the surface of the earth: the plains, the peaks, and all the spaces in between. We have come to accept this pandemonium on wheels, this metallic microcosm, this harbinger of civilization in every country. To this serpent without coloring or scales, the miles are its steps, and the different countries its flights and stages. Its brow is horned like the unicorn and all the forms of terrestrial animality are fused in it, as Jaime Puig y Verdaguer said: it roars like a lion, bellows like a bull, twists around curves like a snake and forges ahead like a dragon.

Lion, bull, snake, and dragon, it charges along, racing, rushing, roaring, and obliterating inertia and all the immovable forces of the earth, in order to wake them to the life of work.

Many tons of coal are its daily nourishment, its boiler is its belly and the flames its heart; the steam is its blood, the wheels its muscles; it harbors safety in its breast, where men of all latitudes take refuge, to be transported across the miles, crossing mountains and cities congealed in the soot of time, amidst great stone boulders that will soon be transformed into arches, columns, and pillars that will support temples of art, science, and peace built by the efforts of the laborer and by the daring of the capitalist.

Yes, they must ever be coupled, in harmonious unity, and just as the steel giant has forged ahead, so, too, will the cause of the working woman gain more adherents with the passage of time. The growing strength of the movement for the betterment of working conditions for women is grounded in recognition of the virtue of freely chosen work, for the only free individual is the one who is self-sufficient. The sun of hope is rising in the east smiling at the woman worker as she takes over the world. Everywhere, she works with faith: in schools, workshops, academies, factories, offices, businesses, writing, teaching, and journalism. This purposeful effort results in the immediate reduction of delinquency and criminal activity.

In our research about women and crime, we have gathered the following statistics: of a hundred criminal cases, seventy-eight were motivated by love, twenty by greed, twenty by pathological or hereditary causes, and two by other factors. Studies of women criminals indicate that there are very few working women in their numbers. In many of the studied cases, poverty and abandonment by a man figure as causes of women's crime, especially when neglect or abuse of children is involved. Even when she is not at fault, it is the woman who is labeled as dishonored by separation from her spouse, one of those "conventional lies" discussed by Max Nordau.[1]

Let me repeat that we are now at an opportune moment, and that we should spare no effort to put the growing current of positive progress on the right track, serving the woman worker ever more effectively as we become better acquainted with her. We do not wish to exalt her fantasy with utopias that will disappoint her, nor to turn her head with unwholesome prospects, but rather to make her love her work, showing her that she need envy no one, not even the high born nor the so-called wealthy, many of whom yearn for a restorative night's sleep, a good appetite, simple pleasures, and sound health.

Once we have examined the differences that exist between the American woman worker and the European, it is clear that the former has all the advantages over the latter. Let us awaken in her heart a fraternal love without continental boundaries, demonstrating with deeds that a strong chain, its links forged together by honor, interconnects good women from every part of the globe. In any case, the woman worker already knows that she should not participate in disastrous strikes nor have anything to do with boycotts or blacklists, for she has already learned from her own experience that "when the wheels are kept turning, busy hands are kept earning." She knows something more, ladies, that when she is putting bread on the table at home, her family is happy and the goddess of harmony presides over spouses who are united by the bonds of love, bonds that are less likely to sunder in modest homes than in sumptuous mansions where the golden glitter dazzles us but where unknown problems underlie the shining surface.

Let us take care to provide education and guidance for women workers, for they are the precious antidote we are able to offer mankind to counteract the poison of social perturbations. Thus may truly civilized behavior prevail in the workplace.

We must admire the astronaut who adventures through space in his dirigible. We must applaud the engineer who constructs railroads on the surface and deep under the earth. And we must encourage the founder of factories, asking him for both equity and justice for workers, and appealing to him to turn over the future well-being of the young American nations to the well established efforts of women.

Let us remind the woman worker that she has no reason to covet diamond diadems when her perspiring brow is encircled by the halo of holy work and of the sublime and universal law. It is our job to provide effective support for the working woman, our sister. Let us "comfort vacillating spirits and troubled hearts." Let us extend the field of action; let us ascertain that her work is properly remunerated since factory owners do exist who pay women less simply because they are women, even though their work is identical to that of men. Ah! These are the ones who forget that the buzz of the bee is more useful than the roar of the lion.

Let us found centers for education and recreation, and societies that protect the rights of women workers without the disruption of strikes, strikes that accord so poorly with woman's true nature, which is gentle, consonant with peace and conciliation.

As women struggle to make the best of their lives, let us inspire them with evidence of the beauty of orderly labor. And may they be even more stimulated by the radiantly beautiful example of the woman worker herself, her enlightened spirit manifest as a halo of true virtue. She is an ideal energy source for the creation of well-being and happiness both in her own home and in our entire nation.

In conclusion, let us turn to those who are most concerned about and most influential in social causes, in order to encourage them to support not only workers but all the needy classes. We should ameliorate their condition by implementing our brotherly and sisterly love. We end with Victor Hugo's message: *Responsibility,* get to work, for your hour has come: improve the human soul!

Cuatro conferencias sobre América del Sur. Buenos Aires: Imprenta de Juan A. Alsina, 1909, pp. 49–55.

NOTE

1. Max Nordau (1849–1923), *The Conventional Lies of Our Civilization,* an 1884 best-seller in Germany, translated very soon thereafter into English (1885), Spanish, and other languages. [Trans.]

Alfonsina Storni

Argentina, 1892–1938

"Alfonsina" has become a legend in Latin America. Her
name has been the topic of songs and stories that tell
of a woman who broke the barriers of her time and
place and who recorded in her bold poetry what her
battles won and cost her. Especially poignant is her dramatic suicide, as she walked into the ocean after a losing battle with cancer. Yet she is also remembered as a
high-spirited ironist who wove together melodrama and
avant-garde poetry and theater to create an unmistak-
able voice that still speaks to the popular imagination.

Storni was a poet who achieved early recognition
in Buenos Aires for her writing as well as her noncon-
formist personal style, yet her story is a typical one of
her time. Like so many of her generation, she arrived in
Argentina as part of an immigrant family and settled in
the provinces. And like many women of her time and
place, she entered the public sphere through her teacher
training, becoming a *maestra* while still a teenager. As
part of a growing group of women who joined a bur-
geoning middle class through professions such as teaching and journalism, she scrambled to find ways to support her writing career without the legacy of family
wealth or patrons. In addition, her status as an unwed
mother closed certain doors to her, a situation she
records in her poetry.

Alfonsina Storni's career coincided with the expansion of Argentina's reading public, and she maintained a steady journalistic production throughout her adult life. Writing both for major newspapers and for more specialized literary magazines, she adapted her style and content for each type of reader. At the same time she published lyric poetry, often love poetry of an autobiographical nature, sentimental short stories, chatty women's columns in major newspapers, and, in more specialized publications, some piercing critiques of women's social lot. Storni's journalistic work can be read as a record of the excitement and the contradictions inherent in new situations for women during the period. Women like her, raised with dreams of romance and family ties, often found the entrance into urban public life a rude awakening. Storni captures vividly the clash between the expectations for women raised by the popular press and cinema, and the often harsh realities for working women beneath the veneer of city life.

Reading Storni's journalism adds a new dimension to her legendary status as a poet, causing us to read her again with new eyes. As she dissects social mores in her women's columns and comments on fashion, conventions, and the vicissitudes of daily life—sometimes under a pen name such as "Tao Lao"—she allows us to see with her the pretensions and delights of an urban society in rapid change, focusing especially on the sphere of women and children. Other histories have not given us this smaller, more intimate theater of daily life. Along with her poetry, her journalistic essays make even more dramatic and important the legend of Alfonsina.

GWEN KIRKPATRICK

An Old Story

There was a time when I had no intention of writing a serious word about feminism. It seemed to me that to talk about an accomplished fact was a waste of time.

But then I came across an article by Carlos Gutiérrez Larreta entitled "Women's Committees," which appeared in the previous issue of this journal. It has snapped me out of my torpor and is inducing me to commit the millionth foolish act of my life.

I believe that my kind friend has written the article just the way he usually recites his certainly magnificent madrigals and sonnets.

He has smoked two or three Turkish cigarettes, read his favorite poets, and then taken a few brightly colored billiard balls and caromed them around with a gold pen.

These caroms are his article.

But in life the brilliant little billiard balls the writer plays with are weighty worlds and the billiard cue that moves them is subject to formidable laws. As we contemplate the implications of these laws our whole being trembles; our faces fall, our tears flow, and we are suddenly saddened and confused by this inescapable, inexplicable Thing.

Only by making a carefree game cunning can one speak of feminism in terms of chivalrous pardon for feminine mischievousness.

I believe that feminism deserves much more than flippant gallantry because it is as important as a complete collective transformation.

Translated by Patricia Owen Steiner

I would even dare to assert that so-called feminism is nothing more than man's managerial failure to achieve by legal means the necessary equilibrium of human happiness.

If every chief of state and every head of the family were capable of knowing, and then satisfying, all the needs of the people under them, there would be an end to all modern problems, including the now-famous problem of feminism.

But life is not an equation perceivable by the eyes of man. However much one looks ahead, one will never see the intimate spiritual depths of each individual whose longings, unsatisfied, become the very struggle required for evolution.

Of this permanent discontent, of this thirst, of this expectation, of this endless movement Eternity is made.

To say man is superior to woman, woman is equal to man, etc., seems to me no more than words, words, words.

To speak of feminism and to separate it from everything like an isolated entity, with no relationship and merely as an arbitrary expression of feminine caprice, seems utter nonsense to me.

To think that "woman wants this despite the fact that we are advising her otherwise" is not to think at all.

What does woman want?

Are thoughts and collective aspirations like mushrooms that sprout up whenever or wherever they feel like it?

Did men dictate that nails would emerge on their fingers?

To poke fun at feminism, for example, seems to me as curious as to poke fun at a finger because it ends in a nail. To arrive at what we call feminism, humanity has followed a process as exact as the one an embryo follows to become a fruit, or that a fruit follows to transform its elements from an embryo, each in their successive steps.

There is as much truth in the embryo as in the stem, in the stem as in the leaves, in the leaves as in the flower or any other stage of its development.

Clearly we have the right to express an opinion about which moment of that transformation appears to us to be more harmonious, more complete.

The writer we mentioned finds that the [ancient] Greeks, such exalted beings, had no feminism.

But this does not have to be the reason for the sublimity of Greece. By following such criteria we would come to believe that it was enough for a population not to have feminism for it to demonstrate its equilibrium.

I could point out to him that the Middle Ages, which did not have feminism, is an example of a barbarous period characterized by its humiliation of feminine dignity under the pretext of a stupid chastity and a religion that was as depressing as it was avaricious.

But in truth we have nothing in the past that can enlighten us about a movement like the present one, the fruit of our own days.

If the time in which we live is compared to some luminous periods of the past, such as [ancient] Greece for example, it is seen as a setback, and we cannot attribute this setback to feminism.

On the contrary, feminism stems from this setback by seeking for "its" support, "its" ray of light, in troubled waters where nothing is visible. And for that seeking, women want to use their own eyes.

Let me make myself clear: Catholic dogma is bankrupt; civilization is bankrupt; everything that has been built up in the last twenty centuries is crashing down with a deafening roar, its balance destroyed, its center of gravity out of kilter.

Men, after repeating the same old things for a long time, are bored with themselves and are demanding new actions, new words, new life.

This is as old as the sun.

We go now from unity to the parts.

Power is distributed, knowledge is distributed, responsibility is distributed.

Man does not know what awaits him when he loses his protectorate, but he wants to free himself from it. Today every human cell wants to feel responsibility.

To disperse, to separate, to divide . . .

This is what things say.

Nonexistent or ineffectual dogma, a hard economic life, imperfect justice—for whom is woman now waiting? What holy word or perception of human justice leads her to accept the idea that she always comes out the loser, without daring to say, "I want to try doing this for myself"?

I understand perfect submission when the hand directing one's life is perfect, when that hand has taken care of and foreseen everything, for then obedience is sweet, slavery a pleasure.

But while everything is changing and an infinity of laws and customs from earlier times are being modified, a group of women, protected by neither state nor man, are taking up the struggle against the new laws and customs.

These are the women who have had to earn their own living, those who are in a position to talk about the bunches of flowers that masculine piety tosses at their feet lest their delicate soles get hurt.

In the struggle for existence there is no truce, no sex, no pity, no flowers. Oh, poet! It's every man for himself. The first one gets the prize, and often the one arriving second, if he's stronger, snatches it away.

At least that's the pattern I personally experienced in my hard apprenticeship.

It is in great part this ruthless aspect of life that has broken woman's submission and that now tries her will, tries her ideas, tries her personality.

She doesn't part company with man, but she has stopped believing in the divine mission that dogma assigned him.

She doesn't turn against man for, as she struggles, she thinks about her son, a man. But she distrusts the state's protection, she distrusts man's justice, and she tends, as I said before, to exercise her responsibility.

It is true that this way of living separates her somewhat from her instincts, but who says that instinct is an end and not simply a means?

Isn't it perhaps true that choice is one of the capabilities that characterizes humankind?

Only the egotism of the species can lead man to believe that *he* is the one uniquely qualified to make choices. I firmly believe that feminism today is a question of justice.

This way of thinking to which woman aspires, in fact, goes hand in hand with the condition of being born free that belongs to both woman and man—the right to exercise free will.

Naturally, in the course of developing her general abilities, woman will do as many foolish things as man has done, and goes right on doing, despite his long experience in directing affairs.

I believe also that perfection is unattainable and that woman and man, as they try to reach it, will both make the same kind of mistakes that have already been made.

But in the feminine exercise of this aspiration to responsibility there is no other justification than the unknown law that governs us, the law that has provided man with all his downfalls and consequently with all the changes through which he manages to survive.

None of us knows where this movement we call feminism is heading, but nothing will detain it.

Meanwhile, before long, women will obtain the suppression of the laws and concepts that have a shameful impact on feminine dignity, laws that a number of stalwart women have already rendered null. To transform words like "shame," "pardon," and "error" into "right of the woman," "right of the mother," and "right of the human being" will be one of the inevitable and invaluable triumphs of feminism.

As for the rest, woman's increased development implies a refinement of her femininity, a greater spiritual grace, a harmony that is only restored by controlled instincts.

This may seem a contradiction to my earlier paragraph, but it is not.

Instinct controlled by clear, conscious reasoning is a very different thing from instinct harshly suffocated because of dogma. Putting instincts in proper balance will be another of feminism's victories.

And if Christ, according to my kind friend Gutiérrez Larreta, had woman mapped out for a different direction, he will see, once again, that neither women nor men now succeed—nor ever will succeed—in comprehending that direction. For although it may be opportune to present myths in articles and essays, these myths are ultimately indigestible for humankind because humankind is so weak, so trusting in an infinite divine goodness that, despite all the gospels, allows mankind to kill, rob, or commit "rosy, silky little sins," in the words of Rubén Darío, who, without Christ's permission, must have been quite a feminist. . . .

La Nota, 25 April 1919

Alfonsina Storni

Letter to the Eternal Father

I don't know, Lord, if you will receive this letter, since I am sending it without any address, in the hope that one of our mysterious postal detectives might get it to you on time.

I am writing to you from a round world its inhabitants call the earth, for at one time they believed that they were the only ones to possess such a precious element. The earth belongs to a certain solar system about which I don't dare to give you precise details; I expect you wouldn't need them for, being omnipotent, you will read my mind perfectly. Besides, I suppose you possess your own cartography of the cosmos, and an ability as a polyglot that I envy. (O Eternal Father, I am saying this because it has been very hard for me to learn certain languages just to be able to say "au revoir," "flirt," "sogno" with the perfect pronunciation that befits a nice young lady from a cultured, refined land.)

Well, then, from the earth, which will be easy for you to locate, I am writing you this confidential and slightly incoherent letter; but what do you want, Lord? Incoherence is not something that a nice young lady from the earth desires, but the trouble is that ideas seem, in their rapid succession, like clothes that we choose to change daily.

But before I go on talking, or rather, writing, I will give you some personal details about myself.

I am a female creature, nineteen years old, very cute and nice. Lord, I

Translated by Patricia Owen Steiner

have blond wavy hair that is attractively arranged, two delicate white hands, a captivating figure and a good heart; this last above all.

But among so many likable things, I have a horrible, disconsolate defect: I am poor.

You ought to know, Lord, that, despite what some beatified souls may be telling you, the poor don't do very well here on earth.

Down here human beings are accustomed to squander all their good qualities on words and sometimes on thought; these thoughts are what human beings call "the ideal." But while "the ideal" floats around like a cloud, people look at each other ferociously, although "the ideal" keeps them from acknowledging even the least bit of rancor.

This is why, Lord, all people desire the well-being of the poor "for tomorrow."

Certain men of great intelligence, whom humans call philosophers, justify these things with very lovely theories.

I myself, Lord, who because I am a woman am prohibited from getting involved in such questions, have forced myself to submit to this prohibition with a certain pleasure, and so I have become blind and deaf to every learned and transcendental theory.

How I wish you would come down to earth for even a few moments to try to work a little justice!

But, meanwhile, as everything is all tangled up and you can't even find the thread to begin unraveling it, I, a very human creature guided by my condition, have resolved not to worry myself about anything that has nothing to do with my personal aesthetics.

Thus, in my double condition as offended poor and as a human being who realizes that everything is going badly and that there is no help for it, I write to you with these confidences.

I've already informed you, Lord, that I am poor.

I've already told you how the poor suffer injustice on the earth.

And if the poor in general suffer, imagine how a wretched girl infatuated with aesthetics must suffer because of weariness with other complicated matters!

Eternal Father: here is a discreet and very serious confidence. Everything is so expensive! Furs, fabrics, shoes, hats, jewelry have gone up in price tremendously.

I have had to do some fancy pirouettes to keep my old outfits up to date: I had some turned inside out, I had others dyed, I had the most expensive ones made over, but, even so, I can hardly keep up with all the dates I have because of my numerous friendships.

Lord, I beg you to pardon me if in the course of my confidences I bother you, but just notice how sincere my words are.

Besides, I want to tell you now that I don't have any very exact idea of what you are.

I know that when men lived like animals they believed that you were the cold that numbed the flesh and the sun that melted the ice.

I also know that when men used to idealize the naked body, they believed you were grace manifested in human form; I know that when men began wrapping themselves in lugubrious black robes, they put a beard on you and seated you on the clouds.

Well, then: as I really don't know what you are, but I do believe in you, if I could be allowed to make you concrete as my imagination sees you, I would describe you as wrapped in expensive furs, yards of silk, luxurious jewels that, with an elegant gesture, you would distribute to the pretty, poor girls on earth.

You will think, Lord, that this confidential letter is disrespectful, and yet if any disrespect exists it is not in the confidences I divulge but in my previous inventiveness in describing you, which I haven't been able to avoid.

Perhaps this confidence may redeem my wild imagination in your eyes and, together with your pardon, there may come falling down on me from heaven golden boxes filled with everything I need in the way of clothes for the winter season, which is so filled with great plans.

O Lord, if you only knew what an enormous torture it is to wear an outfit for two years in a row!

I beg you, Lord, to have pity on my aesthetic anxiety.

There's no justice on earth, Lord.

Why is it that some women get to wear real polar furs, truly aristocratic, while others of us have to resign ourselves to plebeian rabbits, foxes, skunks, hares, and nutrias, all disguised to look like polar animals?

Don't you know, Lord, that many women owe their happiness to the silky skins of some anonymous animal?

I will explain to you sometime in a long confidential talk how, on earth in wintertime, polar animals are used to negotiate the happiness of men.

For the moment you should know that mixed up in all of this is a quality that until now has guided the spiritual and material interest of my type of person: talent.

But, Lord, there's no worse enemy of talent, in matters of aesthetics, than poverty.

That's why, Lord, I have confided these things in you, since, imagining you as I do, it won't cost you anything to bring about, by some gift, the happiness of this lovely girl from earth who calls herself,

LITA

La Nota, 27 June 1919.

Against Charity

Viscountess Astor, who aspires to a seat in the House of Commons in England, and who is a millionairess many times over, has declared that she is opposed to charity.

For a woman this opinion is already quite a statement; for a millionairess it is truly an exceptional thought.

We know well that a rather common idea operates in our imperfect social organizations: create the poor in order to give them charity.

And perhaps there may be some benefit in giving charity to miserable people: such an act, by permitting a comparison, allows a person to relish his own privileged situation.

Viscountess Astor has said that charity humiliates not only those who receive it but also the ones who give it.

This thought, which is not original since it is held by all good-hearted people and responds to a clear sense of what a perfect social organization ought to be, deserves to be placed on posters in our cities where there is a limited—oh, very limited—consciousness of human rights, and where, at present, a rather basic feeling leads groups of good people to believe that the charity drive (including the last big national drive, made to the accompaniment of great speeches, carried out with tremendous effort, with slow, persuasive, insinuating words, with heavenly hopes and the fear and dread of brimstone, and also with all the long procession of lists, raffles, leagues, and festivals) will be able to fill the enormous gaps left by our appalling national institutions.

Translated by Patricia Owen Steiner

I am not saying that these things may not be well-intentioned. They frequently will be. What I firmly believe is that in principle they are shameful.

In a republic, that is to say, in a government where the people are responsible for their governed, almsgiving and charity should be banished.

Wise legislation derived from representatives of the people has the obligation to give each person what, within a democracy, belongs to him.

But perhaps those in the majority don't understand or even realize this, or perhaps it isn't important to them and they don't calculate precisely that they now have in their hands the formidable means of attaining what rightfully belongs to every person: the vote. For, in truth, the vote is something that can be given to all people without any shame, without any hesitation, and can be received without any feeling of anxiety.

La Nota, 14 November 1919.

Alfonsina Storni

The Immigrant Girl

Among the people who come to these lands as immigrants, there is an authentic character: the young girl who comes alone.

This girl is the one who stays in the big cities as the family maid or the servant girl in a hospital.

She is the same girl who at festivals and local dances gets dizzy from the fast rhythms of her native land and, to the beat of the beloved regional music, forgets the feather dusters and casseroles, thus reviving her old familiar surroundings.

The Raise

The city produces rapid changes in the immigrant girl: like a repotted plant that doesn't know what to do with the exotic energy it is receiving, she suddenly gets it into her head to spurt upwards. (In truth, this business of a spurt is only a figure of speech; what really happens is that the immigrant girl puts on high heels.)

Well, then, she has already grown in stature and the completely changed plant continues its constant transformation, which consists of improving its leaves at the expense of its fruits, converting its sap, which was accustomed to send out sober shoots, into a showy excess of greenery.

Soon the immigrant girl takes pleasure in scanty work and external luxury. (When in Rome, shoot Roman candles.) And, day by day, she keeps adding to her costume with blouses of showy silk, the long gold chain

Translated by Patricia Owen Steiner

with a watch "that works," the silver mesh purse, and the bulky beaded necklaces.

This is only in the first stage; in the second, the colors become subdued, the leather shoes are of a finer quality and tend to harmonize with the tone of the outfit. Her model in the first stage might have been her roommate, but in the second stage this model has been replaced by none other than the daughter of the household. And, arriving at this point of her assimilative cleverness, she asks for a raise in pay.

Diminution

Over there on her native soil the immigrant girl had a personality: she was called Mary or Joan or Rose, and she was one of six or seven in a family. She thus became the flower of a small garden, implying hope, possibility, a new household to be formed.

But her life suffered from the weight of tradition as, watchful and watched, she moved between the church that shone white in the distance and the earth that turned black nearby, exhausted and very hard.

The trees along the country path would say: the girl who passes by is Mary or Joan or Rose. But the trees of Buenos Aires only say that the young girl who passes by is a Savings Bank Passbook.

The Letter

The immigrant girl has the habit of coming to you with an envelope in her hand; it is rectangular, like all envelopes, and has writing all over it.

From the dance of its black letters she has only deciphered one thing: her name, which proves that she still exists and that she is called Mary or Joan or Rose.

She hasn't opened that envelope, and she hands it over to you inviolate, perhaps remembering that paternal opinion that women don't need to know how to read—that opinion, substantially shared by her male relatives or friends, that typically left her empty-handed after some years of constant excursions to the bank where she kept her savings.

The Mentality

A case in point: one of the young girls enters into the service of a person who, in training her, gives her this warning: Be careful not to put your fingers in the electric socket, because it would kill you.

But as soon as the lady of the house leaves, the girl suspects that they take her for an ignoramus.

How is it possible that death, a thing so grand, can hide out in such a tiny little round hole?

She certainly knows what makes people die. They die from a stabbing, they die from drowning, they die in bed after a lot of praying, but they don't die from putting their fingers in a hole that looks very much like the ones she made with her index finger in the ground . . . just like this.

And so to have a good laugh on anyone who takes her for ignorant, she pokes her index finger into the socket with all her might.

Life Is Good

Let's just admit that the room where the girl usually sleeps is a poorly ventilated tiny attic room where there's hardly enough space for her cage of a bed and her trunk.

Also, in respect for the truth, let it be said that with some frequency her salary isn't paid at the end of the month, and that her meals are skimpy.

But despite the dim light in her room, and the trunk hidden under the bed, and the friend who swindles her, and the fact that her family is far away, and that the husband comes home late, the immigrant girl sings all day long with all her heart, and if you were to offer her a chance to return to her native village, she wouldn't take it. And if you ask her a little about her life now, she answers you that life is good, and since she says so it must be true.

TAO LAO

La Nación, 1 August 1920.

Alfonsina Storni

Women and Love

I begin this article with my umbrella open. . . . But I beg you, oh divine creatures, not to let anything other than flowers rain down on me.

If that happens, the umbrella will be turned inside out and I will catch them: thanks very much!

Now that I am here with your flowers in my hands and pleasantly intoxicated by their perfume, I can talk about love, and about all of you, and of how I conceive of love.

For the moment let us rejoice that we are still the zealous vestal virgins of Romanticism. (It is lovely to be a vestal virgin; the white tulle hangs divinely and brushes the rosy foot with delicate grace.)

Your imagination thus intercedes between reality and the dream the way a powerful spring dulls and softens shocks.

More flowers? Thanks again. What is love, divine creatures?

Let's descend from the golden Romanticism, where we were, to cynicism; after all, the leap is not so abrupt. The cynic used to be a hopeless Romantic; a kind of medieval troubador who was singing his verses to his fair love, in the soft splendor of the pale moon, and the hounds chased him away.

This cynic, this worldly Romantic, would say to you, "Love is the trap the universe sets for living beings to deceive them and make them perpetuate themselves."

Translated by Patricia Owen Steiner

Let's ascend from a cynic to a philosopher and listen: "Love is, like every existing thing, a relative, visible aspect of the invisible absolute; therefore, every definition would be false." (You understood, eh!)

A skeptic would say . . . no, you can't repeat what a skeptic would say; some Englishmen have given skeptics a terrible name.

A spiritualist would proclaim that "love is the divine part of man that separates him from the beast."

And a poet would assert that "love is the spiritual state that tends to seek the happiness of another being, with an absolute forgetfulness of one's self."

And so, in the great casserole of definitions (a modernistic definition), each of them would try to stick in his spoon and we would end up by not knowing anything about love.

But there you are: there have always been women to prevent this from happening.

From ancient times on, women have had the last word on love: that is, that love should be lived and not commented upon; with the advantage that, to make this understood, they didn't even use words; their actions spoke for them.

In this way women are going to become the true philosophers, since, after all, the supreme philosophy consists in destroying philosophy with life itself.

More flowers? Thanks, thanks, thanks very much.

But now comes the sad part: wicked tongues—I should say wicked pens—declare that you, women, have become the supreme philosophers by chance, as if to say, more or less, that Hernández, the author of *Martín Fierro,* became a genius by chance; that is, without the intervention of his free will and his own intellect; by the simple coming together of phenomena and circumstances quite apart from his will.

It is said against you that you remain attached to life, undoing all philosophy with life, defending love with an instinctive ferocity, idolizing it as the principal reason for existence, embellishing it, adorning it, and magnifying it with the imagination, wanting it to be ardent and serious, submissive and blind, because of your intellectual incapacity to observe life objectively in its true balance and thus have recourse to cold reason and austere thought and thus see reality, which, according to those evil pens, is something quite different from what feminine passion desires.

And so they compare the voluptuous condition of women to that of certain inferior races that live only to make love and to satisfy their passions, and they even claim that the lofty feeling of motherhood is pure instinct.

So you end up, nothing less, as humanity's ballast, the fountain, or the sentimental basic well, into which men fall and are renewed after having been shunted aside by life and after flying over the high reaches of thought, the place to which men return after long journeys, according to eyewitnesses, very cold and like wet hens, to seek in women the blessed warmth of the earth, of life itself.

And don't say now that I haven't avenged you against masculine reason, since you women, fixed to the earth, never have the misfortune of looking like little wet hens.

You may look like something else, even an inverted feather duster if you wear a large hat and a tight skirt, but that business of the wet hens is an image that only squares with men after an excursion through the lofty heavens of ideas. . . .

I am closing the umbrella. In case you're still angry with me, I declare to you now that I am not afraid of you women when you're angry, only when you're subdued and gentle.

A sweet English song goes, "I'm afraid of a kiss. . . ."

TAO LAO

La Nación, 8 August 1920.

Victoria Ocampo

Argentina, 1890–1979

One of the most influential cultural figures of her time in Argentina, Victoria Ocampo was known primarily as the founder and director of a literary review, *Sur*, that was read all over Latin America for more than forty years and that, as Ocampo often said, endeavored to "build bridges" between the Americas and Europe. Her own cultural formation reflected the customs among wealthy criollo families at the turn of the century; taught at home by governesses and taken to Europe for long visits when she was still very young, Ocampo felt as nurtured by English and French as she did by Spanish American culture. Her limited education as a female was unequal to her hunger for knowledge, a passion she expressed in many letters as a young woman. After an early and unhappy marriage, she turned to a life of reading, writing, traveling between the continents, supporting women's rights, opposing dictatorships, and publishing not only *Sur* but an extensive oeuvre of her own.

The essay was her primary vehicle for self-expression; during her lifetime she published ten collections of her essays under the title *Testimonios*, along with numerous shorter works and translations. Her six-volume *Autobiografía,* a compelling story of her efforts to break free from patriarchal bonds and achieve self-realization, appeared posthumously. The first woman elected to the Argentine Academy of Letters in 1977, Ocampo died at

the age of eighty-seven, having become a legendary
figure admired by writers and artists on three continents.

The first selection included here was Ocampo's first
published essay, which appeared in *La Nación* in 1920, in
French as originally written. It shows an early awareness
of her own "otherness" and is an affirmation of the
right to be and think differently—not just for herself
but for all human beings. Framed as a meditation on the
concept of equality, "Babel" is subversive in its rejection
of any single interpretation of truth and its claim that
language is the vehicle for multiple perspectives, thus
implicitly affirming the validity of her own female
voice. As in all her later essays, Ocampo's writing is
highly personal and informal, sharply contrasting with
the authoritative and impersonal style that characterized
many male authors of the time.

The second essay, "La mujer y su expresión"
(Woman and Her Expression), was written as a radio
talk broadcast from Argentina to Spain in August 1936,
just as the Spanish Civil War was beginning. It was evidently directed at a female audience to whom Ocampo
transmitted a powerful appeal for solidarity and commitment to developing a female tradition of self-
expression. Recognizing the male custom of devaluing
women's thought and monopolizing speech, Ocampo
calls upon her women listeners to shed the inferiority
complex to which they have been acculturated and to
begin to change the course of history by bearing witness to their own lives and concerns. Ocampo was
well aware of the dangers of fascist attitudes toward
women—she had already met Mussolini and written
about this—but she did not know in 1936 that Spain's
conflict would force women back into traditional
molds, making her plea for female empowerment a vir-
tual impossibility for yet another generation or more.

DORIS MEYER

Babel

> We suppose that all men perceive and feel objects presented to them in the same way; but we suppose so very gratuitously, because we have no proof thereof. I know the same words are used on the same occasions, and whenever two men see snow, for example, they both express the vision of this object with the same words, both saying that snow is white; and from this conformity of usage a powerful conjecture is deduced about a conformity of ideas. But this is not completely convincing, although one could wager affirmatively that it is. PASCAL

No, this is not completely convincing.

Have you ever meditated on the humiliating failure of the masons of the tower of Babel? I ask you this question in all seriousness. I bet you haven't thought about it for even five minutes. And if you have, you've probably drawn conclusions different from mine. From the time I was eight years old—when, willing or unwilling, I was obliged to familiarize myself with the history and deeds of the Hebrew people—I have often reflected on the story of this tower, and, having reflected frequently, I've done so in different ways. The last time this happened I told myself that the Eternal One, in order to insinuate among these good people the immutable misunderstanding we know about, didn't have to suggest distinct languages to them. It is very probable that the punishment He inflicted was more refined, more cruel. It must have been as follows: Jehovah didn't alter the words of Noah's children, but rather He changed the perception that each of their brains had of those words. The words continued being externally as they had been until then, but internally they became different for each man. The words, then, continued sounding like they always had, but their resonance was distinct in each ear.

Man's pride was great, to be sure, and things had to be set right again. Still and all, I think the severity of the Eternal was excessive on this occasion. Perhaps Jehovah Himself wasn't aware of the dreadful repercussions

Translated by Elizabeth D. Hodges and Doris Meyer

it would have on future generations. But we had better abstain from pronouncing judgments about this, which could be construed as reckless.

Whatever the case, it unfortunately cannot be doubted that the effects of this dirty trick, of which our fathers were victims, are still being felt. As sons and daughters of the masons of Babel, countless generations later, we continue throwing the same words at one another, words whose content differs just as we differ from one another. It might have been better if each of the unfortunate builders of the unfortunate tower had made the good resolution not to permit their children the slightest opportunity to marry the children of neighboring builders, for then, little by little, some groups might have formed that were capable of understanding each other. But those fools became totally and inextricably mixed up with one another. And we will never get out of that entanglement.

These days there is a big word, swollen with emptiness, that we toss around a lot; a word in which, under the pretext of justice, an absolute injustice is hidden; a word frequently used in such an absurd way that we would laugh till we cried, and not become indignant if the sharp edge of the laugh didn't escape the understanding of those who bring it up at every opportunity:

EQUALITY!

In France this word extends its right hand to Liberty and its left to Fraternity, as if to do away with the two of them. As if Liberty could exist where this amputator we call Equality reigns. As if Fraternity could be born where the executioner Equality offers, smilingly, to help poke your brother's eyes out if his eyes see better than yours.

There once was a man, one alone, who gave each word its true and only content. This man said, "Blessed are those who hunger and thirst for justice." He never said, "Blessed are those who hunger and thirst for equality." He promised to satisfy the first; he didn't promise anything to the second, because the hunger and thirst for equality couldn't be satisfied since human beings aren't the same.

In order to conceive of equality, one must be prepared to commit injustice. In order to do justice, one must be able to conceive of inequality.

One must have reached an unusual degree of insanity or perversity in order to aspire to equality as an ideal of justice, to imagine that equality holds "a promise of happiness." In reality, we are all heirs of the masons of Babel because here we are striving to agree on the meaning of words that, individually, we have, or believe we have, understood clearly. I can't hear this word "equality" used in a certain sense—that is to say, non-sense, as I see it—without having rise within me my ancestor from Babel whose vision prevails in me despite subsequent mixtures. And each time I speak of equality, it is undoubtedly and in spite of myself through a piece of his patriarchal beard.

In the fifteenth canto of *Il Purgatorio*, when the guardian angel of the ladder leading from the second to the third circle advances toward Virgil and Dante to exhort them to proceed along their path, Dante looks away from the angel because his eyes are still not capable of contemplating such sheer brilliance without suffering:

> *Che è quel, dolce padre, a che non posso*
> *schermar lo viso tanto che mi vaglia . . . ?*

> (What is that, gentle Father, . . . from which I cannot rightly screen my eyes . . .?)[1]

This is the extent of the querulous question that Alighieri directs to his guide on this point. I confess that this way of seeing things does not displease me, and that if Dante had decided to scream at his companion something like "Put a shade over the head of this being whose brilliance wounds me!" I wouldn't have continued reading. A matter of preference.

Virgil promptly answers:

> *Non te maravigliar, se ancor t'abbaglia*
> *la famiglia del cielo, a me rispuose:*
> *messo è che viene ad invitar ch'uom saglia.*

> *Tosto sarà che a veder queste cose*
> *non ti fia grave, ma fieti diletto*
> *quanto natura a sentir ti dispuose . . .*

> ('Do not marvel' he answered me 'if the household of heaven still dazzles thee; it is a messenger who comes to invite to the ascent; soon the seeing of these will not be hard for thee, but as great delight as nature has fitted thee to feel.')

This answer contains all the sweetness, all the justice, all the wisdom without which human suffering cannot, and will not, find any refuge. Let's examine this reply more closely:

> *Non te maravigliar, se ancor t'abbaglia*
> *la famiglia del cielo, a me rispuose . . .*

Virgil begins by warning Dante not to be surprised at always being dazzled by the celestial family; that is, Virgil shows Dante that the imperfect will inevitably end up being submerged by the perfect, and that it is useless to try to fight against it.

Messo è che viene ad invitar ch'uom saglia

It is a messenger coming to invite man to rise, explains Virgil afterward. In other words, this messenger is not here to hurl his light at your face like a blinding and cruel challenge. He is here to help you find your way and encourage you to ascend, to reach the zone whose brightness clothes him and will also clothe you when your effort makes you worthy of it.

Tosto sarà che a veder queste cose
non ti fia grave, ma fieti diletto . . .

Soon, continues Virgil, the vision of these things—the vision of the brilliance of angels—will not be as painful to you, but rather will be a pleasure. That is, if the vision of these things is now painful to you, it is because you have not yet reached the level at which you can contemplate it head-on. You will reach this when, by dint of your will to self-perfection, you have reached your own splendor. The splendor of others will then be pleasurable, not painful. And in this you will find joy

Quanto natura a sentir ti dispuose . . .

in the measure to which nature enabled you to feel it. This means that there are beings in whom nature placed more sensitivity than in you, and also others with less sensitivity. What does it matter to you! You cannot absorb more enjoyment than what your being is capable of; it would be useless to pour more into you because it would overflow. It should not occur to you, then, to find fault in the fact that others have a greater capacity than you, nor to rejoice because others have less. Once you have completely satisfied your own capacity, you will no longer dream of a better condition for yourself.

Quanto natura a sentir ti dispuose . . .

In this magnificent verse lies the secret of happiness in inequality, the secret of justice in inequality. But the majority of the heirs of the masons of Babel, for once in singular agreement, seem to have decided to pay no attention to it.

San Isidro (Buenos Aires), March 1920

Testimonios, vol. 1. Madrid: Revista de Occidente, 1935, pp. 45–63.

NOTE

1. This and subsequent translated verses are taken from *The Divine Comedy of Dante Alighieri (Il Purgatorio),* trans. John D. Sinclair (New York: Oxford University Press, 1939; reprint, 1977), pp. 197, 199. [Trans.]

Victoria Ocampo

Woman and Her Expression

The first thing I think about as I talk to you, the essential thing, is that your voice and mine are triumphing over my great enemy the Atlantic. Every word heard simultaneously on the two shores exorcises distance for us. And I have always rebelled against distance. For however much it may spring back after each spoken word, however much it may inundate our small silences, however much it may re-emerge as soon as our breath gives out, we know that our words break through the distance. We know that our voices obliterate it. And it is for me a great pleasure to obliterate that distance between us.

I have always seen the Atlantic as a symbol of distance. It has always separated me from beloved beings and things. If it wasn't Europe that I longed for, then it was America.

When I crossed through the Panama Canal and for the first time entered onto the Pacific, I thanked heaven that I didn't have to contend with this ocean, in comparison to which the Atlantic is a Mediterranean. And yet I understand that what is interposed between me and the Orient is not the immense screen of the Andes but rather the ocean whose existence I try not to contemplate. For the Pacific also separates me from countries for which I would feel a sense of nostalgia if I let myself. You cannot truly like one piece of the land without realizing that it belongs to the entire land. For this reason oceans, as symbols of distance and separation, are my enemies. They interrupt the land. Perhaps someday we will make them

---

Translated by Patricia Owen Steiner

into beautiful, fast, safe highways. In the meantime we must navigate them drop by drop.

But let us go on directly to the subject I would like to talk to you about: the need for women to express themselves. Let us try then to forget for a while this happiness at having conquered distance. Let us try to forget that the victory won over distance is transforming the world; an idea that, by itself, would be enough to distract me from everything else during the half hour I have. Let us convince ourselves that this mysterious and momentary victory ought not disturb or surprise us. Let us take extraordinary things in our stride, as we do in dreams.

Haven't I ever dreamt perhaps, without astonishment, that I was living in a house surrounded by a garden bathed half in morning's light and half in the dusk of evening? Today my voice evokes this garden of dreams. While our gardens here are bare, yours in Spain are covered with leaves, and while our rooms are closed up because of the cold, yours echo with the sounds of summer. This idea fascinates me, carries me away, in spite of myself, as did the buzzing of bees or the song of the cicadas during the sultry days of January when, as a little girl, I was in class.

I pursue this idea, in spite of myself, with the tremendous desire of escaping from my subject, of playing hooky—as we say here—of being a truant—as you might say there. But there is no way of doing that, so let me turn to my topic.

Last year, by chance, I happened to overhear the telephone conversation of a businessman calling Buenos Aires from Berlin. He was talking to his wife, giving her some assignment. He began this way: "Don't interrupt me." She obeyed so perfectly, and he took his monologue so seriously, that the regulation three minutes went by without the poor woman having the chance to utter a sound. And as my businessman was parsimonious, the conversation came to a halt with that. I, who have been invited to come talk to you and who am being paid to do it, would like to say to you, "Interrupt me." This business of the monologue does not make me happy. It is to you, and not to myself, that I would like to speak. I want to feel your presence. And how can I know that you are present, that you are listening to me, if you don't interrupt me?

I am afraid that this feeling is very feminine.

If the monologue is not enough to make women happy, it seems to have been sufficient to men's happiness for years and years.

I believe that for centuries all conversation between men and women, as soon as it enters a certain terrain, begins with a "Don't interrupt me" from the man. Until now the monologue seems to have been the preferred means of expression adopted by men. (Conversation among men is nothing more than a dialogue form of this monologue.)

You could say that men do not feel, or feel only slightly, the need for conversation with that other being who is similar and yet different from him: woman. In the best of cases, he has no fondness for interruptions. In the worst case, he forbids them. Hence, man is content to talk with himself, and little does it matter to him whether women hear him or not. As for him listening to women, it scarcely occurs to him.

For centuries, having fully realized that the argument of the strongest is always the best argument (however much this ought not to be so), women have resigned themselves, for the most part, to repeating little crumbs of male monologue, at times interspersing something of their own between these crumbs. But despite her qualities of the faithful dog seeking refuge at the feet of the master who punishes her, the whole performance has proved tiresome and useless.

Struggling against these qualities that men have often interpreted as signs of a nature inferior to their own, or that they have respected because these qualities helped to transform woman into a statue placed in its niche so that it stayed there *sage comme une image*; struggling, I say, against that tendency that leads her to offer herself as a sacrifice, women have dared to speak out with a kind of courage unknown until now: "The monologue of men neither lightens my burden nor comforts my thoughts. Why should I resign myself to repeating it? I have other things to express. Other feelings, other sorrows have shattered my life, other joys have brightened it through the centuries."

Women, according to their environment, their talent, their calling, in many fields and in many centuries—and even in those that were most hostile to women—are trying today, and each time trying harder, to express themselves. And each time they are meeting with greater success. One cannot contemplate contemporary French science without referring to Marie Curie; nor can one think about English literature without bringing up the name of Virginia Woolf, or about Latin American letters without mentioning Gabriela Mistral. As for you in Spain, so as not to leave you out, we envy you María de Maeztú, an admirable woman who has accomplished for young Spanish women, thanks to her authentic genius as an educator, what I would like to see her do for our young women.

I am totally convinced that women are also expressing themselves outside the realm of science and the arts and that they have already expressed themselves marvelously in these fields. I am also convinced that this expression has enriched human existence through all of time and that it has been as important in the history of humanity as the expression of men, although it is of a hidden quality, subtle and less flamboyant than man's, in the way that the plumage of the hen pheasant is less flamboyant than that of her mate.

The most complete expression of women, the child, is a work that demands, in those who are conscious of it, infinitely more care, scrupulousness, sustained attention, delicate righting of wrongs, intelligent respect, and pure love than the work that goes into the creation of an immortal poem. This is because it not only involves carrying the child for nine months and giving birth to a being who is sound of body, but it also implies giving birth spiritually. That is to say, not only living beside them and with them, but before them. I believe, above all, in the power of example. There is no other way to persuade either adults or children. There is no alternative means to convince them. If that fails, there is no recourse.

The child, then, by presence alone, has demanded that the conscientious woman express herself and that she do so in the most difficult way: by living before him as an example.

The essential importance of early infancy is one of the points on which modern science has recently insisted the most. You could almost say that it has just discovered this fact. At this precise moment in life the child is exclusively in the hands of the woman. It is the woman, then, who leaves her indelible and decisive mark on this still-soft clay; it is she who, consciously or unconsciously, shapes it. Man's resistance to recognizing that woman is a being as perfectly responsible as he is himself seems absurd and comical when one becomes aware of the tremendous contradiction that it encompasses; that for centuries, no doubt through ignorance, the greatest responsibility of all has been borne by an irresponsible being. I am talking here about the responsibility of molding a human being at the moment when he is impressionable and of leaving her stamp on him.

The principal difference between great artists and great saints (apart from other differences) is that artists strive to put perfection into a work that is exterior to themselves and therefore outside their lives, while saints endeavor to put it into a work that is interior to themselves, and that consequently cannot be separated from their lives. The artist tries to create perfection outside himself, the saint in his own being.

For this reason, I would dare to say that the artist who is sensitive to saintliness always runs the risk of losing his gifts as an artist. As the zeal to put perfection into his own life grows, the desire to give it life in a work of art diminishes.

It is conceivable that the child has often made woman into an artist tempted by sainthood. Because in order to strive to put perfection in the work that is hers, the child, she needs to begin by trying to put perfection into her own self and not outside herself. She needs to take the path of saints and not the one of artists. The child does not tolerate her trying to impose the perfections on him that he does not see in us.

At this moment in history that is given us to live, we are witnessing a weakening of the power of artists. You might say that at this present time the world has more need of heroes or saints than of aesthetes. The temptation to sainthood, which, it would seem, is fatal to the perfection of the object, stands out all around us.

And for this reason men today are becoming more like women; they are beginning to sense that, in our times, it will no longer be possible for them either to create perfection (which remains beyond human reach) or even the sense of that perfection, at least as they themselves approach it. They begin to feel that every form of art that does not embrace the same requirement of perfection that the child demands is today obsolete.

The work of art, like the child, will be able to correspond, more or less, to our desires, will go, more or less, beyond ourselves, but it will need to be created in the same sense as we strive to raise the child.

God keep me from demeaning artists, whatever might be their defects; their past, present, or future vices; whatever might be their weaknesses. They have been, are, and will be as necessary to us as heroes or saints. Their way is also the way of heroism and sainthood. Even when the beauty of their work, as often happens, is a compensatory beauty (that is, condemned to be realized outside themselves, because it can not be realized within themselves), it is profoundly necessary to humanity. Whatever may have been their personal miseries, what we owe to great artists is some of the best of our inheritance. Take away the contributions of Dante, Cervantes, Shakespeare, Bach, Leonardo da Vinci, Goya, Debussy, Poe, Proust—just to give the first names that occur to me—and how impoverished we would feel! That some of these men personally may have been poor wretches who might be reproached for such and such a defect—what does it matter? They have bequeathed to us what they had of an extraordinary nature. Perhaps they have known no other happiness than suffering for their work. Their work was for them the only way of fitting into an orderly sense of the world.

And this means of fulfillment, among other things, is what men have unjustly taken pleasure in, or have been stubborn in denying to women.

For there are certain women, just as there are certain men, who can know no other happiness than suffering for a work of art.

One of these women, who is one of the most gifted beings I know, a celebrated novelist who writes with a wondrous style, said to me, "I am not truly happy except when I am alone, with a book or paper and pen. Beside this world—so real to me—the other one vanishes." However, this woman, born into an intellectual atmosphere and whose vocation, right from the beginning, was absolutely clear, went through some atrocious years of torment and doubts when she was young. Everything conspired to prove to her that her sex was a terrible handicap in a career of letters. Everything conspired to magnify for her what she had inherited, what all we women inherit: an inferiority complex. We should struggle against that complex, since it would be absurd not to comprehend its importance. The spiritual state it inevitably creates is one of the most dangerous. And I see no other way of struggling against it than by giving women as solid, as carefully conceived an education as men, and to respect women's freedom exactly as we respect the freedom of men. Not only in theory, but in practice. In theory, most civilized countries accept this idea. And in this sense Spain, since the revolution, has progressed rapidly. Unfortunately, Argentina has not advanced that far. Among our people women have not attained, either in theory or in practice, the position they ought to have attained. Men keep on saying to them, "Don't interrupt me." And when women assert their rights to freedom, men, judging no doubt from themselves and putting themselves in the woman's place, interpret this as "licentiousness."

By freedom, we women understand absolute responsibility for our actions and self-realization with no holds barred, which is very different. Licentiousness has no need to lay claim to freedom. One could be a slave and also be a libertine.

As to self-realization, it is, in brief, intimately linked to expression, whatever form that may take. One does not express oneself except by understanding perfectly what one wants to express; or, rather, the need for expression always derives from that understanding. Well, then: the understanding most important to every human being is the one that concerns the problem of his or her self-realization.

That this woman realizes herself by caring for the sick, that one by teaching people how to read and write, another one by working in a laboratory or writing a first-rate novel matters little: there are many different ways to find self-realization, and the most modest ones, just as the most eminent examples, have their own meaning and value.

Personally, what interests me most is written expression, and I believe that here women have a field for conquest and a harvest in the making.

It is easy to demonstrate that until now women have spoken very little about themselves directly. Men have talked at great length about women, doubtless out of the need to compensate, but consequently, and inevitably, as a way of talking about themselves. Out of the gratitude or deception, the enthusiasm or bitterness this angel or demon left in his heart, in his flesh, in his spirit. Men could be praised for many things, but never for a profound impartiality on this subject. Until now, then, we have listened principally to witnesses for women. Women as their own witnesses, a thing the law would not allow since it classified them as suspicious witnesses whose statements are biased, have hardly said a word. It is now women's turn not only to discover this unexplored continent that they represent but also to speak out about men, in their turn, as suspect witnesses.

If she succeeds, world literature will be incalculably enriched, and I have no doubt that she will.

I know from my own experience how poorly prepared women, and particularly South American women, are at this time to achieve such a victory. They have neither the necessary education, nor the freedom, nor the tradition. And I wonder what kind of genius could do without these three things at the same time and still produce valuable work. The miracle of a work of art is only produced when it has been quietly incubating over a long period of time.

I believe that our generation and the one that follows it and the one yet to be born are destined not to see this miracle but rather to prepare for it and to make it imminent.

I believe that our work will be discouraging and that it will remain unknown. I believe that we should resign ourselves to that situation in a sense of humility, but with deep faith in the greatness and productivity of our efforts. Our small individual lives will count for little, but all our lives together will leave such an impression on history that they will change its course. We should think about that continually so that we don't become disheartened by personal setbacks and so that we don't lose sight of the importance of our mission. Our sacrifices are paying in advance for what will only take flower in many years, perhaps centuries. For even when we have unquestionably acquired the education, the freedom, and a little tradition, we will not yet have achieved everything. (I allude to literary tradition, which scarcely exists for women; the literary tradition of men is not one that can orient us, and at times it even contributes to distortions.) We will need to become mature as we attain our education and freedom and tradition. We will have to familiarize ourselves with these advances and stop looking upon them with the eyes of a parvenu.

Thus, what our work buys now is the future for women. It will not benefit any of us personally. But this need not sadden us. (Does it embitter a mother to think that her daughter will become more beautiful than she?) If this holds true, then it is because one can have children without feeling like a mother. The exception that proves the rule.

This maternal feeling toward all future women ought to sustain us today. We have to bolster ourselves with the conviction that the quality of that future humanity depends on our humanity, that we are responsible for it. What each of us achieves in her small life has immense importance, immense power when all our lives are joined together. We must not forget that. None of our acts is insignificant, and our very attitudes add to or subtract from this sum total that we all form and that will tilt the balance.

I have just said that South American women find themselves in an inferior position with respect to women who live in certain great countries. I will add that this is to some degree their own fault. Until now they have resigned themselves much too easily to their condition. Perhaps some naive women may have been afraid of displeasing men, without realizing that they will always please them, despite everything, and that men would be in serious straits if they had to do without women.

It even seems quite probable to me that women will please men more when men become accustomed to seeing them as thinking human beings who are capable of standing up to them and of interrupting them if necessary, not as objects more or less cherished, more or less indispensable to their pleasure and their comfort. More or less, you might say, as warriors' playthings.

If it doesn't happen this way, it will mean that we must begin to re-educate men, realizing that the education that has made them arrogant until now is worthless and doesn't count any longer.

I don't know if what I am saying about my America is still applicable to Spain. In any case, it must have been true in the recent past, for both our good qualities and our defects mostly come to us from Spain.

It is characteristic of our present world that what happens in one country has repercussions from one country to another, from one continent to another. And these repercussions are almost explosive, whether we like it or not.

Your compatriot [Salvador de] Madariaga was talking a while ago about the irresistible growth of international solidarity. He calls it "subjective solidarity" when it pertains to ideas and feelings and "objective solidarity" when it concerns actions and vested interests, and he attributes the world crisis to the lag of the first behind the second.

This judgment on objective and subjective solidarity is confirmed as soon as distance is conquered, that distance of which I spoke to you at the beginning and that my voice quite happily obliterates.

Therefore, with events such as they are today, the lot of women in China or in Germany, in Russia or in the United States—in the end it doesn't matter in what corner of the world—implies an extremely grave consequence for us all, since we will bear the repercussion of its effects. Thus, the lot of South American women vitally concerns Spanish women and women in all other countries.

I would like women all over the earth to be united in a solidarity that is not only objective but subjective. Such an aspiration may seem too ambitious and absurd, but I cannot resign myself to anything less.

I would wish that the sum of all our efforts, of our lives, 99 percent of which remain hidden and anonymous, will tilt the balance toward the good—toward the side that will make women enriched human beings, toward the side where it would be possible for them to give complete expression to all facets of their personalities (not only their physical expression), toward the side that will make men complete human beings for whom the monologue is no longer enough and who, from interruption to accepted interruption, naturally arrive at a dialogue.

Testimonios, vol. 2. Buenos Aires: Sur, 1941, pp. 269–286.

Amanda Labarca Hubertson

Chile, 1886–1975

Born Amanda Pinto Sepúlveda to a middle-class family—her grandfather was a southern landowner, her mother a devout Catholic of English descent, and her father a despotic, Bible-toting Protestant businessman—Amanda Labarca Hubertson has been characterized by Chilean historians and biographers as progressive and visionary. In 1904, at the age of eighteen, she was wed to educator and diplomat Guillermo Labarca Hubertson, adopting his surnames in the *yanqui* fashion. After several trips to the United States and Columbia University with her husband on government scholarships (1909–1911), she returned to Chile to publish *Actividades femeninas en los Estados Unidos* (1914; Feminine Activities in the United States) and *En tierras extrañas* (1915; In Foreign Lands), a "sociological novel" imbued with the pragmatism of William James and John Dewey.

In 1922 Amanda Labarca was named professor extraordinaire of psychology at the University of Chile in Santiago, the first woman to be so recognized in the Americas. In 1928, however, through a series of military juntas terminating in the dictatorship of Colonel Carlos Ibáñez del Campo, she lost her post and, along with her anarchist husband, was exiled to Concepción. From this period, the "Difficult Years" of 1925–1931 in Chile, come most of the pieces included in her *Desvelos en el alba* (Restlessness at Dawn).

Despite Labarca's interdisciplinary interests and background, critics identify literature, feminism, and pedagogy as the three primary foci of her life and work. While some would contend that her work in the field of women's rights and welfare has been more important and valuable than her work in education, other critics have failed to recognize her contributions to the development of Latin American feminist theory and women's social history.

In addition to her numerous pedagogical and feminist writings (1914–1970), Amanda Labarca was also a literary critic and the author of several fictional and private writings that have received scant if any critical attention to date. Critical disputes notwithstanding, recent study of the author's work, reviewed in a holistic context, has uncovered that seemingly private arrangements shaped and affected her life and work in the public arena.

Both of the following pieces are taken from her private diary, *Desvelos en el alba*, published by José Santos González Vera in 1945. The journal entries incorporate theme fragments of articles published concurrently with the "Meditaciones" (Meditations) collection in *Atenea*, the journal of the University of Concepción, from 1924 to 1931. Paradoxically, Labarca believed that her journal, of all her writings, portrayed most genuinely her "deepest thinking and [her] real self." She refers to the essays as "fleeting nocturnal meditations" and "notations on the margins of a life." In fact, they display insights that she would later develop in *Feminismo contemporáneo* (1947; Contemporary Feminism), "El imperio femenino" (1949; The Feminine Empire), and *Una mujer enjuicia al tiempo* (1970; A Woman Judges Her Time).

At first glance, *Desvelos en el alba* seems to be writing engendered by chronic feelings of nostalgia, lost innocence, and crisis, writing in which life problems are raised for both private and public re-examination. A closer look, however, captures the ongoing struggle the author sustained during her lifetime between "dispersion and continuity," desire and fulfillment, resistance and submersion.

"Del valor" (About Courage) and "Páginas personales" (Personal Pages) reflect the ambiguous textual space of this collection of intimate writings, a text in which truth is to be found not in the depths of profound reasoning but in spaces that continue to be constructed and interpreted. It is significant, for example, that the first selection is presented dialogically—two gendered individuals who alternately speak and listen, share two cultures, two traditions, and implicitly two languages. The writer's and reader's commitments, then, become linked to something like conversation (rather than domination), to the production of an evolving series of transformations rather than to the discovery of hidden knowledge.

SANDRA M. BOSCHETTO-SANDOVAL

Amanda Labarca Hubertson

About Courage

29 January 1929

I happened to witness a really provocative incident," one of my friends told me yesterday, underlining his tale with a smile. "Two young women were driving through the center of town; the one who was driving got into an argument with a traffic cop and they ended up at the police station instead of the theater where the women were headed. There the disagreement between the *chauffeuse* and the policeman continued before the magistrate, as bitter as when it started. (The question was whether she had stopped her car a few inches on this or that side of the required four yards.) As the accused woman was starting to give in and the representative of authority was raising his voice, the woman's companion spoke up and began to scold her friend: 'Come on, you can do a more convincing job of defending yourself than that! It sounds like there's sugar-water instead of blood in your veins! I thought you were a brave woman, but now I see you're as cowardly as a man!'"

My friend smiled. "Sign of the times," he concluded.

"Well, you know," I answered, "I'm also one of those women who believe that what they say about masculine valor is very relative. Of course it seems to me that there are two kinds of courage. On the one hand, you have the kind needed for the unimportant, everyday things in life, something like the expression of the confidence people have in their own physical abilities. A woman, an ordinary woman, does not dare to venture out alone, for example, in some isolated place such as the countryside, or

Translated by Carol Maier

at night. This is because she knows she would not have the strength to defend herself in the event of danger. On the other hand, put a man in a situation where moral strength is what he needs in order to confront some
difficulty, and nine times out of ten you'll see him turn into a coward. In
the sufferings that age a person, in life's real upheavals, it's often the
woman who draws on a seldom-used energy she's been holding in reserve, and she turns out to be the one who keeps her spirits up, offers
courage and hope, and endures suffering. How many times have you seen
a man driven to suicide (which in this case is clear cowardice) when his
luck changed, but his widow, a woman who had no previous experience
in business, picks up what's left, raises her children, and assumes the responsibility of carrying on for the family!"

"The other day," someone else chimed in, joining our conversation,
"we were going to El Volcán.[1] There was a young showoff who wanted
everyone to see how courageous she was, and she insisted on driving.
Suddenly a chicken starts across the road.

"'Oh no,' she said, 'a chicken!' She drew back and let go of the steer-
ing wheel. If the guy who was with her hadn't known how to drive they
would have had to pick us up in pieces from the bottom of the ravine!"

"That wasn't too little courage but too much coquettishness. She wanted
the boy to protect her. Women instinctively want the male to be strong
and they give him the opportunity to prove that he is."

"Should we also attribute that to feminine faintheartedness?"

"Of course!"

"No. You're behind the times. Girls these days like to show that daily
courage you were talking about a moment ago, the kind that comes from
confidence in their own physical strength."

"According to Marañón,[2] the fact that women find themselves forced
to assume masculine traits is a sign of the decadence of the race. When
masculine cowardice becomes commonplace . . ."

"No. There we're on shaky ground we'd do better to stay away from . . ."

"Courage—and that word includes both bravery and fortitude—is a
very rare virtue, like all virtues. It's only found in exceptional cases. Do
you remember the life of Spinoza? For me his life is the prototype of
moral courage. This is because asceticism is the best helpmate for bold
resolutions. When a person starts to get soft, cowardice sets in. People
who are incapable of enduring a life of privation cannot afford the luxury
of being brave. This, my friend, applies to men and women alike."

Desvelos en el alba. Santiago, Chile: Cruz del Sur, 1945, pp. 81–87.

NOTES

1. El Volcán (the Volcano) is a popular tourist spot in a canyon on the outskirts of Santiago. [Trans.]

2. Gregorio Marañón (1880–1960), a Spanish doctor and essayist well known for such works as *Tres ensayos sobre la vida sexual* (1927; Three Essays on Sexual Life), in which he advanced scientific arguments in favor of a strict differentiation between the sexes. [Trans.]

Personal Pages

(Selection)

23 October 1924

After some bitter days, the siren with hollow eye sockets is back to haunt me again. Living is a sterile waiting, a slow dying. Why not take one stroke and cross out these hours that carry us inexorably toward old age, ruin, final surrender?

Beguiling chimeras of art, immortality, and love . . . each day I see you recede further and further. Instead of letting me catch up with you, my steps distance and separate us. Chimeras, without you I would have no reason to live.

In my mind I go over my years of bitterness interspersed with brief waves of forgetfulness and happiness. Happiness is so short; pain clings so tightly to my body! I am part of the happiness of the people around me I love, but I derive no pleasure from my own goodness; it does not return to me in joy. I wonder if my heart could have withered and dried out from suffering and from having to put up with so much.

What should I do? What can I do? No matter where I go, I will go with myself, with my memories, my anxieties, my worries. Only by dying will I be set free from myself.

Concepción, 8 January 1925

We should not count on tomorrow for whatever we need to accomplish. What we can't finish in the rush of the moment we won't be able to finish later either, because tomorrow will be just as hectic as today.

Translated by Carol Maier

* * *

Everything you want arrives; but it arrives when you no longer want it.

* * *

There is no place on this earth for ugly women, and we are all ugly when the glow of youth has faded.

* * *

How many anxieties and how many efforts and how many sacrifices, only to discover in the end that we are nothing!

* * *

Before, I was convinced that within me I carried a unique message and that the only reason for my existence, my only purpose in life, was to express it. But I kept postponing it, once because I was in love, another day because I felt too miserable, and then because I had to earn a living . . . tomorrow . . . tomorrow, I'll figure it all out. . . . And now it feels as if that message is lost.

14 March 1929

The hours slip by so gently and pleasantly! In the vortex that Chile has become today, it seems that my home and I have been hurled to some distant backwater, where echoes of all the turmoil are muffled by the time they arrive. A modest happiness, with no high notes, no dazzling colors, created silently with the quiet grace of small things. How different I am now than I was barely two or three years ago!

There is nothing I want, nothing troubles me. When I was teaching, I was torn by remorse for being spiritually inadequate to my task. I suffered because I felt dissatisfied with myself, and that basic displeasure was really what provoked all my anxieties. The daily struggle placed me face to face with things I loved, things I disdained, or things that made me suffer from unfulfilled desires. Now I am a woman who has become reconciled with herself and therefore with the world.

3 July 1929

It felt as if I had been shaken so severely by an inner upheaval that I could not bear anything the way it was. My outlook on the world completely changed color. Why live? Why strive for anything? I was enveloped by a fog of anguish and it was impossible to make out a path in any direction.

I've managed to pull myself together. How? I did not think I had the strength left to sustain desire for anything at all. Life is a continual waiting.

Yet there is something in me that lifts my spirits. I don't know what it is or where it comes from. Will? I don't think I have any. Ambition? Of the huge ambitions I once nourished, nothing is left but live coals. The other ambitions gradually died out as I learned how vain they were. When a person becomes convinced that what the world calls successes are hollow appearances, all the more scintillating when they contribute the least to the grandeur of one's spirit, to one's peace and inner harmony, she leaves them behind along the road. . . .

What is it that's lifting my spirits? I don't know. Maybe a subconscious energy. It rises when I feel most sluggish. And it forces me to take up my cross once again. . . .

5 July 1929

Nothing seems worth striving for today. There is no happiness, whether silent or noisy, whether hidden or found in the commotion of crowds. What we experience is a letup in our suffering, a respite, a few trans-figured moments, a few hours of forgetfulness; but a permanent state in which a person feels at peace with life is something we experience neither here nor anywhere. An endless oscillation between things that please and things that offend, between what we want and what we attain, that's what life is. That and solitude! If this no longer makes us feel so bitter, it's be-cause now we have learned that in the end everyone is alone. Skin is an impassable border. We think we know other people, we think we are bound to them by mutual affection, we think that without their support life would be impossible. . . . It's not true . . . We are islands in an archi-pelago. We will never unite with anyone.

27 November 1930

A year devoid of any spiritual content: the hours crammed together with small worries, tiny pleasures, weak palliatives. A person deceives herself into thinking that she is truly alive and that it's worth the effort to keep shouldering the burden of all her dead hopes.

What is it that has become disjointed in my inner self? Why do I feel discouraged before starting on any project? Why is there a gloomy voice telling me over and over that nothing, nothing is worth the effort. . . ?

At the same time, though, this laziness, this apathy nags at my con-science. I wish I could set myself the task of working, of returning to my novels, to my art, to my quest for expression, to everything I've dreamed of accomplishing. But I can't manage to do it. I haven't even written in my diary.

If I tried to describe my inner landscape, what would I mention first? Fear. Fear of suffering: of physical suffering on the road to old age; of spiritual suffering in this apathy that might be a preview of death; of financial suffering in the uncertain situation we find ourselves living in now. I'm afraid. Sometimes my natural optimism leads me to hope. For what? The unexpected. Although that lucky star has sometimes been eclipsed, it has accompanied me in almost all the important undertakings of my life. Sometimes, though, my heart is convulsed with anxiety. It seems as if I were walking on a quagmire into which I was sinking faster every minute.

Fear first, and then anxiety. Am I coming apart? My drives, my ambitions, my once-defiant inner attitude: where are they? Is this what it's like to grow old?

There is a glimmer of light in my afternoons. I approach it gingerly, because it provides me with some comfort and companionship even though it doesn't shine the way a flame does. It's faint, incapable of producing either crisis or tears or that Happiness—with a capital *H*—that one looks for endlessly. It removes the taste of solitude, of desertion, of absolute helplessness from my life. It erases them; at times it even manages to make me glow like a red sky at sunset, and once again I savor the delight of living, of existing in this world of delectable appearances. For an instant, hope, enthusiasm, warmth, and a miraculous sun, and then gray, gray apathy. Gray.

Instability! Is this something that only afflicts me or is it a condition of today's world? I look around me and it seems as though everyone has become infected with the same imbalance. Is there anyone who feels sure of his situation, of his luck, of his ethical principles, of the path he has followed, of his work, of his fate? Anything that concerns man has always been changeable. But I wonder if today things aren't even more uncertain. A person walking along a mountain suddenly comes to a fall of loose rock, from the top of the mountain all the way down to the bottom. And no firm foothold. That's how I picture this moment in history. Of the world? Of Chile? Or only of myself? I don't know if this happens to other people. What I need—in all this change—is a hub. Something that will keep me from feeling like a stray meteorite about to crash tomorrow on the crust of who knows what planet. A rock in the surf. But I don't find it.

I used to believe these would be productive years in which I would be rich with experiences and could give my words to the world, like ripe fruit. Today it seems to me that I always lived superficially, in spite of my

passions, my tragedies, and my pleasures. I think I've learned very little
from the world; from people, almost nothing; from science, just a bit, and
from myself . . . who knows . . . I still find that I don't know what I want.

29 May 1931

"Life! We are at peace. . . ." Work reconciles me with myself. Leisure is a
luxury I was not born for. There is a force within me that drives me im-
peratively to serve my peers. If I were a believer, I would say that I had
been born predestined.

If someone were to ask me the focus of my greatest ambition, I would
answer without hesitating an instant: to collaborate in the revival of civil
liberties, to collaborate with my entire understanding, with my entire
will, and, if necessary, with my very life. This is the polestar of my life's
course. And I feel, with a faith as powerful as it is illogical, that before too
long I will serve this destiny openly.

My work is apprenticeship and preparation. I want to be spiritually
ready for the day that is to come, for the work that will need my support.
My confidence is rooted so vigorously, so deeply that this inner preparation, this work of gathering insubstantial materials for a future that may
exist only in my imagination, gives me happiness, strength, and will. I feel
young again, because the fields of hope seem limitless once more.

8 January 1933

I write from an inner necessity. I know that my jabbering lacks transcen-
dence: it's just noise made by leaves in the wind. But I need to do it. I also
realize that it's one thing to write for yourself and quite another to sustain
the presumptuousness you need to write for the honor of letters and the
glory of humanity.

This makes me think of something no one has written about: the insanity of a Don Quijote of letters who carries his critic, his Sancho, in his
own spirit; every single minute he is alerted to the futility and the emptiness of his endeavor, but even so he is powerless to resist the direction in
which fate pushes him. That's me, on a small scale. I am not unaware, I
don't think, of my multiple limitations; not even the nastiest of critics—
not even people who couldn't bother to hide their hostility to me because
I was a woman or because of my deep involvement in radical causes—has
ever accused me of the things for which I've condemned myself. Meager
talent, dull intuition, inability to find moving words, timid imagination,

impoverished vocabulary. It's all true. In spite of everything, though, I long to express a wellspring I cannot identify because deep within me its murmur fills my breast, and its voices, which come from the mysterious recesses of my subconscious, urge me to convey its message to my people and my world.

28 April 1933

I have the impression that my inner being has no margins, which is the same as saying I have no channel. At every turn I am lured by diverse temptations: the beauty I feel and its emotion, which I can never manage to express; the love I have not returned, and the other not returned to me because I was not able to inspire a feeling as open, abundant, and long lasting as the love I felt myself; and service to my peers—publications, pedagogy, politics. Also, but to a lesser degree, I am attracted by a calm sense of well-being, by trips, friendship, and the esteem of people I value. . . . All my life I have been waging an inner struggle between dispersal and continuity, between my nature, which avoids boundaries, and my intelligence, which forces me to realize that if I do not specialize, if I do not cut a channel, my energies will be scattered in the wind.

Sometimes I think I can understand my irrational inclination toward X and Z—I have in fact loved them beyond all logic—because of my own nature and a trait they share: they are not divided. They know what they want and their temperament supports their desire with a strong, bony skeleton; it might break but it will not bend . . . Not divided, with no cracks splitting inner constitution from intelligence. But I am like partially kneaded dough in which the water and the flour have not yet been well blended. . . . "This way!" my intelligence told me, and that's how I went as long as I could keep my attention in check. When I dropped my guard for a minute, though, my nature shot off on its own along other paths, not the ones toward which logic had directed me. "What has she done?" people probably say about me. She hasn't accomplished anything definitive. She worked hard, there's no doubt about that, but she never became truly outstanding in anything. It's sad. This is my tragedy: a battle with no victory, between my inner being and the limited achievements of my intelligence.

If circumstances had put me in a different situation to live my life, if I had not had to support myself through mental effort, maybe my work would have been more of a piece; my life would have been more lackluster, less spectacular, more ordinary, but it would have been happier.

Because supreme happiness is harmony between one's being and one's actions, between one's instinctive inclination and one's conscious will.

At sea, 14 September 1936

When every day was pleasant, why did I want the days to pass so quickly? Why was I so anxious to end my trip and start home? Was it love for my family? Perhaps. Because I felt impatient and could hardly wait for the future? I was always eager for the tomorrow that was slow in coming. Tomorrow: one less day of life, one more step toward death. When you love life so much you are really rushing toward death. When you long for today to pass quickly you knock on the door of an enigmatic future, knowing that in the end the only attendant who will open the door for you is the great Mystery: death.

I want to return to my country and my family, perhaps to enjoy things in another way, to have a new set of worries, to work and struggle differently. Am I hopeful? Yes, but for what? I don't know. I feel hopeful, and that's all.

Desvelos en el alba. Santiago, Chile: Cruz del Sur, 1945, pp. 107–131.

Magda Portal

Peru, 1903–1989

One of the most visible and most vocal members of the Peruvian political vanguard during the first half of the twentieth century, Magda Portal was, above all, a pioneer in the struggle for women's rights. A close associate of José Carlos Mariátegui and an early supporter of Víctor Raúl Haya de la Torre's APRA Party (American Popular Revolutionary Alliance), she was persecuted repeatedly by the Peruvian government. In spite of suffering imprisonment and exile, she remained outspoken and firmly committed to the ideals of social justice for all Peruvians and especially equal rights for women, beliefs that were not popular at the time.

Portal's writings include poetry collections, *Una esperanza i el mar* (1927; One Hope and the Sea), *Costa sur* (1945; South Coast), and *Constancia del ser* (1965; Constancy of Being); a volume of short stories coauthored with Serafín Delmar, *El derecho de matar* (1926; The Right to Kill); the novel *La trampa* (1956; The Trap); and numerous political essays. Many of the latter were originally given as speeches in various locales throughout Latin America and subsequently published as *América Latina frente al imperialismo y Defensa de la Revolución Mexicana* (1931; Latin America Facing Imperialism, and Defense of the Mexican Revolution). Her works reflect her active involvement in the political life of Peru. As an essayist she writes in a straightforward and unambiguous manner, often in the form of a political tract whose value is propagandistic rather than aesthetic. As a literary critic she reflects a keen awareness of the social and political uses of literature in her promotion of the new committed poetry (the vanguard poetry of the 1920s) in *El nuevo poema i su orientación hacia una estética económica* (1928; The New Poem and Its Aesthetic of Social and Political Commitment). Unfortunately, Portal is not well known outside of Peru, owing in part to the fact that her writings have not been translated into English.

The first of the two selections that follow, "Andamios de vida" (Platforms for Living), appeared in Mariátegui's seminal journal *Amauta* in January 1927. In this text, written in response to an article by Miguel Angel Urquieta denouncing the work of young writers of that day as "so much effeminate, pseudo-leftist childishness," Portal assumes the mantle of apologist for the new literary wave by linking these artistic rumblings to recent and impending social and political upheavals.

The second selection is taken from a work published in 1933 under the title *Hacia la mujer nueva* (Toward the New Woman), also known as *El Aprismo y la mujer* (*Aprismo* and Women). Written some fifteen years prior to her split with APRA, this volume summarizes Portal's social and political philosophy, in particular her ideas on the role of women in society and the part Aprismo (the APRA party) will play in the creation of the "New Woman." In the essay "Toward the New Woman" Portal protests traditional values that require that women be silent and submissive and asserts that women can achieve equality without sacrificing their femininity.

MELVIN S. ARRINGTON, JR.

Platforms for Living

1. Amauta *and Vanguard Art*

*A*mauta's view of art is eclectic; it subscribes to all of art's credos so long as Beauty is allowed to illuminate the patches of darkness that emanate from deep below the surface. But *Amauta* is a forward-looking publication, and as such it has the obligation, as Haya de la Torre says, to examine values and align its whole moral structure with the winds of aesthetic and ideological renovation, in order to strengthen its position as an organ of the vanguard. It is, thus, on this basis that the new art, as we the youth of America understand the term, will find in *Amauta* its rightful home. It must be reiterated that for us the moribund European "-isms"— of which there remains only what has been recorded in the pages of history—these movements mean nothing more than the first warning cries in the artistic revolution.

It is not uncommon to hear, among those not a part of the proletariat, statements of disbelief and derision regarding the triumph of the new ideological creeds, which signal the dawning of a new day for the brotherhood of humankind. Likewise, among the intellectual bourgeoisie and in the spurious journalism of the Americas the new aesthetic manifestations are being angrily fought against, and they are even being called products of perversion.

Translated by Melvin S. Arrington, Jr.

2. The New Art and the Pre-War Generation

The phenomenon can be explained in this way: the new art—the child of an age of formidable eruptions (the European war, the Russian Revolution, hunger in Germany, China, and Russia, and, lastly, the Chinese Revolution), of great scientific triumphs that have multiplied human activity, erasing mileage markers from the map, confounding common sense and creating a new philosophy—this new art was an inevitable and undelayable outcome of all these occurrences. Like all the new philosophical, sociological, and scientific outbursts that barely grazed the consciousness of the pre-war generation, the persistence of the new clarions—be they called jazz band, burlesque, etc.—mortifies its listeners accustomed to the monastic bells of Romanticism and decadence.

But the new man, born in the midst of these cataclysmic events when the world was going through its greatest hour of stormy unrest, fatally charged his brain with photographic plates of rapid comprehension and synthetic creation, like the moment, the only time in which we live— atom and eternity. The new art undoubtedly emitted its newborn cry in the cabin of an airplane or on the concentric waves of a radio signal.

3. The Vital Meaning of the New Aesthetics

This, which for us has its most perfect expression of meaning in terms of humanity and life itself, becomes something overly subtle, obscured by forced cerebrations for the intellectual diversion of the generation immediately prior to the war. It is precisely for us that this new art has its formidable symbolic meaning: ITS DYNAMISM.

The new art tunes up the cerebral motor, which, being composed entirely of nerves in motion, is a stimulant of energy. The new art always sings of the reality of ACTION—be it of thought or movement—and for our Latin peoples, idle dreamers, there is such a great need for a propellant of energy that will awaken the creative forces of the great future that awaits us.

4. The New Art and the New Ideological Currents

In all the ages of HUMANKIND, art has been a logical outgrowth of the various sociological and philosophical tendencies. It has not been an anarchical, disconnected product, even though art more than any other field has a right to anarchy. Directly linked to the most representative bases of the age, art has been, rather, a mirror forecasting the total panorama that is about to unfold.

And this notion, which falls within the strictest bounds of logic, has not been violated this time, in spite of the fact that common logic has been violated.

The new art—truth, synthesis, the human joy of life, power, and creation—responds to this great postwar age of ours, marked by uncommon triumphs of science and humankind's cry of freedom.

A whole parade of cadavers was necessary for this, as well as millions of hungry ghosts. Art divested itself of the worthless pomp and circumstance of Darío's poetry—Beauty in and of itself is sterile, whereas art should be creative—and by penetrating to the root of life it began its human labor.

Before the war art was decadent, totally sterile and lifeless, an enervating and degenerative blight on all life except the world of artificial paradises. The war with its gashes of blood added more humanity and a greater feeling of life to artistic manifestations, and, as in every chaotic age, art endured its own chaos to escape from literary decadence, finally arriving at the broad, sun-drenched steppes of liberty, which signify the new art, an art not bound to any particular school, an art fraternally linked in thoughts and action to the Social Revolution whose seeds bear fruit in the real world.

It is unimportant that the first ones to fulfill this mission—the precursor poets—deny art's ties to the social movement and disclaim what it is obscurely carrying out. Those who come afterwards and who have already been born into the full HUMANIZATION OF ART are the ones who are consciously fulfilling their double mission of BEAUTY and LIFE.

5. The New Art and the New Artists

But with what right do the "bourgeoisie of literature" demand of this heroic and singularly brave art—I do not wish to repeat the reasons—an absolute product of sincerity and talent?

We, the soldiers of the social revolution, are surrounded by a great number of false soldiers, who at any one time may be traitors and dissidents or simply those who are useless for action. All schools of art have had their mischievous pupils: D'Annunzio, Santos Chocano, etc. The new art is not obliged to cover the earth with lighted billboards calling attention to its wayward satellites. The pseudo-intellectual journalists and other artistic rabble have no right to demand an absolute selection in an art that has just recently pushed its happy plant upward toward the oxygen of Reality.

And to deny this movement in art is to act like the frightened and, for that very reason, incredulous petit bourgeois who refuse to acknowledge the still-distant but unstoppable march of the soldiers of the Social Revolution.

"Andamios de vida," *Amauta* 2 (January 1927): 12.

Toward the New Woman

> This is the new woman: self-discipline instead of exaggerated sen-
> timentality; appreciation of freedom and independence rather than
> submission and absence of personality; affirmation of her individu-
> ality as opposed to mindless attempts to become one with the man
> she loves; the affirmation of her right to enjoy earthly pleasures
> without having to don the hypocritical mask of "purity," and,
> finally, the relegation of love affairs to a secondary position in life.
> Before us, then, we have, not a female, not a shadow of a man,
> but rather a woman-individual.   ALEXANDRA KOLLANTAI,
>   "The New Woman and Sexual Morality"

What kind of woman is the Aprista movement creating? An ambiguous, asexual being who poses a threat to men even though she continues to be held back by the umbilical cord of prejudice, a restraint from which she has violently, but so far un-successfully, tried to free herself? An equivocal, liberated young woman who thinks like a man and absurdly tries to imitate him? A Yankee flap-per, the tomboy type, sports-loving, agile, bold, totally fearless, but unsure of where she is going?

Every profound transformation brings with it violent acts and excesses that enable it to achieve the proper balance, the perfect harmony. Revo-lutions happen because of clashing eras and because of glaring contradic-tions between opposing economic, political, social, or scientific views of the world and society. Without this, there would just be a natural, gradual growth and evolution of the individual and society. Aprismo is a revolu-tion. With respect to women, Aprismo is, if you will, even more all-encompassing, since it wrests women from one spiritual situation and so-cial milieu and places them in another, unlike and adverse to the one in which they have lived.

We might illustrate this movement in terms of a cell door suddenly bursting open, thereby allowing the astonished inmates to walk out in

Translated by Melvin S. Arrington, Jr.

broad daylight, totally free, into a vast, limitless field. Cloaked in the old medieval spirit—which still survives more than one hundred years after national independence and the establishment of a democratic republic— women are suddenly entering an age of unrestricted freedom. They are being shown the road ahead, a road without signposts, and they will have to walk it courageously, alone and free. And since they are accustomed to playing a secondary role, always dependent on men, it is only natural to expect that they will be astonished by the experience. One can logically conclude that this new state of existence will create a new spirit in women. But what kind of spirit? There are no models to emulate. Movies and magazines tell about European and North American women, but movies and magazines serve the interests of and represent the mentality of a particular class. However, such images of the freedom enjoyed by women in more advanced countries will prove attractive, and our women will immediately want to enter that strange, blissful state.

Will this newly created being represent an intermediate stage of development between the liberated woman and the one who is enslaved? Will an ill-defined form lacking distinguishing characteristics, half man— half woman, serve as the bridge to the definitive, self-confident Aprista woman?

Possibly this age of transition, of full-scale struggle and boundless sacrifice, will engender a new modality in the feminine spirit, one unlike the ambiguous nature of those women living in decadent societies who embody the egregious diminution of the social system and spiritual ambience under capitalism. Instead, this new spirit will be manifest in a revolutionary type, a woman who is valiant, energetic, not predestined to the ways of her true sex, in the sense that femininity is synonymous with sweetness. This new being, capable of every kind of sacrifice, will have to struggle, "just like men" and forget that she is a woman. She should be less uncertain, however, than all of the aforementioned types of modern women, because Aprismo is grooming her for her true role in the future, which does not exclude motherhood, the basis of real femininity.

The New Woman, who is just now coming into being, will be the product of the profound contradiction between a mentally inferior age— considerably below the spiritual level of the capitalist countries, where women possess a level of culture and personal dignity unknown to the majority of Latin American women—and a superior stage of development, where new formulations of freedom and justice will open up pathways of opportunity that even surpass those available in capitalist countries. Our New Woman will not be like the flapper, that asexual animal, totally free and slightly irresponsible, who accepts all the gratifications of capitalist civilization and suffers its oppressions without protest other than refusing to submit to its sexual impositions. Instead, she will be a self-assured individual who has followed the road of heroic struggle and who, because of her efforts, has arrived at the point where she can enjoy the benefits of rights heretofore unknown but, by the same token, rights that she has no intention of abusing through licentiousness or otherwise.

For the first time, women are going to assume their just roles as intelligent co-partners of men, not their slaves, as companions in the broad spiritual meaning of the word on the same level as their male counterparts. And the struggle for existence, the push to find better ways of doing things, the constant striving for spiritual advancement, will be no longer the sole province of men but rather that of the human couple, man and woman. Finally, after centuries of losing ground, the couple will once again assume its rightful place of importance.

Thus, the family nucleus will be strengthened, since the woman will no longer be just the discreet female happy in her inferiority, a parlor doll, or a poor domestic servant locked into her daily routines and lacking initiative. The family, with its two firm bulwarks formed by the human couple, will begin to fulfill its grand mission of producing strong children. They will be united by love and mutual respect, by equality and equal sharing of responsibilities, and by the woman's spiritual influence, which will freely manifest itself in the formation of this new consciousness in her children.

If the woman suffers from anything (apart from the denial of all her other rights, including freedom itself), it is from never having had the chance to express her personality. Because of these restraints, she has never been allowed to release, except in a few instances, the great creative force that is in her and the superior impulses of her intelligence, which make her capable of exerting a healthy influence on the shaping of both family and society. She has locked her proverbial timidity in the most remote corners of her spirit, relegating it to the level of the unconscious. The virtues of her true personality can be revealed with greatness at any moment if only offered the proper stimulus.

And so Aprismo will broaden the New Woman's horizons. But she will not lose her femininity in the face of these new opportunities by failing to take advantage of them or by adopting equivocal positions. On the contrary, by framing her revolutionary activity within the lines of rigid discipline, she will continue to advance righteously toward her own liberation, which will raise her to a superior level—in spiritual as well as material terms—and thereby enable her to fulfill her ultimate destiny, alongside her male companion. He, too, will be free of prejudice, and he will understand her and respect her for all her meritorious qualities.

Hacia la mujer nueva. Lima: Cooperativa Aprista Atahualpa, 1933, pp. 50–54.

Teresa de la Parra

Venezuela, 1889–1936

Teresa de la Parra was born Ana Teresa Parra Sanojo in
Paris to an aristocratic Venezuelan family. She spent
her childhood on the sugar plantation of her family in
Venezuela and later split her time between Paris and
Madrid.

Her first book, published in Paris in 1924, was *Ifigenia: Diario de una señorita que escribió porque se fastidiaba*
(*Ifigenia: The Diary of a Young Lady Who Wrote Because
She Was Bored*, 1994). A novel about a girl from Caracas
who falls victim to the schemes of her greedy uncle,
loses her fortune, and has to give up her freedom in order to survive in traditional society, it was both praised
and criticized for the way it depicted modern women.
Her second novel was *Memorias de la Mamá Blanca*
(1929; *Mama Blanca's Memoirs*, 1992). Whereas *Ifigenia*
was a novel of the city, the *Memorias* occur almost entirely in the idyllic world of the patriarchal hacienda
where the protagonist lives as a child.

Teresa de la Parra traveled through Europe and Latin
America. She was an intimate friend of the Cuban
writer Lydia Cabrera and friend to the Chilean poet
Gabriela Mistral. Living in Paris most of her life, she
was diagnosed with tuberculosis in 1932 and spent her
last years in sanatoriums in France and Spain until her
death in 1936.

The three talks she entitled "Influencia de la mujer
en la formación del alma americana" (The Influence of
Women in the Formation of the American Soul), of
which the essay included here is the first, were given in
Bogota in 1930. These were about different moments in
the history of Latin America and the determinant roles
various women played in the evolution of that history.
In the period of the Conquest, de la Parra centers on
the role of Indian and mestizo women, while during the
colonial period she talks about the lives of privileged
women as exercising a certain power from behind the
closed doors and windows of the convents and houses
in America. The third essay, about women during the
period of Independence, was in part a project for a
novel about Bolívar that she never managed to write.
The conferences were published in Caracas in 1961;
they are just now beginning to receive overdue critical
attention for their feminist orientation.

RICHARD ROSA

The Influence of Women in the Formation of the American Soul

First Lecture

It seems to me that I am dreaming, seeing myself here at last in Bogota in front of an audience of intimate and now old friends, without experiencing any of the unbelievable fears I envisioned at a distance, but, to the contrary, feeling the confidence and the happiness of the loveliest moments of life.

For a long time my heart yearned for this visit to Colombia. I responded to the yearning, but only from afar, with gestures and smiles, because, like shy people, even being much in love, I was afraid of coming too close. This autumn the call became a voice, and a voice so urging and promising that, putting aside every fear and trusting in the good star that protects the enterprising, I began to prepare my visit, not wanting to arrive, as you see, with my hands completely empty.

The urging voice I'm talking about came to me in the form of a letter. It was at the beginning of November, and I had just arrived in Paris after a long first trip through Italy. I was preparing to spend a quiet winter in my haven at Neuilly, a winter of reading and perhaps also of work—in Paris you never know—when one morning I was awakened by the messenger-letter from Colombia. It was written by a group of friends who lived in Bogota. They transmitted to me the following invitation: come to Colombia to give a series of conferences about myself, about the history of my literary vocation and about my books. It isn't easy for me to explain to you the state of perplexity in which such a suggestive and dangerous invitation left me. Considering that I had never spoken in public, I was in a

Translated by Richard Rosa and Doris Meyer

sea of doubts and temptations for several days, thinking over the dilemma: How to put together a conference? How to assume the role of author present before a public that perhaps might have liked me from afar because it had not seen me very close? And the literary vocation, so intermittent and fragile? On the other hand, the idea of crossing the sea during long days of peace, of sailing perhaps very slowly up the Magdalena River and through the big jungle and the Andes to reach so many familiar and dreamed-of cities, filled my soul with exquisite restlessness. Through my window, over the golden leaves swept away by the misty Parisian autumn wind, the tropic was calling to me. I already recognized from a distance the Colombia of the first romantic scenes of my childhood: the Cauca Valley, the big hacienda, the bathing pool full of roses, the dog Mayo, Feliciana the black woman; and from there, from the top of the path that led onward, the distant window with its frame of flowers where María still glistened in white waving goodbye to Efraín.

With this bright fantasy of the trip, the question of accomplishing it and of its consequences ceased to exist. One of the more serious consequences was the decision regarding the topic for the conference. Accepting the one that was proposed was almost a duty. When a book has acquired an intimate friendship with the soul of a reader, as happens in every case of intimacy, a sweet thirst for confidence flows naturally from the ears to the lips. I know that my books are much loved in Colombia; I have seen this already, and I say so with the boast of the child who hasn't done anything to deserve love. They are loved with that charming affection, disinterested and domestic, with which we love dogs, flowers, caged birds, and, in general, all familiar and useless things.

I therefore understand that it was natural for me to smile with confidence the day I arrived at this paternal house. Unfortunately, a lack of distance and the abundance of witnesses has not made it possible to create a beautiful story about myself that is truthful to the needs of the heart. Within thirty, thirty-five, or forty years, I'll return to these Colombian cities, and then, as in Ronsard's sonnet, trembling of old age, between the spindle and the distaff, by the hearth at night, I will tell the wonderful story of my youth . . . without the danger of somebody denying it. I will see, reflected in the eyes of my listeners, not the image of what I am but the divine image of what I would have wanted to be.

This promise takes care of the first topic proposed. About the second, that of a literary vocation, I can only tell you that, however much I sought it out, I didn't find it. So much does the literary vocation tend to get lost and desert me that when at times a detractor—for there are always gossips that, for lack of delicacy, tell us unpleasant things—when some detractor once spread the rumor that I was not the real author of my books, I was the first one to believe it happily and comfortably. With my vocation lost, I felt freed of a great responsibility, having also lost the books. After all, what are works accomplished without the vocation that reaffirms them and protects them from us? That my books are not mine now is true up to a point. Aside from my name, which has remained as if by oversight on the cover of the books, I recognize nothing of my own in my novels: the first one, written by a girl of our time, whose whereabouts are now unknown; the second, written by a grandmother, now deceased, who was hospitable and affectionate like many other women still living under the roofs of these good cities of America. Those tales and novels have, to my mind, no other authors than those two absent ones. Situated at opposite extremes of life, they remained with me for some time; one told me of her yearning to live, the other of her sadness for having lived, and when they finished confiding in me, they left discreetly when it was time to edit the books.

About the third topic, that of the books themselves, or, to be precise, that of the thesis of *Ifigenia*—the crucial situation of the modern girl—that one did seem very interesting to me because it lends itself to discussion and urgently requires a solution. I won't avoid that one.

Many are the moralists who, mostly with kind equanimity although occasionally with violent anathemas, have attacked the diary of María Eugenia Alonso, calling it Voltairian, perfidious, and dangerous in the hands of contemporary young ladies. I don't think that this diary is so harmful to the girls of our time for the simple reason that it merely reflects their lives. Almost all of them, especially those born and raised in very austere environments, carry inside themselves a María Eugenia Alonso in open rebellion but more or less hidden depending on how the environment oppresses her, who tells them through an inner voice what the other one told them through the written word. The journal of María Eugenia Alonso is not a book of revolutionary propaganda, as many far-right moralists have tried to see it. On the contrary, it is the exposition of a typical case of our contemporary disease, that of Spanish American Bovarism, of extreme dissatisfaction caused by an abrupt change in temperature and a lack of new air in the surroundings. Whether the moralists like it or not, you don't stop a plague by hiding the cases, as is done in some ports, when at the expense of the truth and of public health they want to get their bill of health at all costs. Plagues are stopped with air, with light, with modern hygienic measures that neutralize the causes of the evil, which are sometimes also modern.

The crisis that today's women are going through cannot be resolved by preaching submission, submission, and more submission, as was the practice during the time when a quiet life could be confined entirely behind doors. Life today, the life of the automobile driven by her owner, of the phone near the bed, of newspapers and of travels, doesn't respect closed doors. Like the radio that so accurately symbolizes it, it goes through walls and, like it or not, makes itself heard and mingles with the life of the home. For a woman to be strong, healthy, and truly clean of any hypocrisy, you cannot subdue her in the face of that new life. On the contrary, she should be free within herself, aware of the dangers and responsibilities, useful to society even if she is not a mother, independent with respect to money thanks to her work and her collaboration alongside man—neither master nor enemy nor exploitable marriage candidate, but friend and companion. Work does not exclude mysticism, nor does it keep one from sacred duties. Rather, it is another discipline that purifies and strengthens the spirit. But mysticism, submission, and passivity imposed by force, "just because," and by the inertia of habit, produce dangerous and silent reactions and a hatred of chains that may have been good in other times; and they embitter souls that, in their peaceful appearance, take their reprisals wherever they can and end by becoming whitened graves. The true enemies of feminine virtue are not the dangers to which it may be exposed by healthy activity, nor by books, universities, laboratories, offices, or hospitals. It is the frivolity, the empty mundane flitting-about with which the girl of marrying age, or the unhappily married lady, brought up in the old-fashioned way and already sick with skepticism, seeks distraction in an activity that, directed toward work and study, could be a thousand times more noble and sacred.

When I say "work," I'm not talking about the humiliating, badly paid jobs in which helpless young women are wickedly exploited. I'm talking about work requiring preparation, in careers, jobs, or specializations adequate to women, and fairly paid according to the talent and the work accomplished. I wouldn't want you, as a consequence of the tone and the line of reasoning of what I've said, to think me a defender of women's suffrage. I'm not a defender or a detractor of women's suffrage for the simple reason that I am not familiar with it. Knowing that it raises its voice to get women to have the same political rights and responsibilities as men scares and stuns me so much that I've never been able to listen completely to what that voice proposes. And it is because I believe, unlike the suffragists, that we women should thank men for the fact that they have shown the self-sacrifice to monopolize political office entirely. It seems to me that, along with coal mining, it is one of the toughest and most unclean professions. Why claim it?

My feminism is moderate. In order to show it and to deal, ladies and gentlemen, with this delicate issue of the new rights the modern woman should acquire—not by means of a sudden and destructive revolution but by a noble evolution that conquers by educating and taking advantage of the forces of the past—I had begun by preparing, in these three lectures, a kind of historical overview of feminine abnegation in our countries, that is, of the hidden and happy influence that women had during the periods of Conquest, Colonization, and Independence. Because I believe a spirit exists truly common to all the countries in our Catholic and Spanish America, and because I believe that promoting it through their union is broad patriotism, I included all our countries in this overview and I called it "The Influence of Women in the Formation of the American Soul."

But, having finished my historical overview, due to unexpected circumstances I had to travel to New York and Havana on the first stages of my trip to Colombia. I thought that I would acquire in those two cities new and interesting information about modern women, an objective for my final conferences, and I actually did so, but at the same time my vocation forsook me at the very moment of writing. In New York you can't work because of the excess of movement and noise, and in Havana even less, because of the *dolce far niente*. I have kept, then, to my selfless women. Frankly speaking, I will tell you that down deep in my heart I prefer them. They have the charm of the past and the infinite poetry of voluntary and sincere sacrifice.

As a brief summary of the recollections of my travels I will only say that Havana is one of the places where one can best see the happy evolution of Latin women toward a more useful and just end without losing the characteristics of femininity and with good results. Cuba has a strong Creole character, traditional and folkloric, that defends it miraculously from spiritual invasions. Its exaggerated "Americanism" has not yet reached the soul of any of its social classes. The people from Havana are dyed-in-the-wool Creoles, despite the presence of the English language, tourism, dollars, and constant traveling. Many Cuban women work and study without losing their femininity or their respect for certain principles and traditions. I lived in the house of a friend's family whose garden was adjacent to the university. Through its doors I used to see the daily comings and goings of as many women as men. And I met a very honorable middle-class family with five sisters twenty to thirty years old. Three of them were graduates of the university and were working in clinics or hospitals very successfully. Two were still studying. All of them were perfectly correct, very beautiful, and feminine; the three who were doctors helped their aging parents and the other two who were studying. Their work didn't prevent them from marrying: two of them had fiancés whom they received at home in the classic Creole custom. The difference of outcome between this education and the traditional education that still prevails in the upper classes in Havana is notable. The high-society girl from Havana, the rich heiress, player of tennis and bridge, dressed by Patou, owner of an automobile driven by herself, sometimes raised in convents and under austere conditions, is generally speaking beautiful, very elegant, and socially charming; but her culture, the aspects of her nature, and especially her moral level, lacking preparation for modern life, is inferior to that of the girl educated by work.

Gabriela Mistral, who may come here in July or August, alluded to this desire in a letter to me in which she calls Colombia "the healthiest place in the tropics." Without a doubt, Gabriela will speak skillfully about this burning issue, which she knows a thousand times better than I do, being a militant in all her ideas. I refer precisely to the idea of establishing a parallel between her life and that of Delmira Agustini—the two best American women poets of our century—in order to demonstrate the redemption and dignity women acquire through work and financial independence. Briefly, I want to outline that parallel.

Delmira Agustini, young, beautiful, brilliant, born in a severe and bourgeois milieu, is the case of the María Eugenia, the protagonist of *Ifigenia,* carried to a tragic end. Because of the powerful tradition that "every woman has to get married," she marries very young in a so-called good match. Soon after the marriage, the drama of incomprehension begins. On one side, the despotic and vulgar master; on the other, the silent disdain of one who feels she's a thousand times superior and yet enslaved. As a consequence: mutual hatred mixed with passion, divorce, and, at last, during one of the interviews of the divorce process, the husband kills her and kills himself—the only way to subdue her and to quench his thirst for domination.

Gabriela Mistral, poor, born in humble and honorable circumstances, without worldly conventionalities, has worked since she was a child. As the days went by, her work and her good Christian faith led her to new ideals that she humanizes and adapts in her work to the real needs of life, and so she goes through the world, suffering and fighting as apostle, socialist, Catholic, defender of freedom and of the noble spirit of the race.

With her experienced voice she will perhaps talk to you of a just and already indispensable feminism. Meanwhile, it is time, if you'll permit me, to go look for my own selfless women, I mean, "The Influence of Women in the Formation of the American Soul." I admit that coming up with this title took a lot of thinking, numerous discussions with myself, and, in general, all the cruel anxieties with which the dilemma of self-expression torments us by tending to lose elegance in order to gain clarity. I didn't know if it would be correct or even if it would sound right to Colombian ears to say "American soul" instead of Latin American, Ibero-American, Spanish American, Indo-American, or Indo-Spanish-American soul. None of these combinations pleased me either in substance or in form. They don't have lightness, they don't have wings, they don't have charm. They sound, I don't know why, like criollo snobbery naturalized in foreign countries, which is the source of many good things but also of many evils and sins against good taste. On the other hand, it seemed to me very sad to have so many and such diverse baptismal fonts. Each one of these different terms contained a formula for disintegration in opposition to the others. I thought at random of the power of words to determine facts, I thought of the sweet intimacy of things related to their names, and I thought, at last, that our anonymous beautiful homeland—so ample, so diverse, and yet so miraculously and mysteriously similar without having had either the embrace of proximity or the fatherly connection of only one name—was being relegated now to the status of abandoned, nameless girl, in great danger of losing her fortune. So I decided to eliminate any composite name and, with a loving smile, just say "American Soul," certain that everyone would understand me.

I believe that as long as politicians, military men, journalists, and historians spend their lives putting antagonistic labels on things, the job for young, simple people, and above all women, since we are many and quite disorderly, is to shuffle the labels in order to reestablish a cordial confusion. I'm talking about the annoying antagonism, the work of the press, not of living language, that has effectively opposed Indo-Americanism to Spanish Americanism. I don't want to talk here about the evil contained in these two formulas, confronting one another like two torches of discord in the same house: on one side, the inhuman scorn of the nonintelligent and insensitive white who still thinks of himself as lord and master; on the other, the romantic Indianism, the deaf hatred the mestizo feels toward the intruding race, the hate that incites daily the popularized and unfair version of the Spanish Conquest, as if made of blood and fire, as if it was only about destruction, as if the conquest of America was an isolated case in the history of the world, and not the eternal and hateful law of all wars and all invasions! This topic has been discussed a lot, inevitably and insistently bringing up the excellent and over-exalted Father Bartolomé de las Casas. I think Father las Casas was an apostle and a saint. He knew how to courageously condemn the spirit of cruelty that incites war and the injustice of the strong against the weak. But, like many leaders of pacifism and socialism, after loving pity and justice passionately, he came to love even more the fire of his own eloquence, which belonged to the school of Savonarola. A brilliant polemicist, he unfortunately lived in an age in which there were no political meetings and no press. His energetic campaigns, enriched with imaginary statistics of mortality and assuming the category of historical documents, have been used as weapons in alien hands—I mean in the hands of Protestants and of Northern races, double enemies of the Spanish Empire—to discredit us systematically. And often they have been used in our own hands to raise discord and to stir up hatred between races.

Other contemporaries of las Casas silently preached mercy and peace. They were the women of the Conquest: obscure Sabines, anonymous workers of concord, true founders of cities by setting up homes, their most effective work was prolonged through generations in their silent enterprise of fusion and love.

As we know, the epic of the Conquest was born of a woman, Isabel the Catholic. Reading Columbus' mind, she brought the splendid commotion of the Renaissance from Spain to America's jungles. From afar, from a spatial and temporal distance, she is the European mother and godmother of our America. Her symbolic figure, later softened by the indolence of colonial life, already contains the characteristics of the classic "criolla matron," our grandmothers of yesterday. In remembrance of them I want to evoke the queen for a few moments in this profile, which José María Heredia used as a prologue to his translation of the Conquest of the New Spain. I do it out of faith and devotion to the race, as one evokes the familiar saint during prayers repeated daily because they're known by heart:

"On 26 November 1504," says Heredia, "Queen Isabel died in her castle of Medina del Campo. A courageous, pure, and selfless woman, she combined the feminine charms with all the masculine virtues. Her soul was superior to that of her age. She loved wisdom and books intensely. An intrepid and astute queen, she conquered Granada and understood Columbus. On her deathbed she dictated her final testament with the serenity of an ancient philosopher. That famous testament, overflowing with faith, love, intelligence, and magnanimity, was the seal of her noble life. Isabel was good. In the midst of the anguish of dying, she still thought of her Castilian people and her children in the Indies with maternal concern. All of Spain cried for this incomparable woman. She had been the best and the greatest of their monarchs. Nature itself seemed touched by her death. There was an earthquake. The sky covered the simplicity of her ceremony with lugubrious pomp. She wanted to rest in the same ground she herself had won. Beneath the storm, the lightning, the thunder, and the pouring rain, a hearse took her to Granada. Isabel's reign was the dawn of Spain's glory, which later sank into the sea with the defeat of the Invincible Armada.[1]

As opposed to Isabel, on this side of the ocean we see the founding women pass by, discreetly veiled by the tales of the chroniclers of the Indies. Their humble lives full of suffering and love are not told. They are hardly noticed. Almost all of them are Indians baptized with Castilian names. Many of them are princesses. The most famous ones go by the names of Doña Marina, Doña Catalina, Doña Luisa, Doña Isabel. . . . They share with their white husbands the governance of their lands, and along with the gift of dominion they teach them to use cotton pants, rope sandals, and palm hats.

The white *cacique*, or overlord, completely adapted to the Indian environment, is not, ladies and gentlemen, a romantic legend; he is a typical case of conversion through the miracle of feminine love. Father las Casas himself, praising the beauty of some Indian women, counts up to sixty who were married to Castilians in the city of Vera Paz alone. Very eloquent and touching is the story of the Spaniard named Gonzalo Guerrero who was shipwrecked with Vicuesa's expedition and lived eight years among the Indians. One of his companions named Aguilar, who had managed to escape and then return to the tribe with enough money to pay for Guerrero's ransom, warned him, saying that he was going to lose his soul by living among idolatrous Indians. Guerrero dismissed him with these words, according to the chronicler: "Brother, I am married, I have three children, and these people consider me a *cacique* when there is war. Go in peace, for my face is tatooed and my ears pierced. You can see how beautiful these three little children of mine are. Please be so kind as to give me, for them, those green beads you are carrying."

And so, in grass huts under coconut palms in the villages by the sea, mixing cocoa with vanilla or cooking cassava bread, Indian women, like tropical Nausicaas, prepare, along with the supper of the newly arrived, the dawn of the colonial age, our criollo Middle Ages. The religion of that period will be an almost unconscious reverence of nature. She, nature, will catechize the new barbarians while they catechize the Indians. Their Gothic cathedrals will be the boughs that line the entrances to their haciendas, rising up in transparent vaults, melodious and stately. Inside will be the abundant blessings of cocoa, coffee, banana, cotton, tobacco, and sugarcane—more than enough so that all men will be brothers. Everyone will give thanks daily with old Don Juan de Castellanos, intoning his Colombian credo of the grateful conqueror (the same one I repeated a few days ago when I entered Colombia through the Cauca Valley and through the Quindío countryside):

> Land of gold, well-stocked land,
> Land for making a perpetual home,
> Land with food in abundance,
> Land of large villages and flat fields,
> Land of bright and serene blessings,
> Land that has brought an end to our suffering.

As often happens in traveling and in enterprises where the heart can be a mediator, our route changes when we least expect it. The Spanish and Portuguese conquerors who left the Iberian Peninsula as soldiers or traders like their Venetian rivals became, without realizing it, the poet-founders of a tropical Arcadia. They came to look for gold and found ideals. After the brutal clash with the generous land they began to discover the gold within themselves. How many obscure adventurers, upon crossing the sea, became, by a miracle of the environment, Patriarchs and splendid gentlemen! Ah! Not in vain do we navigate through the tropical seas, under the fragrant nights full of stars that grow larger and nearer. In the marvel of that spring that spreads over the sea from Europe toward our America, everything promises fortune and love to the traveler. Because of their travels the brutal conquerors often learned to be tender and docile lovers.

The women who play a role in the formation of our American society, imprinting it with their soft and deep mark, are beyond number. I think they can be divided in three vast groups. Those of the Conquest: they are the sufferers, crucified by the clash between the races. Then those of the Colony: they are the mystics and dreamers. And those of Independence: they are the inspirers and the activists. In Mexico, in Bogota, in Lima, in Quito, in Caracas, in Buenos Aires, in Havana they follow an identical evolution, seeming to move about in the same city like neighbors and sisters. Colombia, Venezuela, Argentina, Chile, Ecuador have their collection of female martyrs, the great women of Independence, active and loving heroines. But today I look toward Mexico and Peru to find two humble indigenous flowers who are prototypes of the first suffering women. The Mexican Malinche, Doña Marina, revered and happy at the end of her life, and the melancholy Peruvian princess Doña Isabel, granddaughter of the king Túpac Yupanqui and mother of the first American writer, the Inca Garcilaso de la Vega. The life of this last woman was spent sweetly between love and tears. For all her gentle selflessness, she reaped only ingratitude and indifference. No matter, she took refuge in silence and resignation. Her pain as an abandoned woman, heightened by separation from her son in exile, would inspire, many years later, one of the most beautiful books of classic Spanish literature: Garcilaso's *Royal Commentaries*.

Much has been said admiringly about the political genius of Hernán Cortés, about the extraordinary sagacity with which he negotiated and made treaties with the Indians. I believe, gentlemen, that that mysterious sagacity is named exclusively Doña Marina. In the various chronicles of the conquest of New Spain, at least in the two or three that I know, Doña Marina is credited with the important role of interpreter and mediator; she gave accurate advice and uncovered conspiracies, like the one in Cholula that plotted the death of Cortés and his entire expedition. From what little is said, one can guess how much is not told. It's absolutely certain that the influence of Doña Marina in the conquest of Mexico was more important, her interventions and advice more frequent and subtle than is acknowledged by historians, even by Bernal Díaz del Castillo himself, who talks about her with great affection. They are untold stories because the tumult of military actions overwhelms them. They are little tales not considered seemly amidst the official splendor of history, whose field of action preferably extends over scenes of destruction and death. Harmony, almost always the work of women, is anonymous; it lacks tragic elements and is not the stuff of epics. Happiness, which is less remarkable, is perpetuated not in books but in offspring, in the fraternal fusion of races, and in the humble goodness of tradition that polishes the rough edges of life, bringing smiles and gratitude.

Hernán Cortés was known as a Don Juan. Before undertaking the conquest of Mexico he had already made numerous conquests of a romantic type. [. . .] Sometime thereafter, some *caciques* from the town of Tabasco took Doña Marina as a gift to Cortés, "along with four little lizards, some blankets, five ducks, two gold soles for sandals, and a few other things of little value," says Bernal Díaz. And at the end of the list of gifts, he adds, "After her conversion, that Indian woman who was given to us was named Doña Marina. She was truly a great princess, daughter of *caciques* and mistress of vassals. By her appearance it was evident that she was attractive, outspoken, and self-assured. Doña Marina was an excellent woman, a good translator [*buena lengua*], and a good beginning for our conquest, and because of this Cortés always took her with him."

Sold as a slave by her mother and stepfather, who gave her to some foreign Indians in order to usurp her kingdom, Doña Marina had passed through various masters and cities. During her wandering life, she managed to learn the talent of adapting along with the customs, aspirations, rivalries, and languages of the different peoples who would be conquered by Cortés. Thus she added to her natural intelligence the broad-mindedness gained by travel and the refined touch one acquires by having suffered. She spoke the Mayan and Aztec languages and quickly learned to express herself in Spanish with as much fluency and clarity as if she had been born in Seville.

It's hard for us to imagine the dazzling impression that Cortés must have made on Doña Marina's imagination. Powerful white god, descended from the sun and the moon (according to the common belief among the Indians), ambassador from unknown lands, captain of gods, he carried thunder and lightning in his weapons of combat and ran swiftly on animals that seemed to have wings; his height and his beard declared him invincible, and his presence, according to old prophecies, announced the destruction of the empire and the start of a new age atop its ruins. If for the Indian men Cortés was the Aztec antichrist, and his weapons, horses, and soldiers the monsters of an apocalypse of desolation and death, for the Indian women like Doña Marina he was undoubtedly the messiah.

Doña Marina owed little or nothing to her people. Her mother had sold her to disinherit her. In her bitter moving from town to town she came to know tearfully the condition of the humble women of her race. Consigned to the lowliest jobs, mistreated, sold by one man to another when they were girls as victims for sacrifices—or, when they were grown, as slaves for marriage—they would surely improve their situation under these new masters who worshiped a feminine idol with a child in her arms. In allying herself with such zeal to Cortés and to the cause of the white men against her own people, Doña Marina was obeying the revolutionary imperatives of her love and initiating the future reconciliation of the two races. Albeit in a very primitive way, she was also the initiator in America of the first feminist campaign.

She was "outspoken and self-assured," says Bernal Díaz when introducing her. How much flavor these two blunt adjectives contain, and how much can be read into them! "Outspoken and self-assured," that is, diligent, attentive, witty, and discreet, with a bit of coquettishness and a lot of innate generosity. As Bernal Díaz' lively narrative proceeds, we observe her actions and get to know her well enough to strike up an intimate friendship. She is enthusiastically taken with novelties, like a typical woman and like anyone with a restless and creative mind. Being an idealist, she is credulous. Everything amazes her. She's a likable person, the classic lighthearted woman enjoyed everywhere she goes, because she knows how to fit in and reduce discord with the joy of her presence. The scribes or painters, sent by Moctezuma to give him an accurate account of the invaders, hasten to engrave the portrait of Doña Marina as one of the great mysterious forces. [. . .] There is no mission that she fails to perform, no peace proposal that she does not preside at along with Cortés. She goes about sweetening the bitterness as she translates everyone's discourse. This faith in her intervention, as if it were a secret providence, guides us continuously through the countless crises that Bernal Díaz narrates. There is one critical moment after the fall of Mexico when Cortés seems to have forgotten all the political tact and judgment he had maintained up to that time. He gets carried away with unnecessary harshness. He makes the arrogant displays of a conqueror and offends the sensibilities of the Aztec people, profaning the sacred person of Moctezuma. We sense the disaster that's going to explode; discontent heightens, we feel the "sad night" coming on with the horrible sacrifices of Spaniards to the god Huichilobos; we feel like interrupting our reading and calling on the spirit of mercy and harmony: Doña Marina, where are you?

Cortés' passions were short and violent. His love for Doña Marina suddenly changed to calm affection. Sometime after the conquest of Mexico he married her to a noble Spaniard, Don Juan de Jaramillo. "Doña Marina, who had absolute rule over all the Indians in New Spain," the chronicler tells us, accepted the marriage with resignation. From that long war in which she was the mediator and adviser, she was left with the memory of a great love, the recovery of her power among the Indians, and her son Martín Cortés, Spanish hidalgo and knight of Santiago.

Let's hear how Bernal Díaz del Castillo narrates with a kind of biblical tone the scene in which, through unexpected circumstances, Doña Marina finds herself face to face with her mother, the Indian woman who sold her when she was still a child.

"While Cortés was in the town of Guazagualco, he summoned all the *caciques* of that province to address them on the subject of our Holy Doctrine. Doña Marina's mother and her half-brother, Lázaro (named thus after being converted), were among them. When the old woman saw Doña Marina, she recognized clearly that it was her daughter because of the resemblance between them. The mother and brother were afraid that she would have them put to death. When Doña Marina saw them both in tears, she comforted them and told them not to be afraid; she said that when they had sold her to the men from Xicalango, they hadn't known what they were doing, and so she pardoned them, giving them many clothes and gold jewelry. And she told them that God had been good to her by saving her from the worship of idols and by her marriage to such a gentleman as her husband, and by giving her Cortés' son. Even if they were to make her *cacica* of all the provinces in New Spain, she said, she would refuse the honor, for she would rather serve her husband Cortés than anything else in the world. All this that I narrate here, I saw with my own eyes and swear is true. Amen."

I don't know what you think about this page, but I find it charming. We see characters passing through it just as one does in reels of film taken long ago: they have the same brusque movements and comic ingenuousness at the dramatic moment. We see Doña Marina, another Joseph sold by his brothers, the symbol of mercy, receiving her people who remind her of the sad past. She no more than looks at them and they're forgiven. With generous display she gives them clothes and jewels, things that come from distant and marvelous places. She tells them her fantastic adventures, introduces them to her new family who all belong to the race of the foreign conquerors. Since she is happy, she forgives the evil of the past with a show of generosity.

During his evocative and lively narrative, Bernal Díaz constantly apologizes for his lack of style and the carelessness of his writing. He assures us that he has felt obliged to "distill from his memory those facts that are not ancient stories, nor stories from adventure books, but things that happened yesterday, so to speak." Because men of letters and well-known writers have altered the truth when they wrote their chronicles of the conquest of New Spain, the famous war in which Bernal Díaz fought over a hundred times, it hurts him to see the memories of his youth being abused. In order to restore them, he narrates them as best he can, but he is not a man of letters, only a rude soldier. Once he finishes his true story, he finds it so rough that he will die without having dared to publish it. It is so full of trivial details! And so it is: those details are precisely what remain in memory, as if by some capricious grace, and they contain in their humbleness all the poetry of remembrance: the color of the horses in the expedition, their nicknames, their skills or qualities, the unexpected birth of a colt aboard the vessel, born to a brown mare; the amount of cassava and lard carried by a soldier named Juan Cedeño, resident of Havana, who was said to be rich. Juan Solís—he says—was called "Behind Doors" because of his inclination to listen without being seen. Tarifa was called "The One with White Hands" because he was equally useless at war and at work. [. . .] Such details are numerous and evocative in the flow of facts. Doña Marina's role is also part of this lively tumult. She will be the polestar of his story, which is not exactly history but something loftier and more beautiful: a ballad in prose.

I sense that more than one of you must be thinking that I'm talking like this because of occupational disposition and that it would be better if I confined myself to being a novelist so that I don't speak such nonsense. Well, no. I'm sure I'm not talking nonsense and that it's almost a duty to claim the moral superiority of this kind of narrative. In comparison, historical truth, the other, the official one, turns out to be a kind of banquet for men only where intelligent things are said and eloquent speeches are pronounced without touching anyone's heart because they're so formal. Having excluded women, they have cut off the connecting wires with life. If one looks at Roman times and at the Gospels, which are lively and moving stories par excellence, women play a role of first magnitude—as in this narrative by Bernal Díaz—and not only women but also friendly and brotherly animals. It has been almost two thousand years, and yet the mule and the ox of Bethlehem continue to warm our hearts. The drama of Christ's passion was written by evangelists who were rough chroniclers similar to Bernal Díaz. No writer of the age, not even the exquisite Plutarch, could have recorded it with the same enduring strength. In the Passion story, a rooster has its very important role and women pass by in a hurry following the vicissitudes of the drama, just like Doña Marina. No-body gets in their way; on the contrary: come on forward, all of you women! These are the heroines of the day. It's a street drama in which everyone participates. Described and performed ceaselessly for twenty centuries, the people perform it and describe it again during Holy Week, maintaining the same tradition of love and realism created by the smallest details. [. . .]

I don't think it's possible to write a historical scene any better. I say "better" because, since the moral objective of history is to make us love people or specific things, blending the present with the warmth of the past—making things appear more lovable—will improve it. I don't say this because of the common urge these days to denigrate all authorized and respectable things; rather I believe that, whereas the truth of histori-ans is relative, the truth of tradition or the history of the nonhistorians is absolute, because it gets us closer to reality and in a more charming way. Besides, tradition is disappearing. We have to love it twice as much be-cause of its ideal usefulness and because it's sentenced to death. The press has been devouring it. Memory does not make an effort to retain what is already written, and if it retains it, it's by imitating the printed form. No one today could narrate an action as Bernal Díaz does, or like the anony-mous authors of the old religious verses; they wrote not as we write but as we speak. I was able to corroborate this statement some time ago in my own country. . . .

Once, in Caracas, a group of friends and I wanted to listen to popular songs, and we called on some black singers who enjoyed certain renown. They were men of the plains. Affable and overflowing with regional pride, they offered to sing the most typical music and lyrics of their rep-ertoire. They sang, in fact, music of *galerones*, *joropos*, and *corridos*, scenes from the wars of Independence fought on the plains. Well, there wasn't one word that couldn't have been found in the newspapers. They said "the valorous defender," "the father of the homeland," "the magnificent centaurs," "eponymous hero"; it was, in short, a session in the Academy of History led by guitars and maracas. Since common people know how to inject charm into everything they do, especially when they're not aware of it, that was a very amusing academic session.

Having observed, ladies and gentlemen, that it is not characteristic of orators to put into practice what they preach, I don't want to be less than others. So having made these disquisitions against history, let's return to history. But not for much longer, so don't be afraid.

The Indian princesses, according to their laws or customs, often took up with the Spaniard conquerors. These unions, like Morganatic marriages the Spaniard didn't always confirm with the Catholic sacrament, could be broken at the men's will whenever they thought convenient. Unilateral submission and faithfulness—the eternal law of the stronger— foreshadowed a chronic disease from which our gentle society still suffers. They often went home to look for younger or more prosperous European women with whom to establish a definitive family, as we have seen in the history of Doña Marina. This also happened in the case of the conqueror Garcilaso de la Vega and Isabel, the daughter and niece of the last Peruvian kings, who ended her days alone.

Garcilaso de la Vega, like all the great captains of the Conquest, was from Extremadura. He was related to the most illustrious families of Spain, from the poet Jorge Manrique to the Renaissance poet and soldier Garcilaso. [. . .]

Doña Isabel, his wife, lived in Garcilaso's palace in an environment accustomed to luxury. All the Spanish landowners who formed the Cusco aristocracy treated her with great courtesy and admiration. She received guests, maintained correspondence with the Archbishop, and was extremely favored by her husband. In his splendid palace, an early version of our colonial houses, she occupied the place of a criolla lady with cordial and generous hospitality.

When the deadly war erupted between Gonzalo de Pizarro and the viceroy Núñez de Vela, Garcilaso had to leave Cusco to affiliate himself with the party of the Viceroy. In the large empty house he left behind, Doña Isabel remained alone with her six-year-old child—the future author of the *Florida* and of the *Commentaries*. Seventy years later, old, poor, and secluded in his house in Spain, the mestizo poet Garcilaso described in his recollections of childhood, so full of life and tenderness, his mother's suffering during those years of blood and fire. Persecuted by his father's enemies who wanted to kill them, Doña Isabel and her son hid together in a secret room while the house was plundered and the furniture burned; frightened to death, they lived off the corn that their Indian and Spanish servants secretly took to them. Through the window at night more than once, the child Garcilaso had seen the enemy of his father, the fierce and handsome Carvajal, pass by in the street. With his white beard shining in the dark, the old man in a purple cape and white feathered hat rode his brown mule down the narrow, silent street, dictating plans for war and ordering tortures and deaths.

After the terror ended, Doña Isabel continued in the house with her son, occupying the position of wife and Incan princess. When the landholder came during the holidays of Christmas and Saint John to pay their taxes, her son helped her keep accounts in the Incan fashion, using the *quipu* knotted cords. In the afternoons there were extended family get-togethers with visits from the old Incan princes who managed to survive the killings under Atahualpa and also the war against the Spaniards. In gatherings of relatives around his mother, the child listened to their memories of past splendors, of the celestial forewarnings of the ruin of the empire, and, according to Garcilaso himself, in his own words, "The memory of past losses would always bring on tears and moaning that their reign had become a serfdom." Alone with his mother, she would often tell him in a voice trembling with emotion the legend of Manco Capac and his wife, children of the Sun, civilizers of the world and founders of Cusco. On warm starlit nights his mother used to take him by the hand and point out to him the shape of the heavenly alpaca whose extremities form the milky way; she would show him the spots on the moon and tell him they were the kisses of a love-struck goddess, and she would tell him how the rain comes from a damsel's jug, broken by her brother with a thunderclap.

One day, when the civil wars had concluded, Garcilaso's father returned to Cusco. He was the same great captain, fortunate and wealthy. His son, the mestizo child, went out to welcome him carried on the backs of servants, as was the custom of Indian princes on great occasions. But ah! The father returned married or about to marry a Spanish noblewoman. Thus, after the horrors of the war, came humiliation and abandonment by the absent one—the eternal drama between fidelity and the changes of heart woven by long separations! When narrating in his memoirs that great disappointment of his childhood, Garcilaso, the old writer, does not have a word of bitterness for his father, whom he loved with intense admiration. Nor a wounding word against his stepmother, of whom he does not talk. His pain overflows in the remembrance of his forsaken Indian mother. He seems to seek in the most pristine fountains of mystical idealism an understanding of such ungratefulness. His *Commentaries* are dedicated "To my mother and lady, made more illustrious by baptismal waters than by the royal blood of so many Peruvian Incas." A beautiful filial epitaph, full of hope and forgiveness!

When some years after his second marriage the father Garcilaso died in Cusco, his mestizo son, still an adolescent, went to the Spanish royal court

with the purpose of claiming from the king the rights over land and es-
tates that belonged to his mother. The decision took a long time, and
meanwhile Doña Isabel died in Peru. Garcilaso, left alone and in the
flower of his youth, was surrounded in Spain with admirers and affection;
he distinguished himself in the wars against the Moors, traveled, lived in
Italy, and, upon returning to Spain, became a priest and devoted himself
to a spiritual life. After completing his studies in humanities, badly learned
in his earlier years, he opened his poet's soul to all the currents of the
fifteenth and sixteenth centuries. Along with the Latin and Greek classics,
he studied the scholastics, read the most famous writers of the Renaissance, and translated charmingly the three *Dialogues of Love* of León He-
breo. In the autumn of his life, his lonely artist's soul began to yearn for
his American homeland. It was going to be, from afar, in ripened years,
the true promised land of his spirit. While with his own hands Garcilaso
planted coca bushes in his Cordovan garden and tried to grow the flowers
that he picked when he was a child in the fields of Cusco, he began
to write, in a style full of charm and elegance, *The General History of
Peru*, *The Civil Wars between the Spaniards*, and *The Florida of the Inca*. The
historian-poet of America is really a folkloric narrator. But it is in the
Royal Commentaries where his delightful prose reaches its creative zenith.
Memories of his childhood, memories of memories that others told him,
converge there and unite through love the two currents that will form the
future American nations as they did in his own life. The *Commentaries* of
the Inca Garcilaso, says the Anglo-American writer Prescott, are an ema-
nation of the Indian spirit. In fact, if we listen carefully, under the transparency of the prose a moan from beyond the grave seems to flow with a
sound of tears. It is the echo of the maternal voice that, under the stars at
night, used to tell him the authentic legends of the Incan tradition. Entrusted to the voice for lack of a written culture, these legends would be
forever silenced when the last maternal accents ceased to be heard in the
ears of the mestizo child. But the child, in his old age and in exile, urged
on by nostalgia, would return to his childhood, gather up the millennial
voice with filial love, and encase it religiously in his transparent prose,
making a symbol of it. That trembling of tears, like a distant *quena* or Indian flute, is the gentle lament that in the depths of the race our obscure
and unrecognized grandmothers allow us to hear. Notes of sadness in a
minor key, it is the most authentic and delicate of all the strains that vibrate in our tumultuous American soul. Like Garcilaso, the Spanish mestizo, let's keep it in its Castilian form and, without denying anyone, bless

the harmony of our faith in the future united with our sorrow for the blood spilt and the tears wept.

Obras completas. Caracas: Editorial Arte, 1965, pp. 471–489.

NOTE

1. The English translations of de la Parra's selected quotations from histories and chronicles are ours. [Trans.]

Gabriela Mistral

Chile, 1889–1957

Born Lucila Godoy Alcayaga in the Elquí Valley of
northern Chile, the author chose her pen name, in
honor of two European writers she admired, prior to
publishing her first book of poetry in 1922. Of Spanish
Basque and indigenous American stock, Gabriela Mistral came from a broken home and humble origins.
Starting out as a rural teacher in Chile, she won her first
poetry prize while she was in her twenties and quickly
rose to national and then international fame when she
was awarded the Nobel Prize for Literature in 1945.
Mistral was the first, and thus far the only, woman from
Latin America to achieve this honor. Her many collections of poetry show her fondness for children, for the
indigenous peoples of her homeland, and for the rugged
natural beauties of the American continent—themes
with which she is commonly associated.

Mistral's contributions as an educator and diplomat
kept her away from Chile for the better part of her lifetime, initially taking her to Mexico, then to Brazil
where she lived for six years, and also to many other
Latin American and European countries. Her travels and
friendships around the world were the source of inspiration for much of her writing in both poetry and prose,
though she also wrote many nostalgic verses mytholo-
gizing the Elquí Valley of her birth.

Gabriela Mistral's reputation as a prize-winning poet has overshadowed her prolific capability as an essayist. Her writings appeared regularly in well-known Latin American magazines and newspapers, and they covered a wide range of controversial topics going far beyond those mentioned above. Although she denied her talent as an essayist and claimed that she wrote these short pieces mainly to earn a living, they tell us a great deal about her engagement with the events and people of her time. In prose as in verse, Mistral was a consummate verbal artist. The expressive power and the unique flavor of her literary language defy easy translation.

The first essay included here shows Mistral's talent for capturing the essence of individuals she loved and admired such as Victoria Ocampo, with whom she maintained a long friendship. The two writers, who shared the same birthday (7 April), met briefly in 1930 but became close friends in 1937 when Mistral visited Ocampo in Mar del Plata. This portrait of the Argentine writer, written in 1942, astutely points out Ocampo's very criollo nature and the problems she had achieving written expression in Spanish, given her francophile upbringing and early preference for writing in French. Conscious of those who criticized Ocampo for being *extranjerizante* (a foreignizer), Mistral destroys the myth that Ocampo was somehow less Argentine for being an admirer of European arts and letters. The key to Mistral's portrait is language and the betrayals that cultural upbringing can perpetrate. In Victoria Ocampo's case, her love affair with French gradually gave way to a commitment to Spanish, but it took her many years to find her true voice in writing.

The second essay, written just after World War II, shows Mistral's recurrent concern with relations between the United States and Latin America. Opposed to U.S. government interventions and economic imperialism, Mistral nonetheless felt a great warmth toward the people of the United States, where she would frequently travel and lecture and where she eventually died of cancer in 1957. Her essay is a plea for inter-American understanding that predates some of the better-known essays on this subject by such writers as Octavio Paz and Carlos Fuentes.

DORIS MEYER

Victoria Ocampo

T here must be many Victorias in Victoria since I myself know at least four . . . One is the godchild of France who knows all the phrases, verses, and fairy tales learned from her French governess around whom criollo Spanish was never heard.

And next to the devotee of the Seine and Racine, there is another Victoria who escapes across the channel knowing that the Seine can't give her everything—for example, the strong wind of adventure and a certain freshness of institutions found in a newer metropolis, Paris-like but poorer. This Victoria reaches the other side and sets herself up on the shore, so unlike the first, eager to receive the gusts from the channel or the Mediterranean, not to mention other gifts she can find only there: a poetry less ingrained in the flesh and a prose more permeated with music and grace.

And behind these two Victorias of foreign-leaning mind, behind these two big whims of hers—which some interpret as a vice and others as childishness—there is a magnificent Argentine woman [*argentinaza*] who, as soon as she tosses away the mirror in which she contemplates and distorts herself at will, becomes completely and unexpectedly Argentine and laughs at those of us who fell for her tricks, as if saying to us, What were you thinking? Did you believe, my foolish friend, that one can have a pampa as wide and vigorous as this, and a river like our Plate, and that one can live with Martín Fierro snoozing by the hillside and not carry it in the soul just as in the body? Do you think it's possible to walk with this long

Translated by Marjorie Agosín and Doris Meyer

greyhound stride and breathe with this llama neck and enjoy these endless sand dunes if one is from the Loire Valley and dreams of Piccadilly?

From the moment you realize the hoax or the little white lie, when you see her face or her gait up close or hear an echo of her Spanish anger, all the rest of her black legend collapses, falling on top of us like an avalanche of sand.

And this Victoria will be the one left after the English ivy or the European bougainvillea is ripped away. Before us is the naked stone, the stubborn, massive block of total Argentineity that seems never to have been taken from the quarry; the great woman [*mujeraza*] of the River Plate who, forever after, whatever anyone might say about her, will, for you, be only this loyal image and likeness of her own geography. No one will ever make you believe again in the Victorias of the smoky, fraudulent mirrors.

This criolla Victoria is mistress of all the openness and boldness that name and wealth can give to living, and yet she is consummately timid when it comes to life itself, to speech (she would say "expressing herself"), to spilling her rich human marrow on paper. She seems to protect herself with words, and her word must suffice as mental opinion!

The great literatures she frequents, the best of the classics and the moderns, have given her, with regard to writers and texts, a kind of superstitious reverence and fear similar to what we women and children feel toward complex machinery, or when we imagine the gold cargo of a Spanish galleon. . . .

This is the only way that I—also feeling dazed and daring in taking on this great occupation—can explain the very long road and the scandalous amount of time Victoria Ocampo has taken to convince herself that she has her own treasure to offer and pour out, as wide as the avenue of the Paraná River.

She has only recently begun to suspect what richness she has, but not to understand it with zeal and knowledge, from sea to mountain range. This treasure is from a life of happy submersion, completely soaked in living. The large, Mexican doe–like, woman's eyes of our Victoria have seen the morning countryside and have unfolded the tapestry of a hundred or more cities; her delicate doe-ears know by heart this world's tree of music, which has moved its outermost branches for her. Her enormous desire to capture the nature of places and people of means and experience has made her accumulate the wealth of an essential wisdom and an art of living, which she neither measures nor counts since she's still not convinced that she possesses them. Because she doubts this, and because of her incredible timidity and a superstitious fear that has an Indian-like quality, she has had a foolish habit of seeking ratification, help, loans. In a similar way, in the Elquí Valley where I lived as a child, my girlfriends and I used to play blind man's bluff, but with a twist to it that one of us—I don't know which—invented. The blindfolded girl we turned loose in the orchard, feeling her way past plum trees and vine roots, would suddenly hear us shout, "The river! The river!" And if she was a scaredy-cat—nowadays I'd call her "imaginative"—she'd stop in her tracks, raise her arms, and become very pale or red-faced. She would sense the river there, one step away. . . .

The legend of Victoria will make some people laugh at the comparison. I don't care. In matters of writing, Victoria Ocampo is the frightened little girl of my Elquí Valley.

Smart as she was, she paid obeisance to the Masters and showed that very South American fetishism of book-worship. Thus her tendency to walk a zigzag path, consulting her fake gods, insecure in her intentions and fearful of using her native language because it wasn't taught to her in her infancy.

Pedagogically speaking, I know very well that such a pyramid of superstitious scruples produces a kind of apathy that passes for professional ethics. I know that it's a noble sentiment and even considered a sign of good breeding. But I also know that, for some South Americans, their European idolatry and their doubts about their own spiritual and verbal capacity have wounded them like a paralysis.

I am more than familiar with the symptoms of this criollo infirmity: the river of images is dammed up; one mistrusts the ambient language even though it bubbles with life like the *ceiba* tree; home-grown wheat must pass through triple, foreign sieves; and one goes around every day wasting precious tactile and visual experiences simply because they happened in a mountain village or along a path that smelled of farm tools and cattle.

But this drab and humble treasure was precisely the one that the good Sarmiento gathered up, accepted, and worked with. And the reason for his success was, among other things, his willingness to give credit to his surroundings, to their domesticity, and to write about them, giving them value, beauty, and honor. This was his first concern, or as they say, at his right hand.

To his left side, secondarily, he carried his library, which never became a suffocating blanket because on his right side he carried his Argentine pampa or his Chilean mine or his schoolhouse bumping him at every step, like one holds on to a lover or a child so as not to lose him.

Victoria Ocampo began her work with three books of essays. All three are good, not lacking fine chapters or sections. One of the bad things that can befall a writer is to be successful at going out on the limbs of her being, playing about and distracting herself, and thus delaying her descent to the trunk of her being. It's strange when you can't see a human being whole, like looking at an animal in the water just lying there on its side, or maybe its back, just showing its hide.

Victoria lay back for quite some time on her ingenuous hide, playing cleverly with the genre she deemed most hers—the essay—which, for others, is merely a form of commentary. She did this out of modesty, not presumptuousness as some suggest. The really presumptuous people are those like me who throw themselves into the churning swell of the sea. Victoria tried to glimpse, gloss, skim over the theme of the woman in her debut publication, *De Francesca a Beatrice*. The subject seemed so right for her to express there, in torrents, her own self, or rather, her magnificent femininity. But it didn't happen; she did other things, but not as much as she could and should have. It's impossible to touch Dante without having a gigantic bibliographic mountain fall on you, suffocating and choking you. In this book, Victoria, who is daring when it comes to living but not when it comes to writing, behaved not just reverentially—with tact, hesitation, and modesty—but fearfully. The mountain of predecessors frightened her. Who could attempt to handle, much less lift that continent of illustrious paper? she must have said to herself.

After that would come pamphlets, also the result of timidity, then two volumes of *Testimonios*, which included what was in the pamphlets. But in the second volume of these testimonies—finally!—like opening the shell of a nut, there appeared the almond of her vocation, her ability, her talent. In the essay on Emily Brontë one sees through to the nucleus of Victoria who had spent years of intimate communion with Emily Brontë and Virginia Woolf. Years not just reading about them in European criticism but of having the soul of Emily (the poet and novelist) in front of her like a secret box or capsule that's hard to open and peer into.

The man-genius always intoxicated Victoria, but the woman-genius intrigued her. She wasn't content only to read the biographies and assessments of Emily, which were legion; Victoria insisted on going to see the moors where she grew up and left her trace, however insignificant or supernatural.

Perhaps because she's dealing with a woman, Victoria seems finally to have gained some confidence. It's about time! She is, in fact, very sensitive to the glories and miseries of our sex, to its humiliations and its accomplishments. Her splendid biography of Emily Brontë brought us, her friends, a very special pleasure: that of seeing Victoria free herself from those two thousand ties that were almost like a big soft ball of wool yarn that her Masters—great and small—had wrapped around her.

Victoria Ocampo began to see ahead of her the vast and fertile fields of labor. She awakened to a sense of her own resources: she knew how to write another's life. . . . It was only natural, since she has a memory for people that is fuller and more abundant than a grapefruit tree in summer. Her hands are full and ready to share the knowledge of many types of human beings—the fibers, skin, pulp, juice of many grapes. São Paulo's Museum of Wood doesn't contain more varieties of rare and commonplace specimens than Victoria knows of women of all kinds through her vast experience. She knows the keyboard of the female gender by heart.

Why then did Victoria spend so many years (as did the girl from the Elquí Valley) groping in the dark? For lack of self-confidence, which we might call wisdom but which, in some moral enterprises, could be called a waste of wealth and a left-handed estimate of the tools one has for the job.

We, her friends, who rejoice at her "entry into the subject," have read this beautiful biography in which she fuses herself with her work for the first time. Reading it I remembered the famous Victoria-of-books who casually drops a phrase, just one, about something—a book, a person, a fruit, or a place—drops of pure essence, like those that come from the pine or like myrrh, drops that fall thirty feet from a vegetal heart before landing at our feet or falling into our hands.

Victoria is a temperate conversationalist, never spiteful, sometimes benevolent, and frequently admiring. The cut that she takes on books or other things when she talks strikes me as magisterial because she makes visible the most intimate fibers, even though to do it she must part the outer layers and slice past the comments of others.

It was, then, something from her conversation that, after so much hesitation, she managed to pour onto paper in writing her testimonies. Not entirely, of course, because her writing still shows some "scholarly fears" that aren't there when she speaks.

It would be interesting to find out how her French governess, whom she remembers with gratitude, taught Victoria the classics, and whether her submission to the Masters and her need to quote them comes from that manner of teaching. There's another thing: the fatal attraction South Americans feel for the formal perfection of the French language. Victoria—a passionate person—tends to be a little stiff and cold in her structure, which is not a result of her expression but of an instrument that slightly punishes the faithless daughter of the Spanish language.

In love with the language that rubs elbows with the paternal Latin when it comes to formal perfection, Victoria still is not aware of the bad marriage that results when a passionate woman of Spanish speech expresses herself in French. It's a phenomenon akin to heresy: the unfaithful one lives the tragedy of what people refer to as "a divided love" and what the confessors call the triumvirate of the spirit. Because, really, the other woman, the renegade, continues living next to us, like the mistress beside the lover, but the wife—or, if you prefer, the Mother—is situated in the middle. When the shout of joy comes, it's she who jumps up, owner and mistress of our being that, as flesh, according to age-old custom, controls and governs.

I still remember the part of a conversation in which Anatole France clearly pointed out the risks of a Spanish writer who gives himself to French. This is more or less what he said: that the two languages have opposite and even warring mentalities. What a twenty-four carat truth! Maybe one of the few classics that isn't damaged by Spanish is Shakespeare, whose language approaches the magnificent disorder of our own, its loose abundance, euphoria, and frenzy. Racine may be a counter-Shakespeare. Dante is with us shoulder-to-shoulder in his universality and passion; but again, his almost geometric, iron-rigid form has nothing to do with the frenetic bonfire of San Juan de la Cruz in Spanish, people-language, multitude-language.

For me, the linguistic tragedy of Victoria Ocampo consists in the fact that a heated and passionately tumultuous temperament like hers, when kneaded and molded by a French education from nannies and governesses, ends up acceding to their teaching and example. And to their language: like a first cousin but different, it both fascinates and opposes us. Thus is accomplished an almost inhuman damage, so fatal are its consequences.

But she's happy nevertheless, stubborn as she is. Like a wife who accepts the passing liaison because it suits her or because it occasionally makes her happy, I don't ask myself if it really makes Victoria happy to be with that foreigner, that is, the borrowed language. The subject comes up regularly in her conversation, which would seem to indicate a conflict that concerns her.

That Victoria Ocampo, fertile of body and so rich in potential, full of nutrients like the *ceibo* or the *araucaria*, the Victoria of violent impulse and character as clear-cut as the cordillera peaks, the Victoria of open opinions and familiar expressions—how can she reconcile, how can she go on, *how can she live* with that anti-Rabelaisian, crystalline language that French has become, according to Leon Daudet, who knew the anatomy of his language well? How can she accept the ambidextrism of speaking Spanish and burning to write in a French as smooth as the burnished wood of a *caoba* tree? In what region of her brain or her soul does she suffer her linguistic bigamy?

February 1942

Gabriela piensa en . . . , ed. Roque Esteban Scarpa. Santiago, Chile: Editorial Andrés Bello, 1978, pp. 49–56.

Gabriela Mistral

Similarities and Differences between the Americas

At first glance one notices an abyss between the North and South American continents with regard to the human condition. We all feel the shock of the difference—painful to some and disheartening to others. But if, instead of focusing on the differences with an entomologist's eye, we were to look for a core of similarities, we'd feel better and also discover some surprises.

It might be said that we Americans have four common grounds, four zones of shared reality, or four familiar, unconscious languages. Moral languages, one might say, or long-forgotten points of convergence.

Both North and South Americans believe in freedom, although they experience it differently, the former living it in a constant climate while we fluctuate enormously between highs of fascination and lows of disappointment. But we are all libertarians in the essence of our being, where virginal desire and inclination reside. This is our first similarity.

The second could be the likeness in continental structure. In spite of the Panama Canal nail-clip, the quadrilateral of the North and the near triangle of the South are an invitation to agreement. The two oceans and six coasts have served us as liquid couriers and pedestrian message-bearers before the airplane provided the perfect roadway. The temperate regions of the North are indicated by the meridians, while in the South they are found on our beautiful Andean plateaus. Even the flora and fauna are more alike than dissimilar. Actually, the opposite continent is Eurasia,

Translated by Paul Goldberg and Doris Meyer

whose common trunk never helped two unfortunate peoples to achieve fusion, nor even to look each other in the eye.

The third point of contact is our youthful spirit. The United States is bursting and crackling with young enthusiasm and euphoria. We from the South were born with a larger weight of tradition on our shoulders. I say weight, not lead-weight. Even so, overburdened, we bubble like a pot of stew and scandalize with our untamed ebullience. This means that some metals of tradition were needed at the outset to keep the cauldrons from breaking.

These metals are visibly being forged in the South. The hot steam of youth and creativity that the North wanted to see in us, the resolution to create laws, the determination to rectify mistakes and to make up for re-tarded progress—all this can now be heard and felt.

The fourth commonality between the contrasting Americas is not ap-parent like the others but rather hidden, almost subterranean; it's called Christianity. Both Americas were nurtured by it, and though it may be hard to believe, they shared the same milk, a similar lap, and a lullaby that repeated the same holy verses only in a different rhythm. We were all born here stammering to the same God of the same Redemption and the eight Beatitudes. Had the Mongols crossed the Bering Straits and con-verted half a continent to Buddhism, it would have been a fateful birth, a destiny of war-to-the-death and eventual secession. To our misfortune, both conquistadors and pioneers came from a poisoned Europe, a Chris-tianity cut into mindless and howling shreds. They arrived with divided memories and warlike souls; in all frankness, their religious consciousness was tribal.

Because of this, the Christianity common to both the British and the Spanish was useless to our ancestors. It didn't bring them together, didn't smooth over differences or enable them to coexist, but rather raised walls and opened trenches between them.

Of the four areas of correspondence that could have been firm ground rather than mere bridges—love of liberty, territory, beliefs, and youthful spirit—two are now loudly heard and two aren't yet visible. At the risk of losing the land that sustains us and, simultaneously, our souls, the Ameri-can continent recently had to defend itself with a unified vision and with-out hesitation, and it did so. However, we now know from eye-opening experience that in our mutual task the plow has opened only one furrow, leaving stones, clods of earth, and undergrowth uprooted. Many more furrows must be plowed before the wheat can be sown.

On one side, there is a rich America that worked harder and with greater luck. On the other is an America that has struggled to unite three opposite races, carrying out a very delicate grafting operation that could be either life-giving or fatal. The Anglo-Saxon North didn't spend time or effort on the huge experiment that has been going on for four centuries in the South. It refused to deal with the soul of the Indo-American inhabitant, taking only nature as the field of battle. It wasted no time opening, clearing, and stripping the land by brute force, doing so with the utmost speed and leaving the Indian behind, either defeated or dead. With the land cleansed and validated to the point of being a kind of worldwide agrarian archetype, Americans threw themselves into industrialization with the impetuosity of a champion who doesn't accept defeat under any circumstance.

In the meantime, we Indo-Spaniards in the South pursued an undertaking that was both violent and slow: the attempt to construct democracy out of the *encomienda*[1] and to replace local bossism with civility. This has been both time-consuming and gut-wrenching, a labor of four centuries. No one yet has accurately recounted the valiant effort to unite three races and three souls who worship good and evil in diverse ways with three different consciences that come together with rhythms so contradictory that they don't seem to emanate from the same law of nature.

The North, successful without tragedy and formed in its crucible without major suffering, must see and consider the reality of the South and give us help during our last stage of development.

What we offer is loyalty, a chivalrous virtue still in style and service. What we need is generosity, the kind that goes beyond commercial and political interest to become close cooperation—the authentic Christian coexistence that the Old World never discovered or couldn't achieve.

We want to be understood and then helped, but first and foremost understood. Only in this way will we be effectively helped, without leaving an aftertaste of superiority and stewardship.

The continent must not become a domain controlled by hands skilled at game-playing. Europe just staked everything on ingenuity and malice, bribery and deceit, and lost it all on account of this despicable business, and despite diplomatic appeals. We who witnessed that lost wager have the obligation to do something more honorable and lasting, to work with forged iron rather than the fragile tinplate of annual "agreements" that merely constitute pauses.

February 1945

Gabriela anda por el mundo, ed. Roque Esteban Scarpa. Santiago, Chile: Editorial Andrés Bello, 1978, pp. 47–50.

NOTE

1. A system of socioeconomic domination through which land, along with its indigenous inhabitants, was given by the Spanish Crown to conquering Spaniards who pledged to protect the native inhabitants' souls in return for their labor. [Trans.]

Nellie Campobello

Mexico, 1900–?

Nellie Campobello and the Mexican Revolution enjoy
a sort of drastic symbiosis. The cruelties and the personalities of the most violent years of revolutionary confrontation in the north of Mexico left an indelible mark
on a young girl whose adolescent heroes were not writers or singers or movie stars but warriors, whom she
knew alive and, all too often, dead. And Nellie herself
has left an indelible mark on the Revolution—her
works of fiction and biography, her essays and poetry,
and her choreographies for mass ballets comprise the
only corpus of texts by a Mexican woman offering eye-
witness accounts of the way life was lived and fought on
the plains, along the railroad lines, and in the towns of
Chihuahua and Durango from 1913 to 1917.

Nellie Campobello's most representative and powerful works were first published in the thirties, when revolutionary spirit and national pride were still strong, in
Mexico and in Nellie herself. *Cartucho* (1932; *Cartucho*,
1988) is a collage of scenes of the revolution—short,
poetic, fierce sketches of the men and the actions that
reconfigured the north. *Cartucho*'s narrator also introduces her immediate family—her brothers and sisters
and, above all, her mother, who becomes the central focus of Nellie Campobello's second biographical fiction
of the war years, *Las manos de Mamá* (1937; *My Mother's
Hands*, 1988). In this long prose-poem Nellie sings a

nostalgic hymn of praise to a woman whose domestic skills and personal vitality protected and nurtured her fatherless family throughout the civil war.

Nellie Campobello's works were reprinted in 1960 in *Mis libros* (My Books) from which the selection translated here is taken. By then Mexico's Revolution and its heroes had become, in Nellie's words, at best forgotten and at worst betrayed—undermined by personal political interests that sought to profit from the blood shed by others. It is perhaps this unforgiving partisanship turning "bandits" into "heroes," her nostalgic and subjective regionalism, and the harshness of her criticisms against the "capital" politics and ethics that made Nellie Campobello herself a revolutionary victim in her own country—at best forgotten and at worst betrayed. In 1985, in 1989, and again in 1992, on the anniversary of her birthday, one or another newspaper headline has asked, "Where are you, Nellie Campobello?" The writer, whose lifeline parallels that of modern Mexico, has vanished from public view. In her prologue to *Mis Libros* Nellie Campobello talks about guarding her treasures but hiding her writings, moving them from place to place. She has become to herself a guarded treasure, to us a hidden history. We don't know whether Nellie Campobello, born with the century, is still alive, or whether she, like *her* revolution, has died of neglect and of others' self-interest. We can now only rely on her "polished truths."

IRENE MATTHEWS

My Books
Prologue

I f it were possible to write these truths with arrowheads polished by the copper hands of Comanche warriors, I would do so; and I would do so for the sheer pleasure of feeling myself participating in the landscape where you can still breathe the freedom inherited from our ancestors. The price we pay here for this right is the same—surely the same—as it is everywhere else that men are allowed to use every resource within their reach to unleash their destructive force against their betters.

Ours was a life whose rhythm was subject to violent changes. We lived in one of those highly prized, strategic places where people piled up on top of each other, and I still classify the people there as the baddies and the goodies. I was a pretty happy little girl; I saw how those good men fought against the truly bad ones. So I watched, learned, and understood how the bad steal from the good and kill them; how for the good there is no justice, nor has there been for hundreds of years. For the bad live a long time, their umbilical cords stretch for many miles, they paper their mansions with the laws that they and their cronies manufacture for their eternal protection. To these men, children and youngsters mean nothing; they simply use them and exploit them. They steal their childhood, they trick them, and they convert the majority of them into minions. All of this forms a Mexican panorama, and this panorama blows a smoke screen at the whim of a powerful majority who impose whatever changes may prolong their odious incumbency. Those who wish to be free and to flee from this panorama have to hide or die, and the way they die is unimportant. Or

Translated by Irene Matthews

they have to pretend not to know about a situation filled with deplorable, unjust, and criminal acts, where looting, oppression, and lies flourish, and where everything, absolutely everything, is under control, just as it is in every modern system.

The men who practice this control are graduates and career professionals in pretending, in injustice, in plundering, in lies, and in that ever-so-Mexican institution called *madrugar*—that is, kill your man fast before he kills you. In saying these things, I am not denouncing anything new; very many people have been unable to avoid this situation; others have wanted to scrutinize it, see it and sense it with their own flesh. In exposing my truths in this way, as simple, uncolored facts, I have only wanted to tell why I sought a niche in what I considered to be the best of the panorama, that is to say, in a truly personal freedom, encountered as the result of spiritual and physical anguish. I used to wish for wings, the real wings of a condor: to fly away. I believe that many Mexicans have wanted to have wings, at least once. Many can leave, fly off in a plane, or climb onto a train and give themselves the illusion that they are finding their freedom. In my understanding, this freedom means giving up everything superfluous as well as many other fundamental things of life; it means being the master of your own movements and defending that right as one would defend the life of a child.

I felt my first breath of freedom one day when I sat astride a horse. But don't get the idea that I raced away; no, I didn't gallop off, the horse simply walked, one step at a time, around the interior patio of our mother's old family home, led by the bridle by someone I definitely loved immensely. That stroll, which only lasted a few moments, gave me an almost permanent feeling of well-being. I felt a new air, I believed I had walked through a new world, huge and free. No cross frowns in my direction, no psychological oppression or brutal punishments, no restrictive clothing or any obstruction to the free enactment of mental or physical movement could impede the urge to gain the share of happiness that belonged to me. The pleasure of going to meet the breeze and capturing it on my breath had me constantly seeking an escape window for my overwhelming desire. And so it was like a morning in springtime, like being in a luxuriant orchard where the febrile air was exuberantly perfumed by a huge expanse of flowers. I slipped away from my mother's side and ran to the bank of the river. I walked on the firm damp sand, and, as I pressed my feet rhythmically down, the sand gave me back the outline of my feet, my feet burbling with water. As I looked all around, I suddenly felt such joy that, for the first time in my life as a child, I started to sing a song born of all the particles of light that shone through the pores of my skin—a song I had heard my mother hum as she pottered around our home. This time, I sang it out loud, as loud and as long as I could, and ran off, fast, till I got to a cliff they called Eagle Rock.

Then I went back to where my mother and my brothers were, and I forgot, for a moment, my dancing feet that the sand ate up. But from that day on I knew that the songs we inherit are an instant refuge from sadness. In my case, I still recall them and I know that no one can take them away from me, and I sing them over and over. Sometimes, when that isn't possible, I hum them low, under my breath, and I wrap myself up in them as I go to seek my freedom, which I love more than the waves of the sea and more, much more, than love.

I live on the sands of a desert over which, on what seems to be the nothingness of a sky of blue, I use the points of tiny stars that I have found to embroider—the words I love. Here they will remain in this solitude where, shaded by nature, I am imprisoned by the persistence of a cruel and inhospitable panorama.

In the tender infancy of my existence an infinity of motives had guided me toward what I loved most, something simple and easy: I longed to head toward the highest point, and for me the highest point was exactly what is indicated in the word itself—the act of climbing, outside in the trees, over railings, on the tops of the walls, and, of course, on hills, scrambling up the slopes to reach the summit so as to absorb inside of me the majesty of a solitary immense plain that might speak to me of my ancestors and bring me closer to them.

My land is a place where the adobes still stand upright, and where the fleeting stars fly off from the east and alight, afire, in the north. Its silent people cling to the landscape; their steps are slow, their soft voices speak only in measured syllables. They respect a drawing, they love books, they enjoy poetry. They were born warriors in a land of warriors. They shelter strangers as if they were their own people. If they have a coin or two, they smile, and they smile the same smile when they have many coins. The flowers in that place smell of violets, geraniums, carnations, honeysuckle: the pure scent of the essence of flowers. I love my land with the vibrant love of someone who has forever renounced living there. Of someone who, as she looks at the earth, the color of a Comanche's skin, is unable to kiss the grains of corn that sprout from its entrails.

I practiced horseback riding and understood that the company of my mare protected the fulfillment of my dreams. I had the healthy curiosity of wanting to know where the spirit of the mountain beat, and I sought that place, guiding myself by the breeze that rushed toward me and passed on by, permeating the treetops and emanating a breath that wafted round my ears, caressed my every movement, and penetrated the skin on my face. I recognized that hidden force of nature and could listen to it quietly inside myself. It was something like running along different pathways inside and outside the usual ones and knowing that my physical self was only an instrument under the command of an obsessive desire. Because *freedom* is not just a simple word; it exists in broad horizons and in small and great exertions, for which man uses a technique whenever necessary, following the shortest line, the one within his reach. The ability to enjoy this freedom fully resides in the art of knowing where that straight line goes. This does not mean that curves and indirectness are not also a technique, and that man does not develop them, too, in order to obtain his portion of freedom and other good things. Also entering into the conflict are the imperious visions of latent infantile desires: they seek an escape and huddle together inside the direct gesture that measures out emotion (as one measures electric light or water or speed), until they turn into words and learn the sublime nature of tenderness. I ask myself, "What becomes of unfulfilled desires when you can hope, and when you can see the first evening star?" Contemplating that star forms a part of our freedom, it is an essential part of our smiles, it is what we seek to light up our faces, and to kiss the leaves of the trees tossed by the wind, the wind that shrivels up our faces and beats upon our shoulders: the same wind that, nevertheless, can give me my freedom in exchange for opening up a window or mounting a horse or climbing a hill. And then: let them come, those voices that oppress us and hurl words that form chains around us, words that force us into an apparent calm. But we know that the domineering—or the sometimes apparently docile—actions of our jailers take possession of our visions and smilingly demonstrate that they are going to harness our breath and that we cannot be free. For some spirits the only thing that counts is the comfortable position of the easiest way, the way that conquers without tender words, without effort, without love, but also without reason. Or else because in their being is a gorged vein that seeks release. (It may also be a pinched, strangled nerve that needs distension.) All this gets adjusted so as to excuse the hidden motivations and the apparently simple fact of man using man's technique against man.

I have built my freedom without using words; I have built it simply out of the need to breathe the wind and commit it to my heart.

* * *

With my intrinsically restless nature, and my love of truth and justice for all humanity, I found myself needing to write. I knew that the environment I lived in was not favorable for my desire. I knew that many of the people close to me would not approve of my attitude and would feel displeased when they saw me engrossed in a mission that would bring me no personal benefit—but I knew how to climb trees and hills. Also, I could apply my shortest line. I sought a way of saying this, but to do so I needed a voice, and I went straight to it: the only voice that could give the right tone, the only one authorized—the voice of my childhood. I used its apparent naiveté to display what I knew to be essential: a sincere and direct way of speaking. I wrote alone, consulting no one and seeking no advice. I was incapable of doing so, and if I had, I know that my infantile idea would have been rejected. Although I knew people who had great talent and could have asked them to guide me, I did not dare. I understood that the material I was depending on was not pleasing to those great talents, and I say great talents for they were certainly great even among the very best. I am talking about people who had studied in Europe and in the schools of dictatorship, or who were educated in the schools of the government imposed with the support of the United States. I am talking about that gentleman who, while calling himself a supporter and avenger of the martyr Francisco I. Madero, was actually a traitor to Madero and to his doctrines; a man who took advantage of the many brilliant battles fought by Francisco Villa, whom he also betrayed; about that gentleman whose followers assassinated many, many people from our own families and who stole from the poorest of the poor; about that person who is called a great man and who in his task of suppressing the Ministry for Public Education managed to sack all the teachers so as to avoid paying them. So I was right not to want to consult anyone, or ask permission, when writing about those who I always knew to be the real heroes of the Revolution, the Revolution that carried off our families and fed upon their lives and on our inheritance and our education. Who does not know that in some parts of the north, basic schooling was taking place in homes shattered by the *carrancistas*, Carranza's men? But that is precisely what those who oppress us and punish us day after day don't want to know, negating our parents and negating our selves. That is why I had to write, and tell the truth in the world of lies I lived in. Obviously, not everything was enjoyment; I had to study, do my homework each day, and I also practiced various sports. At school, here in Mexico City, I understood things better: everything could be ascribed to injustice for those who had won the real Revolution.

I was going to a foreign school; my schoolmates were wonderful. Among them my world was full, shining, incredible. How pleasant my life was! I had everything: admiration, love, and success. However, at each step, in the midst of the well-being and the aura of happiness my environment offered me, I never stopped feeling that somewhere waiting for me was a corner where I would pause and say and do what I alone could achieve, despite the fact that I had thrust that idea aside and tried at all cost to hide myself in the circle that welcomed me like a prodigal daughter. Our ballet lessons and benefit parties, the Red Cross and other charity organizations, the obligatory weekend diversions, vacations and horseback rides with a very select group were our world and our chief occupation. Nothing could have been more interesting, nothing more attractive and beautiful. An almost incredible panorama, really wonderful; we could have stayed there: my sister and I were sheltered by two things, our name and our social position. In tall headlines, the newspapers dedicated effusive eulogies to our dancing. What more could a young woman like me ask for?

But in that atmosphere one could not write, and even less could one write about what I wanted to write about. My theme was disparaged, my heroes proscribed. Francisco Villa was considered to be worse than Attila the Hun. His men were all classified as horrific bandits and murderers. I would read this day after day, listen to the hateful lies, and get to know the injustice, the barbarism of those newly rich Mexicans, stuffed with the money they stole from the people so staunchly defended by that glorious man, Don Francisco Villa. They attacked him systematically, with the sole purpose of diminishing him and destroying his character, the character of a great Mexican and a warrior of genius. And I said to myself, "What should I do? Where can I begin?" I selfishly thought about my world, my beautiful environment, my youth, my future. I could get married—that's expected. But at that moment I didn't count. I know that now. I see it clearly, and I am completely content that that is how things should have occurred, although in those days I felt slightly afraid, a feeling that could develop into uncontrollable fear. I understood that telling the truth placed me in a situation of real disadvantage in confrontation with organized liars. I was facing the risk of being demolished by those enemy voices that were always cemented into strategic positions of the highest authority. I could come crashing down from the nice place I occupied, the environment so pleasant for me but not for the heroes of my childhood, nor for the ideals of my parents and my relatives—all of them swallowed up by the Revolution. I could continue comfortably where I was, in my little paradise, where I had no problems and where being happy cost not the slightest effort. But if I knew certain things, it wasn't right for me not to say them out loud. And that is how, without ever quite overcoming my fear, I began to write little by little, in my own way and hiding my notebooks. Finally one day, mostly to prove my ability to write, I put together a book of poems that was published under a pseudonym. I had my helpers: the person who published it, greatest of the greats but as naughty as a nine-year-old, and my little sister Gloria, still a child but a capable, educated girl. The few people who knew about it no longer saw in me the young girl with the impeccable posture of a ballet student; they were surely whispering to each other, "She wants to write; she wants to be a writer."

[. . .] In the city of Havana we met the erudite journalist and critic José Antonio Fernández de Castro, who knew everyone and whom everyone knew. Federico García Lorca was in the city at that time. José Antonio showed him my book of poems, and the great poet came to our house to see me. From a high verandah, I responded to Federico's timid and courteous greeting and to José Antonio, who was laughing like a child. [. . .] The poet's eyebrows were enormous, or so they seemed to me, his face broad, his eyes Moorish, his forehead really beautiful; his mouth showed the bitter signs of constant tragedy. We were never to see him again; soon afterwards Franco's bullets turned him into a statue, but time and distance keep him on a pedestal of love.

We were at the age when people call young girls "dolls," and José Antonio always called us that, even when he wrote to us. He also called us the little Mexican girls, and when he introduced us to the great North American poet Langston Hughes and told him that we were argumentative and capricious, the poet arrived with two metal tins stuffed full of chocolates. But best and most gratifying of all, as I know now, was José Antonio's broad and loving smile like a kind brother. [. . .]

From that moment on, I decided to clarify things, to talk of the things I knew about. But wanting to do so did not make me capable of doing so; I needed a discipline. The historical data I had to write down needed to be told with full care and attention, without falling into a string of incidental anecdotes, nor into aggressiveness, nor into a sentimental, self-pitying plaint. Mexicans like Villa and his men cannot be inserted into a melodrama or treated like characters in some vulgar comic book. I said to myself: it's true that I've written some little poems and had a book published, and that I've written clever comments in an evening paper. I had the intellectual preparation to write silly, old-fashioned stories, carefully stylish. But was that a worthy framework for my heroes? I asked my spiritual brother José Antonio about it, and since he had a special talent for understanding preoccupations of that nature, he told me exactly the right thing to do.

So I immediately started to write *Cartucho*, to tell its tragedy. At last, I was able to talk about the generous sacrifice, joining other voices with my voice and portraying both the exterior and the interior through action. All this was made possible by the divine impulse that moved all those men, to whom charity came as naturally as it did to a saint: as their duty. The charity of my men derived from laying down their lives in the heroic act of reclaiming freedom on behalf of their people. The stories in *Cartucho*—let me make this clear once and for all—are historical truths. They are tragic events seen by my own child's eyes in a city, as others saw similar events in Berlin or in London during the world war; it was the same thing for my little heart that wept without tears. [. . .]

On our way back to Mexico, in our imagination we saw again all the places we had been: Miami, Palm Beach, Tampa, Orlando, Rocky Point—all in Florida—and the beautiful, clean city of Havana, all viewed with the curious and naive gaze of someone who sees things flashing past at speed. And amidst it all, the waves continued to rock our ship, and our imagination followed the waves.

[. . .] When we got to the capital, we noticed the clouds of dust there for the first time, and we also saw something we hadn't noticed before: the people never smiled. I thought that the horrible dust clouds were to blame, at least superficially. I also realized, and this was truly discouraging, that the people I could see were, or seemed to be, somehow obsolete. Their gestures and their ways seemed out-of-time, out-of-place. Their faces did not match the sound of their voices or the meaning of their words. My own perspective was filled with large questions about tacos and dirt and food frying in the streets and garbage strewn over the sidewalks. And about sickness and neglect. I believe that for us all this was like a punishment for the overt pride in our Mexicanness we had shown in the countries we had visited. It is certainly true that the horrible dust clouds, now as then, are only one of the many punishments we have to suffer. Today I do not smile either, and when the season of dusty windstorms arrives, I hide behind my eyelids, too. Nevertheless, the streets of Mexico

City welcomed us. We arrived home: Juárez Avenue, Colón Street, Bucareli, Reforma, our neighborhood, the place of our happiness; we would see our loved ones and once again they would put up with our games and our tricks, our prideful nonsense. But even so we still paid attention to what was going on all around, and my habit of asking myself questions and expressing pedantic opinions became insufferable. Into my mind, in those moments, came the memory of having written for a magazine, the *Havana Review*, my impressions of the city—not particularly agreeable opinions. A self-sufficient pose had helped me to criticize things like a spoiled little girl. And if at that time I had felt myself to be a writer, and very self-assured, vain, and arrogant, when I saw my city again I understood, I understood everything, and the pain of reality cried out inside me. I hadn't known, I was ignorant of that way of being in our Mexico, I had never before felt it as I did at that moment, and I wished deep down that it would be something that passed by and that the pain it caused me would pass also.

[. . .] The voice of one of my brothers said, "Now you're going to see something new in this legendary city of broken stones, something that makes us live completely indifferent to reality. Behind those façades you're so fond of, you'll see the history of the foundations that sustain us. And besides," added Carlitos, laughing ironically, "you know, we are trampling on top of our altars, the real Mexico City is sunk many, many feet below us. Of course, our own architecture is constructed over the temples; and the most interesting thing is that most of us don't know and don't care about such a curious fact. Maybe walking over the skulls and the effigies of our ancestors is just a typical characteristic of ours, perhaps legendary or historical." I asked myself, "The remains of our ancestors under the ground? Skeletons imprisoned in the walls of magnificent underground temples?" And if it surprised me to think that the history they taught us in the schools might also be a legend, I was quite alarmed to realize that the main thoroughfares of the city, Madero and Juárez, Reforma Boulevard, Chapultepec Park, the Cathedral, the Regis cinema, the Olympia, in sum, the little map that has the Alameda Gardens at its center, was the only thing I really knew of the city. I was a savage from the north of Mexico. And I thought I could write, I thought I could criticize!

Knowledge! How difficult it is to be wise! I suddenly understood what it meant to go in search of knowledge, in search of truths, to understand directions in order to know how to use them, to move oneself on the map crisscrossed with lines and get to one's goal. Because it's not enough to have a will to learn, and to wish to learn in order to understand where knowledge stops and pretending begins. You also need to be sly. To mistrust teachers who teach when their own economic problems are unresolved. And I told myself: there must exist teachers born to teach, but the problem is where to find them, since they usually are the ones who occupy lowly positions, teachers who are not political and who don't practice the politics that eat into the schools like bookworms munching on abandoned books. Why had I not had real teachers? Why hadn't all the teachers, rich and poor, built the foundations for a real Mexican education, related to real life, with its real needs, a true education that had its own substance and that also could talk intimately about the universal necessity for historical, scientific, and artistic knowledge? Those little classes, repetitious and without any practical base, highly decorated with elastic theories that lack all real scholarship and that are recited out loud on birthdays to astound one's poor parents—some of them truly ignorant of everything—what use are they to anyone? What use were they to me? The poor schools of the Mexican dictatorship, the truly inadequate schools of the time of the Revolution, and the even more inadequate ones of the time right after the end of our war would offer a highly useful set of statistics, a highly surprising set of statistics. The professional charlatans and the charlatan professionals—the two species—have taken over our environment and continue to proliferate. Some use startling new techniques, others—unbelievably—carry on in the same old way, yet people still exist who believe in them and support their existence.

* * *

I sought the truth at home, in my books, in the daily life of human beings, although I was incapable of analyzing many of their actions and words. And I would continue that way, mistrustful but understanding more day by day from people's eyes. The particles of light in people's eyes (divine light, perhaps?) I love and gather to me like a vast carpet of atoms that irradiate a cloud of unsatisfied aspirations. What a great teacher life is! And how wonderful it is to want to know, to set oneself the task of learning. That's the basis of my present belief that professional titles are worthless when they have been gained merely through makeshift means and pretending to study. [. . .]

We were typical of young women who had grown up in a home created by young brothers and sisters. We were ignorant of certain depressing aspects of marriage, both human and social. And it was better for us that we didn't want to know anything more about that, and that our only interests were the ballet, music, poetry, and, in my case, the world of ideas that jostled around in my brain. For the custom of the Mexican society like ours has always been, and still is, to push young women into the problems of matrimony, into formal engagements for life. That is, to take away their childhood, their innocence, their youth before their due time. I'll say it in one word: they are thrown out of the home. Anyone who knows how to respect children and young people will judge this custom as an act of cruelty and will be astonished that no one tries to reform it. On the contrary, there are many people who, as they act that way, believe they are doing their duty. I, who never looked for such complications, and who had grown up in a somewhat special, somewhat limited environment, never sought such blind entanglements. It seemed to me to be more entertaining, more fun, to write, read, compose poetry, and practice ballet. These things, along with sports and the classes that we—as advanced students of dance—gave in the schools of the Ministry of Public Education, formed our entire universe.

* * *

We had dedicated ourselves for a year and a half, in both the Indigenous School and in the Teachers Training College, to the adorable mission of dance for dance's sake, when suddenly my book *Cartucho* came out. I was taken by surprise: it was as if a bolt of lightning had shot an infinite number of stars at my head. I believed I was seeing a fantastic personage who took my pulse and fixed onto me the unblinking orbs of his eyes, which momentarily, as they stared at me, expanded like electric lightbulbs. I was aghast. I wanted to run away to my corner, hide myself behind a tree trunk. I knew it was the greatest prank I'd ever committed. I closed my eyes, stopped up my ears, and laughed to myself. I had created a phantom and animated it with a great spirit of revenge. [. . .]

In my case, my book *Cartucho* was a humble production, humble for many reasons: its scenarios, its characters, the prose, the special way of revealing those characters, excising adjectives and giving only their historical outline. In spite of that, in a few days my book had become well known, and justly so, by the right people, people who always spoke about it in a friendly way. (I should mention perhaps that General Plutarco Elías Calles read it. Leonor Llorente, his second wife, told me so with her pleasant smile that matched her beauty as a good young woman. "Your book," she confided, "must be really good. My old man keeps it in his desk.") [. . .]

My beloved book excited many other commentaries, but, in spite of it all, I was going to pay very dearly for my tremendous boldness. The lies against me began. They misrepresented me as if they didn't know me, and despite the fact that only sick minds could germinate such monstrosities.

People who had called themselves my friends no longer greeted me on the street, since, according to them and their lies, they wanted nothing to do with the defender of bandits. That's what the organized slander called my heroes. On the other hand, I knew other people who were delighted by the book, and that made me happy. I defended myself as best I could and proved my impartiality by serving causes that could be considered lost in advance. At the same time, I know that having written those pages was useful for history, albeit not for the legend of the Revolution. I had fulfilled an obligation. I continue to admire the real heroes of our armed struggle, those who for ten years kept alive the rebellion of the men who wanted a better Mexico. Those who live in *Cartucho*, if perchance they've gone to a place where their ideals led them, to a world where they can see the things that have happened to us because of the Revolution, I ask them to stop the destructive actions of those who lie and those who are enemies of the real Revolution. I ask them to reinstate reason and respect for the memory of those who died and for those who still live, because they all fought so that our fatherland would reach the state of existence a peaceful country should enjoy.

* * *

Our work at the Ministry for Public Education continued: long and short trips on cultural missions. We were messengers of the art of dance, and other contingents of the fine arts traveled on similar missions. We went from the north to the south, came back and started our beautiful task once more. [. . .]

Our travels confronted us with the reality of one aspect of our life: the painful truth of the structure of Mexican life in the provinces. Who does not know the strange form of justice and the way it is applied in those places almost always governed by local chieftains: through pretense, deceit, dispossession, and theft? All of these, which are brutally present in the provinces, also exist in our capital city life, but here they are administered with more delicacy as we smile at each other, embrace each other, and sniff the wind—brandishing an odd sort of equity along with good manners. When I understood the twisted way that highly complex needs or deeply concealed passions were resolved in the provinces, my whole being trembled like a reed battered by the wind. In the negative vibrations of those failings I was feeling the slow and painful adjustment of one particular characteristic of us Mexicans: in our impulse toward being something better, we accepted all the twists and turns on the way; straight lines still did not seem to exist among us.

I could also talk here about the spirit of imitation that most of us emit through every pore of our skin, in our every gesture, that fills our environment and forms a cloud around the ingenious temperaments and privileged intellects of our country. Its power has no limits. I could also add, although I don't want to, how much our race, with all its qualities, would gain if it abolished its weakness of always falling into imitation: that is, copying what's useless, copying what's easy. I've said that I don't actually say so, I only imply it. If Mexicans would only help one another, we would be singing a true hymn to our race. Our Indian race, our fantastic mixed breed, brimming with resources and with words; as they lose their heritage they only increase their abilities and acts of heroism. For I say to myself: Loving the people is not only shouting along with them on national holidays, or displaying manliness by kissing a sugared skull, or spurring a horse, or swallowing down half a bottle of tequila in one gulp. Loving our people is teaching them the alphabet, directing them toward things of beauty—for example, toward respecting life, their own life and, of course, the lives of others. Teaching them what their rights are and how to achieve those rights. In sum, teaching them through truth and through example, the example that great Mexicans have bequeathed to us, those illustrious Mexicans to whom justice has not been rendered. Is it because we haven't had the time? Is it because we don't know who they are? We should ask ourselves, why *don't* we know?

It was in the midst of these thoughts, born of the environment that surrounded me, that I tried to escape, to find refuge in the most natural place for me, in my mother's skirt. So I went directly to that oasis, to my oasis, and during a cultural trip in Morelia I started to write. Every moment free from my dance obligations was dedicated to my third book, which of course I named *My Mother's Hands*. The title I had chosen for the book pleased all my friends and my family. It was easy for me to find it because, of everything we receive from our mother, her hands are what are most permanently in contact with her children our whole lives long. We understand her eyes, of course, and we talk about her voice and her lap that welcomes us over and over again; everyone knows that. So I know now that I might have preferred a different title: I should have thought of my mother's eyes; but at that moment I saw her hands, I felt them on my shoulders, and her hands naturally converted themselves into my book. The idea came to me because when the month of September came round I went to watch the festivities, the national commemoration I had never seen before. As I watched I realized what the reality was and understood why I had never before observed those outbursts that I consider mere physical expressions, or superficial happiness that produces sorrow. One fifteenth of September Mama had begun her long journey; and I admit that I did wrong in participating in the celebrations. The national holidays are to entertain a people avid for satisfaction, needful of embraces, shouts, bullets, alcohol, and tragedy. I was not in tune with that mood, but my regret led me to reflect over how little we care for the memory of those who have gone. [. . .]

* * *

[. . .] And as far as General Villa is concerned, I've said it already, time and time again: the black legend around him smothers the most innocent gesture of his daily life. Why wasn't he defended by those people who knew that what was being said about him was lies? It's no mystery: they were afraid to. General Villa's enemies were people who envied his triumph, the presidential gentlemen who elected themselves in our admirable and suffering Republic. We, the children of the true revolutionaries, have the obligation to speak and demand that the veil be drawn back. History demands it, since our fatherland is not the property of a few followers of Carranza, Obregón, or Calles. My truth is born of the fear that surrounded us until yesterday. It is the reflection of a presence that appeared permanent and indestructible, a presence that oppressed us for many years. And so books had to be written to tell of hidden historical truths, and many more will appear, and many idols will fall, idols that yesterday took upon themselves triumphs that were not of their making. Those idols represent, for me, the evil ones who stripped and murdered the good.

Of the poems I've written I can say that, since I am a creature of a romantic nature, I know that playing is as sacred as praying, as singing and dancing, and as sublime as loving, in the purest sense of the word. Desires write themselves, clearly and simply, and they project themselves, without any fuss, toward the place where our predilections lie, the place where the impulse to seek out the best of our nature is born. This is our poetry, poetry we can apply to dance, to the way we talk, to play, and to whatever makes us happy. As a very little girl, I read poems; I kept them in my mind and I felt happy, rich, capable of the most difficult physical exercise. I also believe that because I had read them I tried to seek some images of my own, while respecting others' themes, since I believe that every person is master of his own self and exposes that self in his own way, obeying the purity of his own expression. Now I remember that, probably under the influence of the movies, I began to write a novel, and I still have the four pages I crammed with bitter complaints about not finding in myself the state of mind to be a writer, since I didn't know what that was. In the meantime I would throw myself down on the floor, and leaning my elbows on the rug, I'd very seriously scrutinize the poses of my protagonist (the "Countess Diana")—a single woman trying to find a boyfriend.

I understand how sentimental young women guard their memories like treasures: a doll, a relic, dried roses or violets, for example, and a thousand other things. But in my case, while I kept everything else, I hid my writings—and I still do. I also keep moving them from one place to another; nobody would be able to find them. The songs I inherited, the poems I chose from among poetesses and poets I liked, I repeat inside me. I talk to them with the voice I assume in the quietude of sorrow, and I hug them to me as one hugs a child, a baby whose skin rubs against our cheeks.

Mis libros. Mexico: Compañía General de Ediciones, 1960, pp. 9–45.

Yolanda Oreamuno

Costa Rica, 1916–1956

Yolanda Oreamuno—elegant, enigmatic, independent—was born in San José, Costa Rica, in 1916 and
died in Mexico City a brief but intense forty years later.
Although perhaps best known for her experimental
novel *La ruta de su evasión* (1950; The Route of Their
Evasion), she wrote numerous essays that appeared from
1936 to 1948 in *Repertorio Americano*, one of the most
respected and widely read literary publications of Latin
America in the first half of the twentieth century, thus
establishing herself as an original and provocative critic
of Costa Rican life and letters. A number of her essays
are lyrical meditations on emotion or experience; others
are attacks on what she considered outmoded or superficial social attitudes or artistic expression. In these latter
essays, described as bitter and egotistical as well as intelligent and courageous, her stance is typically confronta-
tional, her language refined, lyrical, biting. In them she
challenged Costa Ricans to participate in the modern
world by facing up to the problems of urbanization,
industrialization, and changing gender roles.

The two essays included here show her way of digging deep and speaking her mind. In "El ambiente tico
y los mitos tropicales" (Tropical Myths and the Costa
Rican Environment) she insists that the picturesque image created for Costa Rica by the tourist industry is a
fabrication that Costa Ricans themselves favor because

it frees them from responsibility for their inadequate behavior and history and from taking on the challenges of the modern world. In "Protesta contra el folklore" (Protest against Folklore), a critique of the *costumbrista* literature so well loved in Costa Rica, she exposes a venerable practice that has become shallow through repetition. She attacks the complacency this literary fashion produces in the urban reader surrounded by "realism" but immune to it, who finds "reality" in a tired regionalism, which she reduces to disparaging connotations by referring to it repeatedly as "folklore." Given the high esteem accorded *costumbrista* writing in Costa Rica since the nineteenth century, and the number of writers who practiced it, many Costa Ricans considered her essay an affront. Subsequent literary historians, however, have recognized the pioneering nature of her comments regarding the literary possibilities of urban existence.

In both these essays Yolanda Oreamuno addresses the theme of Latin American identity with boldness and vision. She rejects the evasiveness that is found in facile stereotypes and calls for an authentic recognition of Costa Rican reality.

JANET N. GOLD

Yolanda Oreamuno

Tropical Myths and the Costa Rican Environment

For Joaquín García Monge, who has graciously endured all this.

I f you are a foreigner arriving in Costa Rica, there is, starting at the port of entry, a great figure of guilt that hovers over the country and is blamed for anything that goes wrong . . . and a lot goes wrong: it is "the environment." Its faults, until one reaches the station in San José, are relatively minor: the slow-moving waiters, the dirty food, the frequent stops at rural stations, the prices, and the service. But that really does not justify the bad reputation of "the environment."

The curious foreigner only discovers its large and real sins when, somewhat more familiar with things, he dares to search out the meeting place on the main street below the offices of the *Costa Rica Daily* for a bit of conversation, or, if more adept, he seeks out us "intellectuals" for a bit of literary banter. Then he finds out. We disclose everything. Shortcomings are discussed and described in detail, and we, our inertia, and our lack of ability are thoroughly explained. It is the fault of "the environment."

* * *

This vague and imprecise word acquires in Costa Rica (I don't know if in the rest of America as well) a different meaning from that ascribed to it in the dictionary, in common parlance, or daily activities.

The environment may be blue in the Mediterranean, agitated and violent in the United States, colorful in Mexico, sadistic in Turkey, rococo in Japan (which due to advertising is currently the legitimate heir to a bastard rococo). In Costa Rica it is black.

Translated by Janet N. Gold

By "environment" I understand in general terms the vague but definite atmosphere created by family customs, daily language, local politics, lifestyle, and way of thinking (which often are diametrically opposed). But I don't deny the reality of its influence or its vast radius of action.

In Costa Rica these meanings are invalid. "The environment" is something very large, very powerful, and very hated that allows one to do nothing, that muddies the best intentions, distorts vocations, aborts large ideas before they can even be conceived, and keeps us twiddling our thumbs always waiting for something sensational to come and erase this gloomy and ominous shadow.

But if we want to be truly honorable and accountable for our point of view, we must recognize that this position of comfortable stasis is our own fault, that we carry "the environment" within ourselves, and that we are the ones who make it, capitalize on it, and maintain it. This does not negate that there is a kind of influence, always capable of being overcome, that comes from the mediocrity of the cradle, the mediocrity of our economy and our politics. What I refute is that the term is exact and the charges justified.

Two accusations that assume the character of national maladies do merit serious study: the almost complete absence of a fighting spirit and the willful ignorance of any dangerous quality that could, at any given moment, jolt us out of our passivity.

This antiaggressive spirit is manifest in a provincial fear of all things large and a sporadic preference for things small; the willful ignorance acts as a simple process of elimination, not of the bad to make room for the efficient but rather of dangerous competency to make room for the inauthentic and inoffensive.

The reason for all this comes from our past. . . . Our people did not form themselves by themselves, civilization came to us as a gift, and culture continues to arrive as a product that is imported and still suffers from prohibitive taxes. We inherited European civilization like capital made by foreign hands, foreign hands that came to exploit, never with the intention of settling down here, and if they did settle it was as parasites because there was very little to explore. Rather than a quick rape yielding ample profits, our conquest was a slow, long-term bourgeois enterprise undertaken with scant capital. We remain scarred by the total absence of the spirited blood that audacious Spaniards of cape and sword left behind in other lands, and by the mediocrity of the small business, with few dangers but with few rewards. We get a morbid little thrill when we plunge, always shored up by timidity and the possibility of turning back, into those projects that present few risks; we manage with some difficulty to be in style, yet we are. Every day we commit infinitesimal sins that we atone for with even slighter remorse and by falling into some even more insignificant but stylish sin. Constant recidivism does not tarnish our immaculate honor, and we can loudly condemn the great countries for the great sins that we never commit.

Even the landscape is an accomplice to our psychology. Huge precipices from which water cascades and bellows, immense and hostile sandy deserts, frightening cold, all these end north of us; we cannot even lay claim to real tropical inclemency. Our landscape is a tableau. A delicately lovely tableau. The little house rests lazily in the corral, corn field, or coffee grove, as clean as a whistle; the trees are always green, and there are not even bothersome distinctions between summer and winter to make us think seriously about climatology. We suffer neither from horrible droughts nor from immense floods. The mountains are always desperately blue; October and January are rich and fertile; there is quite enough land (and quite poorly parceled out) so that this parenthesis does not seriously affect our beatific tranquility. The little house painted white, with a bright red-tiled roof and a furious blue stripe at window level, remains gently lazy, endlessly and romantically enamored of the consistently green fields and the never-dry river. The concept of the grandiose, the immense, the sensation of primitive fear, accompany the disproportionate landscape of the north, while here, to the contrary, savage fear becomes simple precaution. Only further to the south, on the coast of Peru, I recall, does the sensation of aridity, of impotence in the face of nature, of vigorous and virile struggle with the unknown, begin again.

This not needing to struggle brings with it, consequently, a desire not to provoke a fight, to flee from it. We prefer to be nonconfrontational: we abstain. He who presumes to hold his head up above the general level is not decapitated. No! He is gently brought down to ground level and slowly, without violence, is positioned at the appropriate height. If you write a strongly worded article today and shock the critics, and you are foolish enough to maintain this tone in the next article, if it appeared yesterday in the newspapers with bold headlines, tomorrow it will appear delicately placed on the literary page, the day after tomorrow in the sports section, and if you continue it will end up on the society page. . . . Quickly, without a fight or a fuss, you are silenced. We don't even like sensationalism.

Hospitable Costa Rica receives with open arms the political emigrants of all America, the victim of this or that tyranny. Reporters pay him a visit, they take his pulse, and if they see that the gentleman insists on his innate rebelliousness, they gently ignore him, and he just as gently becomes completely anonymous. Great political and literary figures, revolutionaries and demagogues have spent periods of exile in Costa Rica, and of their stay there remains nothing more than . . . a name on the immigration lists.

Besides our willful and studied ignorance (I maintain), we have the subtle power of the *choteo*. *Choteo*, or verbal banter, is a deadly weapon (deadly as a camelia!) that one can carry without a permit and brandish with impunity. It has the finest lyrical flourishes and biting ingenuity; it serves to demonstrate ability, to make one appear learned, precise, philosophical, and erudite. It takes on various characteristics: it is medical empiricism, literary empiricism, sociological empiricism, and Freudian empiricism. What's more, against such a fine and elegant weapon there is no defense. You find it in the mouth of your best friend, in the hand of your colleague, in the morning and evening papers, everywhere. And what's more: you are brave and subtle and "tell it like it is" if you know how to use it effectively. You have the incontestable advantage of not having to respect anything or anyone, and no great profundity is required to exercise it. I believe it is the only real technology of which we can boast, and its "professionals" the only experts we have in abundance.

At this juncture we arrive at the "tropical myths." Costa Rica, the unfortunate Costa Rica violated by travel agencies, has three important things: pretty women, color, and demoperfectocracy, in strict advertising order. The beauty of our women proliferates in the imagination of the "Kodak" tourist: beautiful legs, dark eyes, brown bodies, delicious mouths. . . . Color, or rather local color, consists of Negroes with taut and sweaty skin, bending in fake poses over plowed furrows, Indians who practice strange medieval-criollo rites, permanent sunshine, zero rain (which is not the same as below-zero rain), and palm trees, lots of palm trees . . . so many and so visible that they can be the easy object for even the most inexperienced amateur photographer. Demoperfectocracy is a bit more complicated and subtle: the president strolls through the streets without a bodyguard, shakes hands with any anonymous citizen, and gives press conferences every day, without the newspapers' feeling they have to publish a special edition to commemorate the event.

Contradicting the tourist agencies and the creators of these lucrative "tropical myths," I will tell foreigners the truth: Costa Rican women are beautiful, very beautiful . . . (this fact can remain in the advertisements); the Indians, of whom there are about three thousand living deep in the interior of the republic, maintain no exotic rites, and, though some speak their own language as well, they all speak Spanish; it rains nine months of the year in the most desperate way imaginable (which disputes, as one can see, the idea of permanent sunshine and "eternal springtime"); it is extremely hot on the coast, and our landscapes are ideal for painters, picture postcards for the family, and hopeful spinsters (this can also remain in the ads but with the noted corrections). We do not have perfect democracy, nor have we ever (this cannot be used in full for the ads).

Without entering into a more profound analysis of our "Costa Rican" democracy (which is quite different from democracy per se), I want to note that there are two divergent concepts of democracy, as there are also two ways of living it. There is active, evolving democracy and the passive democracy of the bill of rights of the republic. Ours is the latter. There are, as well, two ways of living it: one (for us, so far, in the future) putting it into practice with everyone, without distinction of social, economic, or political categories, and the other self-applied without justification. We live the second and we sing of the first in the national anthem. To add insult to injury, we frequently act as if we lived in a true democracy, acting with the freedom that this implies, and when we do so, it is discreetly brought to our attention so that we are made to question the bill of rights of the republic.

This way of acting degenerates into a visible impoliteness and an absolute or almost absolute lack of responsibility. We act with ourselves in mind and very often haven't even the remotest or most simplistic understanding of fellowship; we lack cohesion, connections earned through suffering and work; we lack collectivity. The maximum representative of this nefarious tendency is a type that can be called the "local talent."

The "local talent" is boastful, discusses the news of the day as well as his neighbors' conduct, is always in secret but never substantiated contact with the official sources of political news, is a know-it-all, a speculator, and a gossip. He exists to an extent in almost all our great politicians and . even more so in the soul of our ordinary citizens. He would be harmless if he did not lack, as noted earlier, a simple sense of fellowship, and if he did not consider our little world, our politics, and our economy as being isolated from the rest of the universe, separate entities floating in the ether, and if he did not contaminate with his virus this politics, this world, and this economy that he diminishes.

Against all this, a reaction begins; one feels it nudging tentatively and at times taking infantile steps. We try to orient our mute and unselective vitality, and that dulled muscle moves hesitantly along those first virgin paths. This is where the search for folklore comes in. With delight we discover our racial inheritance, with the same pleasure with which a fourteen-year-old girl watches her breasts grow; the folk singer bursts forth like a caged bird, sometimes copying foreign songs; the door is firmly closed on the furtive exodus of indigenous artifacts; we begin to study the poor people's joys (without paying too much attention yet to their sorrows); we have more respect for the language of the countryside; and as we go we are finding our way.

Along this path of struggle we can easily overcome our pathological or learned inertia; through an open and simple sensibility we can grasp the truth of the landscape, and there, in the land and in the people joined in sorrow and movement, what is indigenous calls to us. It is one way. There are many open to us.

The mistakes, the sins caused inevitably by any step forward, frighten our nonaggression, and our puritanism trembles when faced with the mortal sin, the fundamental and decisive sin of giving ourselves to the future. Countries are not born with original sins as humans are, but they must commit them in order to move forward.

Costa Rica discovers her puberty, her virgin sex trembles, and the future calls her to convert her into an authentic and brilliant sinner.

San José, 1939

Repertorio Americano 36 (11): 169–170.

Protest against Folklore

For days I have been trying, with the very best intentions, to finish a novel—a very good one, many say, the critics describe it as marvelous—which has definitely exhausted my patience.

In the ranks of those books that attempt to get to the heart of the American agrarian problem—the suffering of the Indian and the exploitation of the peasant—this book is not only true, it is complete and, at times, even brilliant. In spite of finding in it some literary absurdities such as the presence of a Lady of the Camelias, plump and consumptive, and a crudely drawn Robin Hood, if I examine calmly the aesthetic expression, I can recognize that the book is . . . good.

Nevertheless, to arrive at this conclusion I have had to suppress something powerful in me, a definite and tenacious opposition that prevents me from finishing it happily and exhaling at the end an exclamation of satisfaction or sympathy. So I have searched patiently within myself to determine the source of this violent reaction, and I believe I am able to articulate it.

The cycle of American folkloric literature scales heights of unsuspected magnitude, it extends powerfully through many decades and leaves engraved, in luminous letters, names that I will not repeat, since they are so well known. Every nationality has felt the historical imperative to make known the painful truth of the suffering of, respectively, the Indian, the deculturized Indian, the peasant farmer, the half-breed, and the native of

Translated by Janet N. Gold

Spanish blood. The lexicon is swollen with words peppered with the indigenous *atl*, *iztl*, and *chua*; we learn turns of phrase and feel the suffering as if we too were barefoot, with calloused palm and primitive mind. Geniuses work at drawing from the shadows humble figures that become realistic and colorful at their touch. And thus it has been for a very long time, through numerous artistic renderings. From every American ethnic group come one or more magnificent voices.

The efficacy and good will of this work, whether spontaneous or deliberate, is indisputable. The intensity of this rending cry has shaken consciences, it has given birth to generous initiatives, and various wonderful realities have subsequently taken shape. American folkloric literature, energized through suffering, replete with individuality, is a done deed.

But I hold that the climax of saturation has arrived, and I accuse folkloric literature of being one-sided. I believe that more folklore, seen as the only artistic current possible in America, signifies decadence. If, when they write, our authors feel the impulse to redeem, they have before them industrialization, which arrives with giant steps with its following of penury, crisis, and abundance; they have the cruel adaptation of our multifaceted and fantastic mestizo population to a scientific, mechanized reality. In what other flesh can the change from languor to forced activity, from a dream state to unexpected knowledge, come about with more rending than in our American flesh? The revolt against the anonymous face of merciless progress must be more cruel than that against the palpable presence of the criollo exploiter or the half-civilized overseer. This reality exists for those who find suffering a literary inspiration. And if we surrender before beauty, the urban landscape—at times situated in the heart of a voluptuous world of primal vigor and ferocity—attains visual forms of inconceivable brilliance. The civilized life of our continent, not separate from the Indians, the peasants, or the natives of European blood but hand in hand with them, is as rich and worthy of attention as the panorama offered by an exclusionary folklore.

Our writers, with very few and usually unworthy exceptions, won't condescend to get out of the valley that, for being so frequented, has become literarily and emotionally secure. In the modern asentimental environment, it is very hard to squeeze a tear from an audience desensitized by the proximity of tragedy. But the remote, distant portrait of the peasant, in which readers from the city have no direct participation and for which they hardly feel guilty, inspires sympathy without remorse and therefore more readily. By now all this ought to be so simple as not to tempt us.

On the other hand, the city, the office worker, the growing bureaucracy, the semioriental sybaritic life of our bourgeoisie, the way our respective nationalities have adopted tendencies and fashions previously very European and now very Yankee, cry out for a voice, an accuser, a rebel, and someone to discover new beauties and old suffering. The very particular idiosyncrasy of our worker—so sadly molded to the factory and innately ill-equipped to assimilate its rhythm—demands, with all the force of an existing reality, a powerful, faithful, and talented hand to portray it.

With the "excess of folklore" factor we advertise one element of our society that, although very powerful, is not the only one, and we feed the myths of the dominating foreigner and his traditional greed.

Speaking of literature, I confess that personally I am fed up, in capital letters, with folklore. From this corner of America I can say that I am quite familiar with the typical agrarian lifestyle of almost all the neighboring countries, yet I know little of their other urgent problems. The local-color devices of this kind of art are worn out, the aesthetic agitation they used to produce no longer occurs, the scene is repeated with numbing synchronicity, and emotion flees before the inevitable boredom of what is seen time and again.

We must end this calamity: the cheap devotion of the local-color writer, the abuse, the sloppiness, the one-sidedness and one-way vision that are the equivalent of artistic blindness. I think that from now on I will refuse to review poems, paintings, and books that foolishly insist on this theme. I will make a final effort to finish the book that was the source of these conclusions in the hope that it will be the last I encounter, at least for a while, whether it be good like this one or bad like the rest.

I would hope with this to encourage some questioning and to fortify the protest that perhaps others like myself have considered but not dared to articulate. I am grateful to folklore for what it has contributed, I salute it as a past glory, and I look forward to the renovating breath of works in step with the modern American movement, so I may pay homage to them from a better literary future.

San José, March 1943

A lo largo del corto camino. San José: Editorial Costa Rica, 1961, pp. 93–97. Originally published in *Repertorio Americano* 40 (6).

Rosario Castellanos

Mexico, 1925–1974

Rosario Castellanos, Mexican author, teacher, feminist, and diplomat, was born in Mexico City in 1925. Her childhood as part of a landowning family in Chiapas, near the Guatemalan border, led her to a lifelong interest in the dynamics of race, class, and gender in Mexico. Through her writings, she became an early spokesperson in Latin America for the feminism of the 1960s and 1970s. As a young woman she studied philosophy at the National University in Mexico City. After a fellowship year at the University of Madrid, she returned in 1952 to Chiapas, where she spent two years in educational outreach work among the indigenous population. By this time she had already published several books of poetry. For the rest of her life, she combined significant literary and journalistic efforts with other pursuits: first, continued involvement with educational projects in Chiapas; later, teaching and administrative posts at the National University and visiting professorships in the United States; and finally, the Mexican ambassadorship to Israel between 1971 and 1974. Married to Ricardo Guerra in 1957, she was the mother of a son, Gabriel, becoming a single parent when her marriage ended in divorce. Castellanos died in 1974 after an electrical accident in her Tel Aviv home. Her eleven books of poetry were collected in *Poesía no eres tú* (1972; Poetry Isn't You). Her other works include two novels, *Balún-Canán*

(1957; *The Nine Guardians*, 1992) and *Oficio de tinieblas* (1962; Rites of Darkness); three collections of short stories, *Ciudad Real* (1960; Royal City), *Los convidados de agosto* (1964; The Guests of August), and *Album de familia* (1971; Family Album); and the play *El eterno femenino* (1975; The Eternal Feminine). Her essays are key to understanding her feminism but so far are less studied than her other works. They comprise four volumes: *Juicios sumarios* (1966; Summary Judgments), *Mujer que sabe latín* (1973; Woman Who Knows Latin), *El uso de la palabra* (1974; The Use of the Word), and *El mar y sus pescaditos* (1974; The Sea and Its Little Fish).

Castellanos' essays range from analytical pieces on academic subjects to chatty newspaper columns on her own domestic struggles. Like much of her writing, they often reflect her life and concerns, and it is thus not surprising that the condition of women in Mexico and elsewhere is a frequent point of departure. In some essays, she examines the contributions of such significant women as Virginia Woolf, Simone Weil, and Simone de Beauvoir. Elsewhere, she discusses the women in Mexican history who have been termed archetypal— Malinche, the Virgin of Guadalupe, and Sor Juana Inés de la Cruz.

In "Costumbres mexicanas" (Mexican Customs), originally published in 1964 in the Mexican newspaper *Excélsior*, she gives a contemporary Mexican setting to her denunciation of traditional social practices unfair to women. As in other works, she decries the devaluation of women and their exploitation within Mexican society. Although ironic and slightly caricaturesque, the essay conveys her awareness of women's psychological experience. Castellanos' satirical approach is in keeping with her theory that undesirable social structures are better combatted through ridicule than through tears or indignation. But the seething anger that lies below the surface of her prose is nevertheless apparent.

MARTHA LAFOLLETTE MILLER

Mexican Customs

I'm not yet able to put it all into words. In the first place, my observations are just casual. Then too, I'm held back by the thought that we're dealing with a matter of no importance: an attempt at living together. Can anything be more commonplace, more natural for all of us, from the moment we're born and join first a family, then a social group, and finally a marriage?

This last item is the problem. Because it's a question of choosing the proper partner—that individual we're not afraid of swearing undying love and fidelity to.

I've mentioned choosing, but I think that to be more exact, I must change the verb. Because, in this country at least, women don't choose. We sit passively down to wait until a man casts his eyes toward the corner that our modesty has afforded us and discovers the marvelous qualities that adorn us. What follows is predictable and subject to fairly strict rules: the progressive stages of the male's approach, our conventional standoffishness, our attempt to hide our terror of losing this opportunity, because no one has guaranteed us we'll have another. At times, of course, the opportunity is so puny that we have no choice except to refuse it. But we're generally satisfied with little: with someone who holds a steady job, who enjoys a certain measure of health, and whose appearance isn't decidedly repulsive.

His moral qualities boil down to his acceptance of two ideas: that marriage is a valid institution, one not to be toyed with, and that within that

Translated by Martha LaFollette Miller

institution the wife has a place she must be granted. But what is her place? That, it seems, depends on the circumstances. If those "entering into the marriage contract"—as society pages so delicately like to express it—are wealthy, the wife's place may be that of a decorative piece of furniture that can be displayed not only to visitors in the home but also transported, for exhibition, to parties and other gatherings. She is expected to avoid any activity that might spoil her figure, though she is permitted to devote her spare time to works of charity.

Since this woman is an object almost totally out of touch with reality, we will not bother further with her but will consider instead the wife of her husband's employee. Of course, she too aspires to being decorative and is obliged to fulfill that function. But she has fewer means and less time at her disposal, because she not only performs all the domestic tasks in her household but also brings joy to the home each year with a visit from the stork. It is difficult, amidst diaper changes, bawling babies, the antics of those old enough to wipe mommy's expensive skin cream on the rug, and the alarming hisses of the pressure cooker, to maintain not just one's equanimity but one's resemblance to a human being. The wife little by little starts forgetting the most elementary principles of civilized life: she doesn't comb her hair, for example. And when her husband returns from his demanding duties at the office, he beholds—from the lofty vantage point of his own impeccable grooming—a disheveled woman. Isn't that good enough reason for him to turn to his buddies, go out and raise hell, hire mariachis to play, so they can help him forget the disaster at home? If the husband has a practical bent (and the money, of course), he sets up a second household, where he can always find waiting, arms open and clad only in an enticing negligee, the "other woman." That other woman whose existence looms largest in the mind of the wife whose husband leaves her at home alone with the classic excuses: the meeting with the board of directors that for technical reasons gets longer and longer; the open-ended dinners with old school chums; the sudden unexpected business trip to that branch office, whose accounts are muddled . . . and on and on. If the wife, alas, has been blessed at the baptismal font with a lack of imagination, she will take such alibis seriously; she will even earn his thanks by meticulously packing his suitcase or by ironing that special shirt or by digging out of the trunk where the family heirlooms are kept the cuff links that once belonged to that uncle who (if he'd only led a more orderly life) would have made them millionaires by dying (as in fact he did) a bachelor and intestate.

But the nights are long and women possess few means of amusing themselves. After putting the children to bed and blotting them out until the next day, they turn on the television set. There they become vaguely aware of an intrigue going on in some exotic country full of palm trees and natives, where a fair-haired young man distributes punches, foils the bad guys' evil schemes, and ends up with the booty and the blonde.

The woman yawns. She thinks it's time to go to sleep, so she gets into bed. But when she turns off the light a certain uneasiness creeps over her. Sleep doesn't come, and to pass the time, what could be better than one of those magazines designed especially for housewives? She turns the light back on and rummages through the newspapers until she finds what she is looking for. There it is, on its cover a seductive young female, with shining eyes, shining teeth, shining lips, and hair shaped and trained by the best hairdressers in the world. The woman regards her in the same way that someone damned to Hell might view an angel. Half irritated, half distracted, she flips through the magazine. Pastries in vivid colors to tempt the poor woman, who had so nobly skipped dinner hoping to trim even half an inch from her waist! Paris fashions that neither her figure nor her budget would ever permit her to wear! But at this late hour she's alone and she can dream. Yes, she strolls down the paths of a park with a dog on a leash; she attends a cocktail party and an elegant reception and awakens the next day with no trace of fatigue, spreading about her the folds of that marvelous dressing gown that both veils and reveals the charms that her successive pregnancies (which pregnancies? She had entirely forgotten them) had temporarily eclipsed.

Dear lady, at this critical moment, close the magazine and go to sleep. You will dream pleasant and impossible dreams. Because if you turn the page you will find your portrait. And little by little you'll recognize yourself. Your husband's absences, my dear, aren't really necessary; his excuses are false. Because you have failed to take care of yourself. Faced with choosing between being a wife and being a mother, you have chosen to be a mother, abandoning your man to the innumerable temptations that besiege him. And that, my dear, is costly. And you are paying for it now. But you must not lose control of your emotions. Men stray, it's true. But they come back. It's a natural law, as unvarying as the migration of birds. Don't spoil his return by making a scene—with tears, jealousy, or recrimination! Instead, double your sweetness and understanding; do your best to improve your appearance; find a way to make the children invisible during those brief moments when your husband is at home. In a pleasant, cozy, and—above all—legitimate home. Because you, dear, arouse deep feelings of guilt in your husband, since you drive him to improper behavior. And as for the "other woman," don't hold a grudge. Contrary to what you may think, her life is no bed of roses. Her situation is ambiguous, and she knows that in the long run she's bound to lose out. It's simply a matter of time. When have pleasures not ended in boredom? As for you, try hard and you will win. Yes, my dear. You will win this time. And the next. And the next. And the next. Your cardinal virtue is patience, and if you practice it, you will be rewarded. When he's ninety, your husband will be all yours (that is, if he's managed to sidestep entanglements, and you to put up with his shenanigans). We assure you that no one will fight you for the privilege of preparing him for burial.

25 January 1964

El uso de la palabra. Mexico City: Editores Mexicanos Unidos, 1982, pp. 28–32.

Carmen Naranjo

Costa Rica, 1930–

Carmen Naranjo is a dynamic and controversial presence in Costa Rica whose work in the cultural arena,
through political posts and publications, has achieved
extensive diffusion in Central America. Her international renown, however, is attributable above all to her
sixteen volumes of poetry and fiction. Her novels have
won numerous awards and include such works as *Los
perros no ladraron* (1966; The Dogs Didn't Bark), *Camino
al mediodía* (1968; On the Way to Noon), and *Diario de
una multitud* (1974; Diary of a Multitude). In both the
personal and professional spheres Carmen Naranjo is a
leader in the arts and a catalyst for social change.

Naranjo has many years of public service to her
credit, including positions as ambassador to Israel, minister of culture, United Nations delegate for children's
affairs in Mexico, UNICEF representative in Guatemala, director of EDUCA (Central American University
Press), and director of the Costa Rican Museum of Art.
She was instrumental in the drafting and passage of the
Law for Social Equality (1989), a milestone for women's
rights in Costa Rica, and she is a frequent contributor
to national periodicals, as she engages her compatriots
in dialogue on topics of cultural concern.

Although Carmen Naranjo's voice was heard as early
as the 1960s, it was in the 1970s, a decade of cultural in-
novation and expansion under the governments of José

Figueres Ferrer (1970–1974) and Daniel Oduber Quirós (1974–1978), that Naranjo became a force to be reckoned with. Her essays of that epoch are frankly and assertively optimistic, especially her seminal book written for UNESCO, *Cultura* (1978; Culture), in which she defines culture, suggests ways to maintain and promote it, and calls for a cultural politics.

Her essay "Crisis cultural en Costa Rica" (Cultural Crisis in Costa Rica) was originally a speech given at the National Theater when she was director of EDUCA. It is a mature reflection on Costa Rican reality from the perspective of "an indefatigable advocate for culture." In a very tangible way Naranjo's essay is both a response to the observations, queries, and challenges of her four volumes of essays written between 1967 and 1988 and a confirmation of the thematic unity of those essays. She reiterates the definition of culture first proffered in *Cultura* ten years earlier. Her acerbic critique of the Costa Rican's use of inauthentic language in *Cinco temas en busca de un pensador* (1967; Five Themes in Search of a Thinker) is still a central theme, as Naranjo laments the hypocrisy and lack of trust it engenders. She is harshly critical of politicians who consistently fail to address the real needs of the people, and who have failed to adopt a cultural policy such as the one Naranjo tried to establish in the 1970s. Her denunciation of the sterility of formal education in Costa Rica and the degenerative effects of unregulated mass media speaks of disillusionment with educators and leaders who have lost sight of authentic cultural values in the face of a growing materialism and consumerism. These same issues, which were a bone of contention when Naranjo was minister of culture (1974–1976), are seen here as having a direct relationship to the economic crisis being faced by the country today.

ARDIS L. NELSON

Carmen Naranjo

Cultural Crisis in Costa Rica

C osta Rica's principal problem is culture.

This affirmation is as passionate as it is valid for whatever view one takes of the cultural life of a country.

Culture is passion. Anyone who denies this is denying the power that emanates from those who dedicate all their creative forces to maintaining the cultural heritage of a people.

Born of passion, culture finds passion all around it. Any critical point of view about culture naturally incites alternative or even conflicting views, which in essence is healthy and constructive. I applaud in advance those who disagree with me, because if their point of departure is a desire to affirm our culture in order to make it grow, we are on parallel paths. We may walk together in silence or we may argue and shout, but we share a common goal for our country.

I am not thinking of any particular administration as I organize these thoughts. To criticize our culture based on the measure of a four-year platform would be ridiculous. Besides, there has not been a single government in Costa Rica that has defined a cultural policy. Since the country's beginnings there has always been a group of people who have fomented culture, from the transcendental to the showy temporal event. The mere fact that we have a Ministry of Culture does not automatically mean that we have a cultural policy.

Culture does not abide officialism. Rather, it is generated by a people and is of the people. A government, nevertheless, can and must stimulate

Translated by Ardis L. Nelson

awareness of that culture and encourage its diffusion and enrichment by all possible means.

If a nation seeks to raise the standard of living, well-being, and general wealth of its citizens, it must include in its plans for development all that the country is looking for in the cultural arena.

There is nothing more closely tied to the efforts toward development than culture, because it is the most basic and essential capital. We have seen many public works for which enormous human and economic resources were expended that did not fulfill their function nor improve well-being because the cultural condition of the population was not taken into account. We have also seen housing projects transformed rapidly into slums because the inhabitants were not culturally prepared for the new housing or because its construction did not take into consideration the customs and lifestyle of its residents.

Although culture represents the most crucial problem in Costa Rica, it lacks a government policy and is rarely given priority in critical analyses of the country.

In order to not merely continue patching and mending and never finding the source of the problem, it will be necessary to reflect on these issues conscientiously. Otherwise we will be doomed to a destructive path that will take us ever farther from needed solutions rather than leading us to a confrontation with our real problems.

Costa Rica's crises touch all of us: educational crisis, political crisis, institutional crisis, social crisis, economic crisis, moral crisis.

As we analyze these crises we find in each one a cultural basis.

First, let us ponder the concept. What is culture? We understand as culture all that contributes to the heritage of a people and manifests itself as communication, tradition, national identity, beliefs, and artistic expression, whether popular or individual. Culture includes such important factors for all peoples as language, customs, the expression of religious belief that transcends reality, and the wealth of creativity that enriches a people's heritage.

And what is befalling our morals, our values? In simple terms we have divorced saying from doing, that is, we have severed the relationship that ought to exist between word and action. From the religious, ethical, and political points of view, the Costa Rican has found two noncoinciding paths: opinions flow as if all were aspiring speech-makers, but attitudes never agree with speeches. Language, as it is used and abused today, limits expression. We speak with eroded words heard by others as eroded thoughts. We do not believe each other because our language has lost its validity. Words reach us as a dull sound that neither communicates nor inspires nor demonstrates the concept that was meant to be transmitted.

A culture without a valid language is a culture in decline, because it results in a lack of trust in written and verbal values, and even in the material world. Life has become a stage on which we act with two faces and two languages, one for public consumption and the other, quite different, for our private lives. We don an appearance that bears no relation to reality. This farce is so common that people no longer believe in anyone or anything. This incredulousness implies neither criticism nor value judgment but rather conformity in the face of the irremediable. If culture is to prosper and be a growing force for the people of Costa Rica, a simple, sincere, and legitimate language is urgently needed, one that eradicates the illusions of promises and formulas that do not work.

We Costa Ricans must make an effort to restore true communication to our language in order to overcome hypocrisy and reinstate those values that are in danger of extinction.

The endeavor is monumental since the most influential people in public life play with words. And every language requires the backing of a real attitude, every word needs the backbone of truth, and every expression must be linked to decisive action that favors its success.

Day by day it is becoming more and more evident that only an austere and accountable ethics, only a sincerity shaped by action, can enrich and reaffirm our language so that the integral values that dignify the Costa Rican materially and spiritually may prevail.

In the face of this crisis, another of political character stirs.

In a country like ours the political crisis takes several tangents. On the one hand we are a nation in search of our own development. Nevertheless, we do very little to support a culture that encourages individual and social development, strengthens the desire to improve, foments solidarity among people, and promotes bold attempts at creativity, which in turn incite successful outcomes.

Like it or not, our governments have been utterly paternalistic. They design solutions for urgent needs, forgetting in the process to teach and stimulate people to resolve their own problems. Thus, we see a concentration of public works in some sectors, providing partial, regional protection, and total abandonment of other regions. Both those who do and do not receive consideration expect the government to provide all these services, because they ignore the possibility of their own initiative, a combination of effort and creativity, and follow only the path of pressuring the government to fulfill their needs.

Underdevelopment produces underdeveloped governments as well, ones that prefer a deceivingly calm ferment to an open recognition of needs, demands, and initiatives in which government may lose its primary role as benefactor. In the midst of underdevelopment a democracy such as ours ends up being largely a system of governmental and partisan self-defenses that calculates concessions and favors, not in a dialogue that gives representation to the people but rather in an allotment of benefits that may favor certain groups, according to the concerns and preferences of the politicians.

Our democratic culture has been wasting away by degrees as well, because it lacks the spirit of change. People no longer believe in the criticism one political party makes of another, when they are in or out of power, because the criticism does not provide an objective analysis in good faith or a serene appraisal of their proposals, which might lead to the well-intentioned and profound reform the country requires. It is only a question of blowing one's own horn in an exaggerated and negative way that capitalizes only on blunders. The defenders use similar means and only point out their successes. Thus it would seem that we live in a country where it is impossible to make a mistake, where the only way to survive politically is by circumventing comprehension with false words and a falsifying language.

For years our political campaigns have abandoned sincerity in favor of publicity schemes that sell a candidate using catchy slogans. The result is what we have called a noisy fiesta, a pageant of flags beneath a chorus of shouts and horns in which the Costa Rican, his conscience clear and without purpose, marches with resignation to vote for the lesser of two evils.

Our political campaigns have become shows. That is why the clowns have so much fun as they participate in the battles and later tell jokes to tame the pride of the winners.

The democracy of an underdeveloped country runs the risk of its culture becoming a game in which the people participate, but only as passive recipients. The diverse spectacles tend to diminish and invalidate both individual and social worth rather than endow the people with creative opportunities.

How beautiful it would be if, on election day, we went to the polls in silence. After having analyzed the advantages of each candidate's serious and profound discourse, we would listen to the voice of our conscience and vote for the best, convinced that he would foster positive circumstances for the general well-being of the country. Now that would be political culture.

And the political crisis, in its cultural aspects, does not end with the shows that entertain us superficially. It has entered the institutional arena. We have a set of laws that are not respected and the most agile is he who discovers the loopholes necessary to make them inoperable. We have almost a whole galaxy of institutions, with their backs turned to the needs of the people, bureaucratized, worm-eaten by their own organizational and administrative problems. Institutions closed in by their own artificial and technical jargon, only opening their doors when some pressure group forcefully demands an answer. Institutions full of comforts and luxuries are an affront to the growing poverty of the country. The internal culture of these institutions is concerned with expanding technical facilities for its own purposes, but those projects benefit very few and rarely have meaning in terms of the larger problems of the country.

The visible signs of all this are worthy of the best theater of the absurd: a national economy in crisis because it cannot support increased public spending; a Ministry of Finance obliged to impose restrictions to avoid excess spending on the rest of the administration, which does not voluntarily and rationally observe this rule of public finance; a general idea that the state patrimony is at the service of the whims and pretensions of the leaders in power; an importance given to the influence and favoritism that politicians confer on their associates; a lack of political definition in all areas because the idea in force is the opposite of "Don't put off until tomorrow what you can do today." Thus we have improvised administrations that are put to the test by dealing with emergencies, sometimes exaggerating them, because so many urgent demands of the past have been consistently buried without the least bit of foresight for those of today and tomorrow.

The people observe and learn. Their political culture is an accumulation of expressions such as "Thank goodness it's not my problem!" And little by little they become indifferent, passive, frustrated, until one day they are jolted by a clear and urgent indignation. On that day they will discover the political culture that we have been imposing on them and that thwarts those who had confidence and faith, at least in their own efforts.

The next link in the chain of crisis is education.
Even on the most elementary level at which the basic tools for learning are first introduced, a valid and creative education always invites and

accommodates dialogue in which culture is affirmed. It is a kind of learning that prepares one to think, create, and contribute, for it is based responsibly on the need to be useful, to serve. Within this permanent and continuing pattern of learning, a sediment of discoveries and rediscoveries leads to an austere lifestyle as in the olden days of this country.

But over a period of many years we have been isolating our people from their cultural life by the easiest means: the belittling of their creativity.

Our educational system has become rigid and formal, separated from social, religious, and creative traditions of the family and society in general. This type of education is invalidating, and instead of producing people capable of serving in different fields where they may be able to shape and motivate creativity, individuals come out of this system demanding recognition and privileges, without ever finding the path of mission and service.

This enfeebling education, which sometimes continues even through the university and postgraduate levels, operates as if absolved from any duty to the country's culture. It always offers solutions or alternatives that detract from the good of the people or that prohibit acting on their behalf. Thus we see the insatiable exhaustion of resources on the part of the educated, who do nothing to replace them or create new sources. They consume the cultural wealth in the sense of extinguishing, corroding, and impoverishing it, without thinking of the fervor it took to germinate it, its historical inception, or the careful cultivation of its growth.

Added to the disadvantages of a formal and rigid education is the fact that the country has not acted responsibly with regard to mass media communications, neither in regulating them nor in using them to promote culture. The media floods the populace with materialism and commercialism, closing people into a circle of defensive and violent egoism characterized by vulgarity and pedestrian dreams. We are already seeing the consequences of that weakness: children with no imagination, dulled before their first thoughts develop, people caught up in their eagerness for prestige, demanding privilege and denying social responsibility, rejecting the least effort or mission of service to their country, and almost always indifferent to the contribution implicit in personal and national achievement.

We are left with a narcotized society, one that has stopped thinking and has accepted a mind-set based on the constant barrage of slogans, stereotypes, and frivolities, all calling for consumption above and beyond their normal needs and reasonable possibilities.

This society, in its clamoring for luxuries with worn-out clichés, opens the door to economic crisis. How can we not succumb if they continually and feverishly show us how to consume, and at the same time incapacitate us to produce? A cultural explanation is therefore the only valid way to describe the constantly growing imbalance between the quantities we consume and the small amount we produce. There is never enough money, there is no economic plan that works, and there are no healthy colons. In truth we are consumers. Our cultural lesson has been one of obedience to repetitive sounds, images, and propaganda. They have destroyed our culture of thrift, modesty, solidarity, and honest work, all the factors that give satisfaction in terms of our human development.

This series of profoundly dangerous crises is due to the fact that we have separated social and economic improvement from bettering ourselves culturally. For this reason we now have a deepening of the breach between favored minorities and marginal majorities; a growing state of poverty that exacerbates the national reality; an increase in violence and prejudicial radicalism; and a continual wavering in development plans, always resulting in benefits for only a handful of people.

We live in an era of the miracle of mass urbanization, invented by poverty in the worst of conditions, without basic utilities, with improvised housing. Rural poverty moves into the city, and in record time puts up houses and organizes streets.

If attention were paid to real needs, perhaps that potentially creative force would have a better fate. But, lamentably, we keep on glorifying physical works without situating them in their true light. Their purpose is to help develop the country. They are not ends in themselves. What we need most is a people ready and able to use these projects to their fullest extent. Here the optimal advantage can be achieved through culture, because culture provides the potential to manage new installations as a means to their integral absorption.

It is a sad comment, but when it comes to culture we have been playing house. Fix things up a little here and there, a bit of recognition for some and maybe others, a bit of support for such and such activity and a bit less for others, an interest in certain arts and jobs, and a let's-wait-and-see attitude for the others, a touch of fear in the voice that fully and freely devotes his or her life to cultural creativity.

But in the most basic and essential projects true courage has been lacking: the university radio station, a labor of love, has barely gotten off the ground; national radio has good intentions but goes forward in fits and starts. It seems that public television has not yet found a way to anything of transcendental value. A lot of effort went into these stations with hopes of their supporting our faltering culture, but we are still waiting for them to produce something of lasting benefit.

Costa Rican culture has given us things of much beauty and value. It gave us a hardworking, basically honest laborer who longs for the restitution of an approach once typical of Costa Rica, yet so foreign to us today: "Take the bull by the horns and the man by his words." [. . .]

But this culture is seriously injured and is losing the orientation of its compass. Nevertheless, culture is eternally disposed to being impregnated. In the fields fertility is a seed that can become a tree, carried by the wind, a traveler, a laborer, or the rain. Culture is also planted and fertilized, stimulated, affirmed, cared for, and defended. The seeds are the study of letters, the apprenticeship in music, the understanding of art, the acquiring of abilities, the affirmation of human values, the expanding of horizons, the introduction of improvements in the home and community, the practicing of thought, the learning to do, and teaching what one knows. The seeds grow and grow, creating a culture that excels and is voluntarily integrated into the very essence of being.

Even in the most hostile of environments those individuals who have a desire to create manage to do so. They set themselves against those who join the masses in mediocrity, those who take the easy and irresponsible road of imitating models and living according to those models. The people who want to create also manage to follow their creative bent despite all the difficulties. The Costa Rican creates, invents, imagines, works, cultivates, produces, thinks, and learns, in spite of all that erodes his or her cultural life. This cultured Costa Rican, laborer or farmer, young or old, teacher or poet, intellectual or artisan, has advanced while still conserving traditions and values. We cannot leave him alone, at the mercy of an avalanche of negativity that threatens to fall on him. We must support and sustain him, give him the esteem he deserves, and follow his example. It is this creative and hardworking Costa Rican who should be the living image of the country, not the politician of the day. It is he whom we must serve and help, so that his culture may prevail, flourish, and enrich us all.

They say that every analysis should offer at least the outline of a solution. They also say that in this solution one must include the what, the who, the how, and the when of it.

The what is represented in culture by all valid mediums of creation, born of an empowering education and full of free experimentation and practice. The what is as expansive as reality and dreams, as long as it feeds our people's hunger for culture. The what combines actions, even invents them. The what is the instrumentation of an infinite wealth of possibilities. The what is always open to meet the real needs the people bring forth in a genuine and spontaneous manner.

The who includes all Costa Ricans. No one should be alienated, because our culture requires everyone's support. Each one must contribute according to his or her capacities. Each one is obliged to teach and to learn. The more a Costa Rican evades this responsibility the more our culture suffers.

The how is pure motivation, the desire to do, to study, and to learn, even when it goes against the grain of established methodology, for that is the pathway to invention. Precisely the exclusive use of traditional techniques in teaching has restricted the scope of achievement.

The when has no temporal confines nor circumstantial barriers. In order that the cultural heritage be amply shared, vigorously ameliorated, and perceived as it should be, education must become a national movement in which we are all accountable agents, offering multitudinous opportunities to children and adults, not only in schools but in any other type of free education open to the public as well, the goal being that the majority of the people develop to the fullest their capacity to work, create, and appreciate.

Culture offers us an opportunity for change, one that gradually and incessantly incorporates itself into our lives in a way that cannot be denied or taken back. Of course it brings with it the immediate cry of injustice and a demand for the recovery of our losses, but it is also certain that these claims are made with a clear awareness of the country's historical unfolding and the stability required to achieve these social goals. Culture gives this liberating equilibrium.

There is a truth I cannot forget to mention as an epilogue for whoever would like to keep it in mind. León Felipe expresses it marvelously in poetry. To conclude these remarks, let us hear his poem:

> I don't know very much, it's true.
> I just tell about what I've seen
> and I've seen that man's cradle
> is rocked with stories,
> that man's cries of anguish
> are drowned with stories,
> that man's flood of tears
> is covered up with stories,

that man's bones
are buried with stories
and that man's fear
has invented all the stories.
I know very little, it's true.
But they've put me to sleep
with all the stories
and I know all the stories.

Estudios sociales centroamericanos 46 (1988): 15–20.

Margo Glantz

Mexico, 1930–

The essays of prolific Mexican scholar and writer Margo
Glantz represent a significant contribution to contem-
porary literary and cultural studies. The child of Jewish
Ukrainian immigrants, Glantz occupies a prominent position in Mexican intellectual life. She has served as director of literature at the National Institute of Fine Arts
(INBA) and cultural attaché for the Mexican embassy in
London, and she is a professor of graduate studies in
comparative literature at the National Autonomous
University of Mexico (UNAM). Margo Glantz engages
both canonical and little-known works of Spanish,
French, British, North American, and Latin American
literature in a complex dialogue about culture and the
tradition. Her "I" is the reading eye of the scholar and
the transforming eye of the artist, which see language
and literature as necessary but treacherous figures of
"interpretation" between the human subject and the
world, and between self and Other.

The two short pieces that follow represent two different kinds of meditation on a common preoccupa-
tion: the writer's propensity for approaching the world
through books. *Doscientas ballenas azules . . . y . . . cuatro
caballos* (1981; Two Hundred Blue Whales and Four
Horses) is a lengthy creative essay that inscribes a
densely intertextual rereading of two enduring cultural
signs in the Western tradition. The sections chosen for

translation show the poetic structure of this and other
books such as *No pronunciarás* (1980; Thou Shalt Not
Take the Name), in which Glantz utilizes principles of
fragmentation and association to fashion a nonlinear and
highly ludic writing.

"Mi escritura tiene . . ." (1985; My Writing Is . . .)
was previously published in a special issue of the *Revista
Iberoamericana* dedicated to Latin American women writers. It refers back to the earlier piece on whales through
an autobiographical reflection on the role of literature
in the writer's apprehension of real relations and in her
creative process. While the essay begins by seeming to
reject the "read" in favor of the real, within its few
pages Glantz comes back full circle to her own point of
departure: the privileged status of paper whales and the
name of the rose in the construction of our human
wor(l)ds.

Margo Glantz has also produced numerous works of
literary and cultural criticism, including studies of Tennessee Williams and of French and Mexican literature of
the nineteenth and twentieth centuries. In the field of
colonial literature Glantz has recently published a book
entitled *Borrones y borradores* (1991; Rough Drafts), and
she has books forthcoming on Alvar Núñez Cabeza de
Vaca and Sor Juana Inés de la Cruz.

BETH E. JÖRGENSEN

Two Hundred Blue Whales

(Selection)

L ong ago young ladies corseted their waists with whalebone, whaling ships roamed the seas searching for the spermaceti, Melville sang the whale's terrible praises with Ahab, and perfume makers used the ambergris to fix the gentle aphrodisiac in their fragrances. Today only 200 blue whales are left in the world, and each year they pass through the Gulf of California, foretelling like Jonah a useless Babel of white spouts.

Only 200 blue whales are left traversing the globe like ships, with their soft silky skin intact, always calm, so calm that not even their color can harm them. Now they return and pass through the Gulf of California because they are brave in spite of their name. There they nest and surrender themselves to the pleasures of mating and suicide. Perhaps by the time I finish writing these lines only 198 blue whales will remain on earth.

Don't worry, though, because the 500 sea turtles that still live, and their offspring, may grow and change form according to the law of the evolution of species. In that future time there will be only 200 Holstein cows left in the world.

We must go back to the whales, to their bones, to their illustrious mouths that house prophets. It is dangerous to forget their large eyes and their beautiful, round blowholes that spew forth a true reading of the gospel and a question mark of foam throughout the seas and the circuses. How could we forget them when they are enormous caravels stripped of their riggings, and their faces show the face of Jonah or his brother, Melville? White whales live among harpoons, hiding their semen like the

Translated by Beth E. Jörgensen

huge Saint Gertrude bulls who store it in tepid, sacred horns: the whale encircles her potent belly, and her gigantic womb fulfills the words that come to us from Conrad, the circus, and Collodi.

I like the whale because it doesn't resemble the pelican, and, unlike the birds that nest on the coast, it repays the sea's fertility.

On their shining backs algae sparkles and the Sargasso Sea rests. Whales are beautiful even when they are reduced to bones and used as corset stays or when they turn into splendid white brooches scorched by the foam and the sun that Joseph Conrad condensed into the typhoon of his words. I like whales for their intelligent, silken skin or for their fragrant, damaged texture and their oblique, humorous eyes. I like them for their voices, because they were the mysterious sirens that fascinated Jason and Ulysses. I like them because they disdain even the sea, keeping it for their grave when they kill themselves, leaving their bones to float, dazzling rafts, refuge for the shipwrecked. I like whales, but also snails and even the pebbles and the crabs that riddle the sand with holes. I like the giant sperm whale whose oil becomes a burning, unfurled sail on the whiteness of the masts and beams. I like its tame look in the Disneyland exhibits, although I like dolphins less because of their dangerous kinship to absolute monarchs. I like whales because they relapse into sirens, and I like them for their salty, aquatic, mammalian bestiality, for their impetuousness and their clamor, for plunging to the depths like the sperm whale, for flooding the huge sandy coves, for taking refuge in national parks, for their premature extinction, and for the vast, pacific blueness with which they break the cosmic, primiparous waves of their bodily exile. [. . .]

The course of the Tigris and that of the Euphrates are geographically alike; only Melville knows the path of the whale. His knowledge surpasses the whale's primeval morphology. If one pays close attention, his fecundity is surprising and the endless pages (which speak to us and repel us from their unbearable whiteness) go heaping up riches.

The Pequod stores spermaceti in its hold. Melville narrates beauty by shattering it into classifications or describing, inch by inch, its strange, impertinent, and majestic face, until Moby Dick comes along and, in a single night, destroys Job's prosperity, plunging Ahab into his coffin and fulfilling the prophecy of the devil, he who appeared in the ship dressed like the enemies, he who covers his head with the white turban and disturbs the Seer's nights.

Call me Ishmael, says Melville, and the enemy is his first cousin, purple, incestuous, immaculate, the umbilical vertebrate of the world. [. . .]

Without touching it, just by watching it or writing it, Ishmael senses his task. He was saved to speak of the suffering of the whale, submerged after the attack, injured and bloodied, sending out a labored breath and a choking red spout as his only visible sign of pain. Ishmael, or so he asks to be called, has sworn to speak, and his speech is lost in the silence of the page scribed with the perfect pen carved out of a tiny fragment of the great jawbone. Its faltering breath defines the writing and allots the chapters, curtailing the story with mutilated images of the beast, distributed anatomically in each of its parts, while the protagonist, the long-awaited, blonde, and smiling Moby Dick, appears. On land Mary and the child and other crews wait, and the preacher recalls Jonah before the sailors' graves, reciting litanies to comfort their widows; the burning, perfumed spermaceti filters through the darkness. Women tighten their useless waists with the polished baleen, the nets that make the whale legendary because of the tiny pelagic organisms that nourish them. Ishmael listens to the omens and turns toward the tavern. The monstrously tatooed cannibal is waiting for him, and the voyage begins again, the same as always, until the whales become extinct.

On the prairies the buffaloes have died and the longhaired Indians take up oars.

Melville whispers: the whale is the pelvis of the portolanos. [. . .]

There isn't a single drop of water in the sea that doesn't respond to the mysterious forces that cause the tides; the tides respond to the attraction that the sun feels for the moon or to the sweetness of a drop of water that looks at itself in the most distant star.

Man is dangerous but not infinite like the moon and the whale.

Man is dull of ear and his brain is small. The whale is perfect and in its inner circumvolutions a satin intelligence branches out like white coral seen through a lens. We know almost nothing of its fate. [. . .]

Fitted into his pirate's leg Ahab navigates by the charts harpooned into the crow's feet that surround his deeply circled eyes. Ahab throws his pipe into the sea, and Stubb smokes his while he eats a whale steak (cooked medium), the same way that the shark, in a kind of Elizabethan feast, devours the immense flesh tied to the ship's keel like a figurehead. Ahab turns the ship over to me and I calm the people who are frightened by the omens. I spent the winter on the bridge.

Call me Ishmael, Melville told me, and I obey, loaded down with lamp oil, remembering that in all the farms the candles were lit by my efforts. I continue keeping watch from the tall mast and the salty horizon relaxes me; I doze off barely held upright, I am fascinated by the passing danger of falling and touching the dangerous and exalted waves. I meditate sleepily and the meditation swells and returns me to the sea where I mount the grayish back of one of the smaller whales, the bottle-nosed one, deformed and intermittently furrowed like the skin of the sailor who stands watch on deck through the night, in rumbling and reeling guard duty. Melville approaches the Galapagos Islands; I live on the mast subjecting the gulfs and the trident to my control. The shipwrecked wait while mute narrators embroider the sea with their sorrowful mythology. I keep on watching the constellations that shine in the night, looking from the fish to the bears and from the whales to Andromeda. [. . .]

It is said that Noah couldn't make room for the whale.

And Job had three thousand camels, five hundred yokes of oxen,

five hundred asses, seven thousand sheep,

and not a single whale.

But his inheritance is consumed by fire, wasted like mutton fat, and God commands that the whale be punished and filled with hidden spermaceti like in a mine so that greed would make men voyage and make them capable of destroying it like Job was destroyed.

The lord was tempted and in turn he tempted Ahab, the cursed one, cursed because neither dogs nor earth would drink his blood.

Poor maligned whale, above all maligned when your name is sperm whale!

Covered with inscriptions and snarled fishing line, the white whale receives new scars and Ahab loses, besides his leg, his eyes.

That view from the main mast condemns me to resemble the prophets. I am not Jonah or Jeremiah; I am Cassandra. Voices perforate me; harpoons pierce Moby Dick.

Doscientas ballenas azules . . . y . . . cuatro caballos. Mexico City: UNAM, 1981, pp. 7–12, 22–40.

My Writing Is . . .

My writing is connected with whales and monarch butterflies. I could say that, apart from my parents to whom I owe life itself, whales and their creator Melville, and monarch butterflies and their creators Mariana Frenk and the conifers of Michoacán, are the agents of my writing. And now, as I write this down, it seems even more certain to me. I don't know much about nature; storybook animals interest me most, like the ones that Borges collects in his *Book of Imaginary Beings*, but my animals are true to life, real, like the characters in the novels of Conrad and Dostoyevsky, because, as they say, "reality surpasses fiction." I don't share with them (or with other authors whom I have always admired: Faulkner and Flaubert, Stendahl and Proust) the profound intimacy that they had with human beings, whom I almost always approach through a book and not with the skin. That is a misfortune—also a boon. Because of it, inscriptions brand my flesh, and from these signs I forge a writing little by little, piece by piece. Or perhaps that is only true until my last published book, *Erosiones* [Erosions], because now things have changed. I have taken two definitive trips, trips that have led me to the source, the origin. Before, I used to travel to cities, to museums, to stores like Bloomingdale's, to movie theaters, to restaurants. This time I traveled to an encounter with nature. I headed for Michoacán, near Angangueo, where there is a pine forest. There the monarch butterflies nest after an adventure of thousands and thousands of miles by air. They hang in the trees, they nestle together, they soar up, they take on color and life,

Translated by Beth E. Jörgensen

waiting to perpetuate their species without caring at all about our wars and our destructions, and flying off at the sun's slightest provocation. We arrive very quietly, we the men and women who come to see them, to spy on their secrets, to sniff out the color of their wings, to wait until they fly toward us and pause a moment on our hair, especially on blonde hair. (What else, monarch butterflies love light, just like Quetzalcoatl!) Then they continue flying until they alight on the pine boughs and bend them under their weight, making a thick, dense, almost repugnant stain on the landscape, and, all of a sudden, fly off again toward the light, duplicating the yellow of the sun. I took that trip and another one to see whales and seals (I didn't really want to see the seals, but I saw them in spite of myself because there they were on the rocks, near the pelicans, the same color but with different skin and shape). The whales were the important thing. I have always been fascinated by their ambiguity, their mammalian way of returning to the water—from whence we all come—their stubborn persistence, their seafaring condition. All of that, yes, but it was all a lie taken from books. I looked everywhere, I knew the information, collected it, fragmented it, and made my collages of letters until I had composed two hundred whales, and blue ones no less, but they were just paper, like paper tigers.

Two Voyages toward Reality

It can't be helped, reality wins us over in the end. The whales behaved with utmost restraint. They didn't destroy my (motor) boat although they destroyed Ahab's (row) boat, and the boat of a European ambassador who ventured out to see them (without her husband), and one of them, irritated by the noise of the jet set, split her yacht in two.

I saw them showing off, their backs dirty and scratched, the calves close by. The noise of their spouts as they surfaced to breathe warned us of their presence. The noise of the motor warned them of ours. Immediately they submerged, and we could see the fluke gracefully entering the foam. Far off others played at being acrobats and let us see their triangular heads among the waves. Multiple aspirations: their spout and my emotion at seeing them, combined with the alarm I had already felt when admiring them in photographs or studying them in the encyclopedia, or when anxiously following the adventures of their white incarnation, when Melville dressed them up as Moby Dick.

I also met a sea captain born in Acapulco. He shepherds North American tourists out to the desolate rocks of the Isla de la Raza, where hordes of penguins take over the sands to lay their eggs in astonishing quantity until not a single empty space is left. Occupying their spot with mathematical precision and without injuring their wings but changing the color of the grains of sand, they look like the birds that Darwin discovered in the Galapagos.

And I sailed through the waters where the Japanese and Korean boats sail in their efforts to destroy our flora and fauna, because they go along killing sea lions, poisoning the mother-of-pearl beds, until the mythological peninsula, ancient California, full of mangroves, black coral, roadrunners, vultures, and cave paintings, turns into an even more brutal desert than Cortés found when the seas of his misfortune forced him to sail to the gulf that bears his name.

There are no more pearls now, only black coral. The pearls come from Thailand and are cultivated in Japan, which left us without white pearls. Now they sell them wrapped up in tissue paper like contraband, sickly, deformed, discolored pearls. And in its southern reaches the long narrow peninsula has two hundred thousand scorched inhabitants spread out over ranches and piled up on the capes where the caravans of cowboys head day after day, even though they don't play Wild West anymore or kill Indians or bring sheriffs: they just come with their trailers to camp in designated areas. They bring everything along with them: their refrigerators, their cans, their purified water. They buy gasoline from us and leave us their trash. The enormous rocks that separate the Pacific Ocean from the Gulf of Cortés stand with untouched strength and harsh, enduring beauty. So they will remain, forever, I hope. The hotels with a sea view crop up on the rocks; the terrace crowded with tourists who drink artificially colored and flavored daiquiris, wear shorts and tee shirts and ridiculous dark glasses. The whale passes by; the waiter points it out to me. I can't see it, there are too many distractions. The sea breeze is cold, the daiquiri goes to my head, I stop. Meanwhile the whale has gone down under the waves and I can't see it, I can't see it, I give up, my whole adventure has entered through my eyes, my passivity in action is as great as the one that rules my readings; I attend the operation *Twenty Thousand Leagues under the Sea* from the showcase window; I kill Moby Dick and I am lame like Ahab; I ride with D'Artagnan and I wear the necklace of his queen; I burn down Jane Eyre's house, I complete her journey; and I rewrite myself in another sea, the *Wide Sargasso Sea*. I end up like Proust in a stifling, cork-lined room, and there I gladly bid farewell to Odette, today when I have understood that she wasn't my type. I share with Borges the idea of the tiger (although I substitute whales or monarch butterflies—just origami ones), and I return to the point of departure, to that key, galactic place, which rushes me headlong into the infernal circle of writing and reading. I have made the obligatory visit, with pleasure, of course, to real-life beaches; I have admired the animals outside the zoo; I have seen the whales jump the same way that Proust looked at the cathedrals, only after having understood them by the letters of their name, and experience corroborates that I remain in the name of the rose.

It can't be helped. We all get the world we deserve, and mine is not Conrad's, or it is when I stay quiet, eyes closed, submerged in the immense sensation of a far-east sea. It's not Melville's world either, or it is when I read *Moby-Dick* lying in a hammock, looking toward the sea with the breeze and the sun in my face. Bernal [Díaz] had to resort to writing to demonstrate the truth of his past; Casanova sensualized his exile and converted his library into a bed. Today I take notes on a scriptural process, I describe an ailment, I diagnose it and prescribe a book, in that endless anthropophagy through which I digest the fragments and reincorporate them into the eternal circulation of writing.

Revista Iberoamericana 132–133 (July–December 1985): 475–478.

Rosario Ferré

Puerto Rico, 1938–

Rosario Ferré was born in Ponce, Puerto Rico. The daughter of Luis Ferré, a former governor of the island, she studied at the University of Puerto Rico, where she was active in literary and sociopolitical dialogues through the journal *Zona de Carga y Descarga*, which she cofounded and directed in the early 1970s. Ferré earned a doctorate in Hispanic literature and has lived and taught both on the mainland and in Puerto Rico.

Her first book of poems and stories, *Papeles de Pandora* (1976; *The Youngest Doll*, 1991), was outspoken in its satiric portrayal of Puerto Rican society and established Ferré's talent as an outstanding writer of her generation. This work was followed by three volumes of children's stories and a book of poetry entitled *Fábulas de la garza desangrada* (1982; Fables of the Bleeding Heron), as well as a novel, *Maldito amor* (1986; *Sweet Diamond Dust*, 1988); a book of fables, *Sonatina* (1989); and several volumes of critical essays, among them *El árbol y sus sombras* (1989; The Tree and Its Shadows) and *El coloquio de las perras* (1990; The Colloquy of the Female Dogs). Time and again, in a variety of genres, Ferré criticizes the moral and social decadence of a bourgeois society rooted in male domination, yet she also retains close emotional ties to the island that is the inspiration for much of her writing.

"La autenticidad de la mujer en el arte" (Woman's Authenticity in Art) is one of thirteen essays published in *Sitio a Eros* (1980; Eros Besieged), and it forms the theoretical basis for this collection of essays in which Rosario Ferré analyzes the art of writing by various well-known women and their relationship to the creative process. Each of these writers—among them Flora Tristan, Mary Shelley, George Sand, Alexandra Kollontai, Julia de Burgos, Virginia Woolf, and Tina Modotti—challenged the traditional mores of patriarchal society and inscribed a female voice, subverting the status quo of their time.

In "Woman's Authenticity in Art," Ferré points out that women have internalized a male hegemony that circumscribes their own potential and compromises their artistic integrity. She believes that women who voluntarily choose a domestic role can indeed be happy, but such a choice should not be based on a fear of independence or an easy option regarding personal identity. Women must free themselves from external and internalized limitations; instead of merely replicating masculine behavior and concepts of power, says Ferré, they must question the very constructs of power vis-à-vis gender, economics, religion, morality, and politics. Only through this process of examination, both societal and personal—including confronting their own eroticism—can women find their true voice.

JOY RENJILIAN-BURGY

Rosario Ferré

Woman's Authenticity in Art

In *A Room of One's Own*, Virginia Woolf says that if a sixteenth-century woman with a literary calling (Shakespeare's sister, for instance) had tried to fulfill it, she would have gone mad, committed suicide, or ended her days in an isolated house on the outskirts of town, perceived as part witch, part enchantress—an object of fear and derision. Today, a woman with a literary vocation probably won't go to these extremes, but her lot is still anything but easy. Her life has become a vortex of conflicting forces trying to destroy her to the extent that she persists in fulfilling her inner voice—that is, her literary vocation.

The contemporary woman writer is different from the sixteenth-century one in that she can exercise her vocation with relative freedom; however, compared to a man, it is still much harder for her to become a good artist, and this is for a simple reason: it is more difficult for her to become a whole person.

First, her freedom is considerably restrained, which limits the experiences she might have that could enrich her work. For instance, a woman is not familiar with the mechanisms of economic and political power; and in a certain sense, this limited access results in a fortunate situation, since her duty is to oppose them. Second, her role as wife and mother tends to make her a dependent being, both in her economic survival and in her sense of identity.

The initial problem—that is, the problem of her material freedom—is an external one and is relatively easy to solve, because during the last ten

Translated by Joy Renjilian-Burgy

years the feminist movement has energetically confronted this problem. The successes of this movement indicate that, at least in terms of law and labor contracts and the opportunities offered by society, woman's dilemma is in the process of being resolved.

The second problem, that of her interior freedom, goes much deeper and is harder to solve. It could be divided into two parts: on the one hand, the emotional and psychological sanctions that social mores still impose on women and, on the other hand, the sanctions that she is accustomed to imposing upon herself.

The woman who is successful in her profession, whatever this may be, is taking advantage of those opportunities provided by society on a public or a rhetorical level. But woman's right to equal opportunity on the public level is one thing, whereas it's quite another to achieve it on a private level. The truth is that each and every woman who is professionally successful is immediately viewed with distrust by the majority of men. There exists a kind of tacit judgment that a woman who succeeds with her mind will consequently be a failure in bed and in the home. For her, success will bring conflicts and only under exceptional circumstances will she be fully able to achieve it.

Most of the time, a woman is forced to choose between Prince Charming and her vocation. For this reason, when they are about to be economically, intellectually, or scientifically successful, so many women find an excuse to quit and leave things unfinished. Solitude is a painful dilemma that a professional woman frequently has to face.

However, the problem of a woman's interior freedom has a second and more painful reality than material freedom. A woman who tries to break with conventional modes of behavior rarely needs to be punished by the law or by social mechanisms. Much more efficiently than any tribunal, she punishes herself—she feels horribly guilty. This is partially due to her education; while a man is educated with a view to his own fulfillment, a woman is educated with a view to other people's fulfillment. A man is educated as a worldly being, to be successful, to realize his dreams, and to become a professional or an artist, whereas a woman is educated to teach her sons how to be successful and her daughters how to sacrifice themselves so that their brothers can achieve success. Solitude and domestic anonymity have traditionally been the fate of a woman, whereas a man sets out to conquer the world.

However, one must acknowledge that this education is not the only cause for the lack of coherence that usually defines the feminine personality. She sometimes treats her role as wife and mother in an intolerant manner so as to justify the emptiness of her life and give herself meaning. Other times these roles are embraced with relief by women for whom, after so many years of dependence, the responsibility of independence and of facing the consequences of their own actions would be a terrifying trauma. When a woman assumes the role of wife and mother as an authentic vocation, it becomes a desirable condition. What cannot be forgiven is that she be condemned to know love only under these circumstances, when love has the potential to be much more than that. Love also is professional work done lovingly, with the possibility of developing human capabilities to the utmost degree.

For the majority of today's women, to be the artisans of that indispensable home paradise is a poor substitute for the complex wonders of the world. Education has shown them that changing diapers and watching out for the physical well-being of their families are not an equivalent alternative to the practice of art, politics, or science.

There's no doubt that the fundamental problem for today's woman is the integration of her personality, with all the satisfactions and sufferings that maturity and independence bring with them. I am not referring to the kind of imitation of men in which women sometimes engage when they appropriate the masculine mentality of money-making and power-seeking with more zeal than men themselves, and thus despise all that refers to feminine vision. A woman's role should consist precisely of questioning the practice of that power—moral, religious, or political—as much in countries with government-controlled capitalism as in countries with private enterprise, while she simultaneously continues to reflect upon her own identity, searching to know who she is and what she is like.

Today, a woman with a literary vocation enjoys greater opportunities to become a writer because her own struggle for self-knowledge helps her to attain that goal. As Rilke said in his *Letters to a Young Poet*, nothing can be more disastrous for a writer than to speak in a false voice. How can a woman writer sound genuine if she still doesn't know who she is or what she's like? If they want to become good writers, today's women writers know that, above all else, they will first have to be women, because in art, authenticity is everything. They will have to learn the innermost secrets of their own bodies and how to talk about them without any euphemisms. They will have to learn how to examine their own eroticism and how to derive from their own sexuality a latent and rarely exploited vitality. They will have to learn to explore their anger and frustration as well as their satisfaction in being women. They will have to cleanse themselves and help cleanse their readers of the guilt that secretly torments them. Finally, they will have to write in order to understand themselves better and also to teach their women readers to do the same.

Woman's authenticity will also imply a reexamination of the nature of love, because her guilt is rooted in love. In the final analysis, what does love mean for a woman? What is that great good for which she has been forced to renounce the world for centuries? Is love the only end in her life? Must it be irreplaceable and sanctioned by the respectability of procreation and private property? Doesn't a woman, just like a man, have the right to profane love, to transitory love, even to demonic love, and to passion for passion's sake?

Like Anaïs Nin, I too believe that passion is the defining nature of a woman; that passion, however, tends to be both her greatest strength and her worst weakness. The education to which she has been exposed—the anonymity, poverty, self-denial, and spirit of sacrifice—has given her depth, a capacity to dream and to be moved, a faith in the fundamental values of life that a man does not generally embrace. And, paradoxically enough, it is that same passion that convinces her of the existence of a Prince Charming who never arrives.

The current responsibility of every woman writer is precisely to convince women readers of that fundamental notion: Prince Charming does not exist. He doesn't have any reality outside her imagination, outside her own creative capabilities. And if she ever hesitated and felt compelled to believe the opposite, she should recall the words of Diotima, the wise woman from Mantinea, when she asserts in Plato's *Symposium* that love is plural and never limits itself to only one body. "According to Diotima, [a lover] should realize that the physical beauty of one body is akin to that of any other body, and that if he's going to pursue beauty of appearance, it's the height of folly not to regard beauty, which is in all bodies, as one and the same. This insight will convert him into a lover of all physical beauty, and he will become less obsessive in his pursuit of one single passion, as he realizes its unimportance." And even if only once Prince Charming were to materialize before her, implacable and frightening in his perfection, she would have to convince herself that she has invented him; otherwise, the price she'd have to pay for his reality would be simply too high.

In *A Room of One's Own*, Virginia Woolf points out that woman's disturbing situation is the major reason why there have not been great women writers throughout history. Not a single woman has written like Shakespeare, says Virginia Woolf (with the possible exception of Jane

Austen), because a woman's situation prevents her from writing objectively and with all obstacles discarded, with that kind of absolute transparency a literary work acquires when the writer is completely distanced from the writing, while at the same time having become one with the written work. This may be true, and it may be that, for various reasons (some of which I have already mentioned above), there are no women writers comparable to Shakespeare or Cervantes, but it doesn't make sense to say that the cause of this fact has been a lack of objectivity.

In the case of passion, anger, laughter, and arbitrary subjectivity, I differ radically from Virginia Woolf's opinion and tend to think more like Anaïs Nin. Like her, I believe that a woman should write in order to reinvent herself, to dissipate her fear of loss and death, and to confront daily the effort that living implies. For her, both good and bad passions find room in literature: "I also mean the evil earth, demons, instincts, the storms of nature. Tragedies, conflicts, and mysteries are always something personal. Man invented indifference and indifference became fate."

Just like every artist, a woman writes as best she can, not as she wants to or as she should. Whether she has to do it in anger and in love, laughing and crying, resentfully and irrationally, on the very brink of madness and aesthetic stridency, what matters is that she do it; she must keep writing. She must devote her body and soul to persistence, not to objectivity, not to letting herself be defeated by the enormous obstacles facing her. She must keep writing even if it only helps open the way for those women writers who will come later, and who will be able to write in tranquility and not in anger, as Virginia Woolf desired. Just like Anaïs Nin, I think that passion has great power to transform and transfigure the human being from a limited, small, frightened creature into a magnificent figure sometimes capable of reaching the heights of myth. "All my moments of courage and vision were born out of passion," declares Anaïs Nin. "The barrenness that came afterwards doesn't interest me."

Sitio a Eros, 2nd ed. Mexico City: Joaquín Mortiz, 1986, pp. 34–39.

Julieta Kirkwood

Chile, 1936–1985

The name of Julieta Kirkwood has become practically
legendary in the history of Chilean feminism. Born in
Santiago in 1936, her untimely death of cancer in 1985
was a significant loss to the intellectual history of her
country.

Kirkwood was a professor of political science in the
1970s at the University of Chile, and in 1976 she became a member of the faculty of FLACSO (Latin American School of Social Sciences). At that time she began
to work intensively with groups of women and to for-
mulate a body of thought that would be published posthumously by FLACSO as *Ser política en Chile: Las femi-
nistas y los partidos* (1986; To Be a Political Woman in
Chile: Feminists and Political Parties). A second edition
was published in 1990 by Cuarto Propio, a feminist
publishing house in Santiago, with a different subtitle
taken from a suggestion made earlier by the author:
Los nudos de la sabiduría feminista (Problems of Feminist
Knowledge). Kirkwood worked on this book up to the
time of her death; it has had a major impact not only in
Chile but in Latin America in general. Feminist-oriented
scholars and critics consider it a penetrating analysis of
social and political issues that have relevance beyond
Kirkwood's Chilean milieu. Within Chile, it has become a classic text of feminist intellectual history. Another collection of her notes and writings-in-progress

was published by Cuarto Propio and Ediciones de la Mujer under the title *Feminarios*.

Julieta Kirkwood is remembered by her friends and colleagues as a vital and devoted member of many women's groups. Stories of her involvement in them are circulated orally and have become part of the Kirkwood legend. She was a founder in Chile of the Circle for Studies on Women and also of Casa de la Mujer/La Morada (Woman's House/The Dwelling), a well-known center of feminist support services and cultural activities that occupies a lilac-colored house in the Bellavista section of Santiago. Kirkwood was also instrumental in the founding of La Librería Lila de Mujeres (The Lilac Woman's Bookstore).

Active in the Chilean socialist movement during the dangerous and difficult years of the Pinochet dictatorship, Kirkwood did not live to see the hoped-for transition to a democratic government. But as she said in her prologue to *Ser política*, "Against you, patriarch of patriarchs, I oppose my whole being, even with my silence." *Ser política* was intended to be part of a collective female effort to break out of traditional silences. In her prologue, Kirkwood also said, "I hope my daring will stimulate the publication of the hundreds of works, essays, stories, and poems that so many women for so long have hidden under their beds and in dark closets. We need confrontation and the interplay of ideas—opening up, millions of bits of light coming from many small ideas."

MARJORIE AGOSÍN AND DORIS MEYER

Julieta Kirkwood

Feminists and Political Women

Beyond recognizing some evidence on the superficial level and formulating certain tentative hypotheses, it is not yet possible to discuss seriously and completely the relationship between women and politics. For this reason I will only attempt a simple, personal essay regarding two modes of feminine political action and behavior. I am referring to women who are feminists and to political women.[1]

Over the past decade one can track the emergence and growing visibility of a new sociopolitical presence in the Chilean democratic opposition: women's groups. With varied backgrounds, dates, durations, and memberships; with secular or religious origins; with single- or multiclass characteristics, but always having in common the great novelty of being constituted and generated fundamentally by and/or for women, these organizations span the widest possible range of activities and objectives.

Groups have arisen to promote urban and rural needs; groups for reflection and personal growth; for studying the condition of women; for promoting solidarity and/or self-help; for political education and action; for neighborhood support: for the homeless, for *arpilleristas*,[2] for the unemployed, community dining halls and soup kitchens; in support of national meetings for the permanent defense of human rights, the backing of claims submitted by relatives of political prisoners, the "disappeared," the exiled, the dispossessed; for the defense of public health, to alleviate the impact of drugs, the abandonment of children and young people, etc.

Translated by Doris Meyer

Based on this broad spectrum of groups constituted wholly or primarily by women, it would seem that we are looking at one singular and new concept of organization in Chilean civil society. So it would appear.

Nevertheless, a closer sociological glance will uncover subtle variations, small differences between some groups and others, in structure and process as well as in the content, principles, and objectives that each one of them sets forth.

In some, one discovers a small variation or mutation in the formality of procedures: the structure seems to dilute its hierarchy, the vertical order of leaders-to-group becomes diffuse, the meetings open and close with chairs arranged in a circular, level pattern; the leadership is lost, mixed in a shared circle of responsibilities and tasks. There are no constant, separate speakers among a body of passive listeners; the initiatives, proposals, and criticisms simply come from the group itself.

A similar change occurs in language: the topics on the agenda relate to the experience of those attending. Private matters, the woman herself, become the focus of discussion and group debate. A new combination of politics and everyday life is achieved. Terms are de-categorized and inverted in their order of importance. Participation has become a social, real, and concrete activity.

The members of these groups possess to a varying degree the quality of being *feminist*.

In the organized groups at the other extreme, which are still in the majority and more influential in the political sphere, the rupture of form and content has yet to manifest itself. Established codes for making politics [*el hacer política*] are more common and adhered to more strongly in their procedures and topics of discussion. We find "directives" and "executive decisions" clearly and succinctly spelled out by the deliberations of the "governing board" as opposed to the female membership-at-large. The processes for mobilization, the tactics, strategies, and functions are all defined without in-depth discussion; the issue of priorities has already been resolved. Therefore, the major difficulty becomes *how* to mobilize and get things done, not the background rationale and justification, which are not seen as problems of greater relevance.

The priority word in this case is *politics*, and within it, the word "woman" is emphasized in a line that is clearly and unmistakably linked to the situation of the nation, the family, and children. There's a certain disdainful rejection of any focus on individuals or topics considered "too feminist." In these groups the term "woman" will always be qualified by social class, by the topic of concern, the crisis, the family system. It's not an independent term. Woman is not conceived of as a separate entity.[3]

Despite these polar differences, both styles of organization doubtless converge in a wide spectrum of political commitments and events. They work jointly on programs and protests, they develop and support proposals and stand politically unified on democratic objectives. They also mobilize jointly and in large numbers at events of their own and at national demonstrations.

Perhaps for this very reason, when ideological confrontation does occur it appears to be charged with misgivings and stereotypes. Discord becomes a solid vortex that opens and totally separates what were movements, blocks, closed ranks. Discussion seems to end, along with the possibility of agreement.

What gives rise to this disharmony? Distinct, unreconcilable projects? Matters of style, of social class, ways of interpreting the world? Looking at this breakdown, I perceive a more profound complication than just an occasional nonmeeting of minds. With more optimism than clarity of approach, I will try to examine this discourse and analysis.

Both feminists and political women might seem to agree on one aim: to achieve the recognition of the historical-cultural possibility of the emancipation of women. Where there does not appear to be full and absolute agreement is in the area of ends, objectives, methods, theory, praxis, and the priorities that a global emancipation of society assumes. Let it be said, then, that there is no agreement in the full course to be followed to achieve this social liberation.

Every explanation is arrived at from a unique value system. One of them, in general terms, refers to the necessity of doing politics *from a woman's perspective*, out of her own sense of lack and alienation. The other one, the traditional one, would be simply *the inclusion* and the massive insertion of women in a given political program prior to the identification of women's needs, in the assumption that these will be incorporated in the future.

The explanation for this bifurcation into two poles is found in our recent history. Ever since the first political gatherings of women, in which all manner of groups and feminist political intentions were found, two types of assertions can be constantly identified, no matter what the themes and occasions:

One can be summed up in the phrase "There is no feminism without democracy," which means, in other words, that the only possible mobilization for women now is to support the struggle in opposition to the authoritarian government; that the unique problems of discrimination against women are secondary to this priority and can be dealt with later or *only* if that priority is not compromised. This affirmation is sustained by political women.

The second assertion, opposed to the foregoing one, inverts the terms and affirms that "There is no democracy without feminism." Rejecting other priorities and contradictions, it affirms the fundamental nature of all oppression that implies the domination, discrimination against and subordination of women in the public or private spheres. It also points out that, by not taking the private sphere into account in a process of change, women have been overlooked and cast into a conservative ideological and political position. They back this up with statistics for women's participation and affiliation with the most conservative and status-quo philosophies.

This assertion denotes the possibility of joining together to discuss and identify *all* the forms of oppression as part of a new synthesis, not stratified from without. Penetrating further the discourse that arises from this second proposal, one could say that feminist thinking comes about through thinking about democracy—at first, unsuspectingly and as part of a reevaluation and reexamination of its tenets. Before long, reflection leads to the perception of a wide and profound difference between democratic values (such as equality, nondiscrimination, freedom, solidarity) and concrete reality as we know it and live it.

Seeing the difference between theory and practice, we women recognize and observe that our day-to-day experience is *authoritarianism*. That women live—and have always lived—under authoritarianism within the family, which is their recognized place of work and experience. That there, what is structured and institutionalized is precisely the undisputed Authority of the head of the family, the father, based on discrimination and subordination by gender, through hierarchy and vertically ordered discipline, imposed as natural, and thereafter projected onto an entire social fabric.

This leads us to observe that there are *two areas* or spheres of action in relation to the political that are decisively separate, mutually exclusive, and based on sexual gender—a "natural" division not originating in the authoritarian regime reaped by democracy. To the contrary, it precedes it in the order of civilization.

These spheres, as previously noted, are the *public*, with its control of politics and its possibility of acknowledging and seeking liberty, and the *private*, solidly situated in the domestic realm of the necessary.[4] The work of women, as a group or cultural category, is found in this private sphere, in the "excluded from . . . ," in political marginality.

From the perspective of political parties with greater or lesser incentives for change, women's political participation is always seen as a problem of obstacles, either to their joining or to their supporting tactical-strategic plans. From the feminist perspective, the situation necessarily has to do with the meaning and significance of making politics, as we mentioned, on the part of those whose identity has been fundamentally denied.

Once it is stated that *the private is susceptible to being seen politically*, as a problem of social dimensions, two phenomena simultaneously occur. In the first place, we perceive the close relationship between the political and the public, and who the real subjects and actors in politics are, if we look at the topic with an eye to democratic reform. In the second place, we see a widening and complicating of the political field by the incorporation of the sphere of the necessary and of women as new subjects and actors in a politics that has been affected by this change.[5] New themes, new ways of approaching social, political, and economic problems will be involved.

There will be a rethinking of human production and reproduction, including domestic reproduction; of accepted practices and meanings of social participation and exclusion; of the incorporation of nontraditional demands into political programs; of the invisibility—causes and consequences—of certain conflicts such as sexual and domestic violence, prostitution, abuses in family planning, etc., in view of the fact that, from a feminist perspective, these problems and conflicts are considered *true violations* of women's human rights.

There will also be a consideration of the role of women as political subjects with individual rights, contrary to the culturally and politically induced conservatism inevitably resulting from a mode of authoritarian-patriarchal-historical behavior. Possible ways to effect a cultural change in attitude will be examined.

Now, to confront these phenomena will entail more than a few challenges for feminist activists. I will mention two of the most recurrent and difficult problems [*nudos*] for feminism to broach and resolve, assuming that this is the mode of making politics from a woman's perspective. The arbitrary selection of these two kinds of problems, among so many others, responds to their greater potential for giving meaning to the orientation and political practices of women's groups. I am talking about the problem of *knowledge*, followed by the problem of *power*.

These problems are part of a living movement brought on by the demands of a transformative and unavoidable revolution—if it doesn't turn to destructiveness, which is also an inherent possibility.

The problem of knowledge has been around a long time and much debated, especially when it is coupled with the privilege of wealth, the innocence of social poverty, or the urgent responsibility to act and stop interpreting. We have chosen to look at the problem of knowledge from a Foucaultian perspective. Foucault affirms that to speak of knowledge from a position of marginality is to speak, at the same time, of a will-to-knowledge [*un querer-saber*]. This will-to-knowledge is contrasted to the violence of declared ideas put forth by the party that appropriates the truth and displaces its adversary into error, where it is left (idealistic violence, Sartre called it).

There is, then, a need to develop or recuperate knowledge for oneself, from a feminist perspective. The will-to-knowledge arises when a lack of correspondence is observed between values espoused by the system and the concrete experience of real human beings.

For women, the values of Equality, Fraternity, and Democracy are actually lived as inequality, oppression, and discrimination. The will-to-knowledge is similar to rebellion. Obviously, *we don't know this* right away. There's a long and difficult road to follow before recognizing it in one's own consciousness. Fundamentally, this is because official, transmitted knowledge always adopts a benevolent, positive appearance, while in reality it functions in accordance with a whole game of repression and exclusion: exclusion of those who don't have the right to know. And when the latter, from the private sphere, through work or necessity, accede to knowledge, they do so in a conforming attitude. They accept knowing *only* a certain number of things and *not* others. For example, which one of us women hasn't said or heard said "we women aren't interested in power"? This is pure political conformism.

That women may struggle for power is not accepted as true. "It's an error," they tell us in varying tones of voice. And of course it is, in the sense of knowledge as understood by the party-in-power.

A first consequence of this unrecuperated knowledge of power is that we women accept not ever struggling for power; in fact we disdain it. A second consequence is that we generally organize, set forth, and produce the struggles *to obtain* something: health care for mothers, for children; employment for our spouses, etc.; yet we don't struggle to reintegrate ourselves, to acquire, to make our own the exercise of those rights *for us*.

What has happened with regard to women, as with other marginalized groups, is an expropriation of knowledge. And perhaps for that reason, on occasion when women do recreate knowledge, it has an air of "bricolage." Concepts are taken from other kinds of knowledge and contexts and given a different meaning. The reappropriation, at times irreverent, has no other sense than that of changing the same notes for a different tune—in a new key that sounds better. It's not a new truth in its own right.

The conflicts among feminists produced by this marginal situation with respect to knowledge are serious and threatening. In a certain sense, *there exists no alternate eternally valid model* for questioning the paradigm of patriarchal knowledge in which we have been robed and adorned.

Nevertheless, *everything we do* and undertake with our paradigm in perpetual revision *has near and far-reaching effects* on many other women. It is thus here where we incorporate the idea of political responsibility.

A considerable part of this reappropriated knowledge, with the difficulties inherent to the act of opening spaces and expanding concepts, has been expressed in feminist research. This research has discovered and studied flagrant abuses against women. Yet rarely, and only with great difficulty, do these abuses constitute the basis for concrete demands within the movement. Perhaps they're not considered very political, like the slave-drudgery of domestic work; the over-exploitation of informal jobs; the prostitution of adults and children; the practice of abortion with the sinister results of its clandestinity; civil and federal incapacity as citizens, given the level of domestic violence. Or even being "dependent" and "unimportant," not to mention other obstacles beyond the public sphere of economics and politics.

Feminist action often separates itself from what its knowledge uncovers and deciphers. In any case, it's important to remember the close tie between the two. Now let's look at the problem of power.

What significance does this problem have? How is it related to women's action, knowledge, and politics? Perhaps what is most important about the theme of power within feminism is precisely its *absence*.

In the problem of power and its practice, we women are the principal absentees. The discourse of power is only valid in the patriarchal sphere and is expressed with rapid derivation from public, political power—the power of the State, and, in its social dimension, the power of certain groups, classes, and sectors. These are the accepted paths. For the private (female) sphere, one speaks of "another power," the power of the home, of affection. "They're the most important," we're told. And there we are: with real difficulties in assuming power when we enter the public sphere. If there are troubles between us women, we ascribe it to someone's trying to take power. We give it a bad name, a negative ethical connotation, and we don't want to talk about the matter again.

But what is power? How can we break the padlocks and advance in this problem?

In the first place, power *doesn't exist* as such; it is *exercised.* Exercised through actions and words. It isn't an essence. No one can *take* power and store it in a safe. To hold power is not to have it under wraps, nor to preserve it from foreign elements, but rather *to exercise it continually.* To transform it into actions and to make others act and think. To take power is to take control of action—the idea and the act—an act frequently grounded in force and violence. Perhaps this is why we reject it and distance ourselves from it.

As a result of years and years of patriarchal culture, the desire for power (that is, the desire to know—the desire to act) has been totally obstructed in women. They don't seek it for themselves, they exclude themselves from the possibility of taking it, and they don't even discuss it. Women see it as something *beyond* (beyond what and where?).

The road glimpsed on the horizon by French students in May 1968, which enabled them to question power on a large scale, must become ours. It involves, first of all, a de-subjugation of our own will and consists of a *de-legitimation* of what is denied to us, a denial imposed from a situation of privilege. This situation of privilege, for us women, is patriarchy.

Then, it must be an effort to liberate one's own subjectivity by means of an attack on culture, on taboos and sexual limitations, arbitrary overpowerment, or categorization. We must return sexual practices to the area of freedom of choice.

Finally, we must establish communitarian practices to break down the normative value of individuality. A good example of this is the proliferation of groups of women that undertake multiple tasks with the common understanding that they are rejecting atomization and privatization of personal and family relations.

To conclude this point, let's remember that one can't speak of power without mentioning its necessary counterpart: political responsibility.

A project brought into being, from the time it takes shape, no longer belongs to us; it follows its own dynamics. And this produces certain effects. On the one hand, an action [*hacer*] that has come into being [*acto*] acquires a life of its own, an independent existence. On the other hand, from the time we launch it, we are responsible for it—an inescapable quality of political action.

Another problem worth pointing out is the *feminist political problem*. This arises from the fact that every place, home, organization, or group related to women—even though it may not have been previously expressed or understood—is, by nature and almost objectively, a *woman's political space*. This is explicitly and implicitly accepted beyond circles of militant feminists; I refer in particular to women from partisan political organizations who have not always supported programs for women's liberation but who nevertheless have seen in women a field to be cultivated or incorporated into political agendas at many levels.

This quality of women's political space has been understood by partisan political women *even before* we feminists became aware of it. Accustomed as we are to the scant interest they express in attending group undertakings and feminist workshops, we tend to attribute their general presence in women's meetings to hidden motives involving manipulation and partisan control.

The perception of political space and the suspicion of being threatened immediately transform that space into disputed territory, fought over like conquerors' booty. For political women, there's a certain impression that this space is full of women but politically empty. It's easy and natural, therefore, that it be viewed greedily like a playing field to be mapped out and strategically won over. [. . .]

This form of expression, of *nonfeminist militant participation* in feminist spaces, produces the following dilemma for feminists: Is this a simple unwarranted intrusion or is it an express intention to have a dialogue? And is the latter possible if perspectives have been previously constituted? This problem might appear unresolvable.

Initial feminist reactions are not long in coming and take two paths: some want to defend their own, close ranks around exclusively feminist concerns, so as to *move ahead* in the elaboration of a political program and strategy. Others prefer not to fall into a closed group, a ghetto, and want to widen the appeal and encourage many women to practice dialoguing, arguing, participating, with the risk entailed in any opening-up (weren't we once one of "them"?).

The debate on this point can become more thorny or bear fruit, but I'd like to refer to another point that can be detected behind the feminists/political women problem. I persist in believing that behind all this (call it manipulation, intrusion, whatever), there is a solidly structured enigma that is very difficult to untangle. I have always been very impressed by political women who, in their cultural and ideological way of being, show a marked satisfaction for the *results* they can accomplish by rigorously applying their analytical methodology and their globalist explanatory theory. Nor have I ever believed that the radically rigorous is the only alternative to a feminist critical way of thinking. It seems preferable to me to choose the happy path of always testing things out, being able to seek out different interpretations for conflicts and the nuances of problems.

Neither the problem of power, nor that of knowledge, nor that of feminism and politics can be fully examined in these few ideas. I have only tried to go a little beyond the maneuvering and functioning of certain concepts and actions. I prefer to come down on the side of a way of thinking that recognizes the diverse ideological positions and solutions offered for the problem of women and politics. After all, gender subordination has been defined in different ways that have consequently provoked different solutions.

A positive basis for analysis and comparison might be found precisely in the mechanisms that the two groups have developed among themselves for posing problems and solutions. This would avoid the continuation of a cold war–type situation, or a war of nerves in which each pole appears to undertake actions or spread information that is alarming to the other side, obliging them both to be constantly attentive and always there, preparing for what might be a real war or devastating confrontation.

From "El feminismo como negación del autoritarismo" (Feminism as Negation of Authoritarianism) in *Ser política en Chile: Los nudos de la sabiduría feminista*. Santiago, Chile: Editorial Cuarto Propio, 1990, pp. 218–233.

NOTES

1. I use the term *políticas* in the strict sense in which this category of women refer to themselves. I do not intend to imply any statement or partiality regarding the validity of this term.

2. *Arpilleristas* were Chilean women who did original patchwork embroidery, or "tapestries of resistance," as Marjorie Agosín has called them. They were sewn together in bright colors and depicted scenes of community life during the repressive Pinochet dictatorship. The women generally worked in collectives and used the income from their international sales to support human rights and the families of the "disappeared," victims of the regime. I would like to express my gratitude to Marjorie Agosín for reading my translation of Kirkwood's essay and making suggestions for its improvement. [Trans.]

3. Simone de Beauvoir points out in *The Second Sex* the effects of the ideas of "alterity" and "dependency" tied to women's being, as defined by traditionalist philosophy.

4. See Hannah Arendt, "The Human Condition," on this subject.

5. On the concept of "necessity," see Agnes Heller, "The Theory of Necessities in Marx" and "The Sociology of Daily Life."

Cristina Peri Rossi

Uruguay, 1941 –

Born in Montevideo, Uruguay, Cristina Peri Rossi has
lived in Spain since 1972. While she is best known for
her prose fiction, she began her writing career as a journalist in Uruguay, where her outspoken criticism of that
country's government forced her to go into exile. Peri
Rossi received her first literary prizes in 1968 for a collection of short stories, *Los museos abandonados* (1969;
The Abandoned Museums), and for her novel, *El libro
de mis primos* (1969; The Book of My Cousins). Among
her highly acclaimed works of fiction are *La nave de los
locos* (1984; The Ship of Fools), *Una pasión prohibida*
(1986; *A Forbidden Passion*, 1993), *Solitario de amor* (1988;
Love Solitary), and *La última noche de Dostoievski* (Dostoyevsky's Last Night), published in 1992.

Peri Rossi has also established herself as a poet: she
has published several collections, including *Evohé*
(1971), *Descripción de un naufragio* (1975; Description
of a Shipwreck), *Diáspora* (1976), *Lingüística general*
(1979; General Linguistics), and, most recently, *Babel
bárbara*, winner of the 1991 Ciudad de Barcelona prize.
In her prose and poetry, she gravitates toward themes of
politics, resistance against oppression, love relationships,
lesbian sexuality, and language. Her prose fiction has
evolved away from the notable early influence of Julio
Cortázar to culminate in a unique expression of psychological realism and linguistic fantasy. Or perhaps the

reverse is equally true: she fuses mental fantasy with sharp, observant narrative voices to create hallucinatory textual worlds that feel uncannily familiar.

The essay is a genre that Cristina Peri Rossi cultivates with the elegance of her prose fiction and the passion of her poetry. Whether she writes about art, literature, politics, or social issues, Peri Rossi displays a profound understanding of culture, power, and representation. Following in the tradition of the creative writer as intellectual commentator on her society, Peri Rossi observes through a critical and compassionate eye. It could be said that Peri Rossi writes from a marginal subject position in that she is an exile, a foreigner, a lesbian, and a politically committed writer. At the same time, she occupies a position of authority as a recognized author, and the themes about which she writes in *Fantasías eróticas* (1991; Erotic Fantasies), her recent book of essays, have found increasing acceptance in contemporary culture, having transcended their function as taboo to become, in some instances, an integral component of mainstream chic. *Fantasías eróticas* is one of several recent contributions by Latin American women writers to the growing body of feminine erotica. In her fiction and poetry, Peri Rossi has approached themes of sexuality and eroticism with remarkable imaginative fluidity (*Solitario de amor*, for instance, offers haunting evocations of the beloved, a woman, as told from the perspective of a man). This essay collection extends her discursive powers into the realm of film criticism, popular culture, literary criticism, the confessional mode, and erotic writing. Intended primarily for a popular audience, these essays nevertheless may be inserted into the general rubric of cultural criticism of a fairly elite order. Peri Rossi's commentaries focus on canonical figures such as Plato, Ovid, Beethoven, Wagner, Freud, and Bataille, but they also interrogate such subjects as "outlawed" sexualities (fetishism, prostitution, transvestism, homosexualities, sadomasochism, pornography), formations of pleasure, and sublimation of instinct.

The first selection from *Fantasías eróticas* is taken from the Preamble, an autobiographical sketch in which the author illustrates the performative nature of gender presentation, lesbian sexuality, and erotic attraction. The second selection centers on a male erotic practice of the modern age: the manufacture and consumption of inanimate sexual surrogates (inflatable dolls). Cristina Peri Rossi's observations on sexual fantasies—irreverent, lyrical, sometimes playful and sometimes moralistic—constitute a link to her fiction and poetry, where she has already proven that the best creative writers are no strangers to desire in all its expressions.

ROSEMARY GEISDORFER FEAL

New Year's Eve at Daniel's

On New Year's Eve in 1989—I despise calling it *Nochevieja* "Old-night": that makes me sad—I decided to stop in and have a drink at Daniel's. Daniel's is one of the oldest places in Barcelona for queers, and one of the few for women only.[1] It is futile to search for it in newspapers or in exclusive guidebooks: Daniela, the owner, prides herself on not advertising her club anywhere. She believes that in this way she can select the clientele better. Daniel's is a bar of scanty dimensions with a small dance floor, and a billiard table on the second floor that hardly anyone uses. Perhaps for this reason it offers a warm, intimate, and welcoming atmosphere. The owner knows the majority of women who go there, alone or with another woman. Further, she knows their personal stories, their loves, their sorrows, their joys and frustrations, the problems with parents, husbands, or children. Sometimes she gives advice to one who has asked her for it, but, in general, she remains reserved: Daniela loves discretion above anything else in this world. Part of this discretion is her not listing the club in newspapers or magazines. This way she assures her customers of anonymity, if necessary.

The door is never open at Daniel's. To get in one must ring the bell (next to a metal plaque that says "We reserve the right to refuse admittance") and wait until Daniela, or one of the girls, looks through the peephole, and afterward, if the customer is accepted, the door finally opens. There are always a few girls who help Daniela tend bar, serve drinks, or spin records. They are very young and they exude that deliberately

Translated by Rosemary Geisdorfer Feal

ambiguous appearance that has signaled the style of a certain age and sexual alternative. In fact, anyone could confuse these girls with an adolescent of the male gender. They wear their hair very short and combed back, sometimes with a touch of gel; they are very thin, have no breasts to speak of, and never use makeup. But something in their soft gestures, in their gazelle-like movements, reveals with certainty that they are girls: rebellious adolescents who live alone or who share an apartment, emigrants from obscure villages far from the big city, which they left behind one day to escape provincialism and rigid ways of life. Daniela looks out for them, like a protective father or mother.

I believe that Daniel's is the oldest private club for women in Barcelona. I discovered it in 1976, and since then it has changed very little. Now it has psychedelic lights and American billiards, but nothing else is new.

I haven't gone to Daniel's more than a few times: three or four at most, despite which, on the last night of 1989, when I rang the doorbell, Daniela recognized me and looked glad to see me. I went there that evening precisely because I thought that it would be a most special night. I was right: Daniela told me, as soon as I walked in, "Stay until three in the morning. At that time, we'll turn out the lights, light candles, and drink a toast with champagne, courtesy of the house."

I feel a good deal of affection for those people who refer to their business as "the house": a prolongation of the maternal home, a protective womb that frees us from outside hostility. And it seems to me that Daniela is such a homebody that the place resembles a collective dwelling, for women only, without men. (Daniela is rigorous about this: not even gays are admitted. "They are also men," she says, "and, at times, some of the worst.")

That night, the place was very crowded. The New Year had already begun, and as soon as the women were able to get out of their commitments they flowed into Daniel's as if it were a liberated territory: liberated from social or orthodox customs, from family obligations, from conventional attachments that lack fantasy or passion. I sensed that once they arrived at Daniel's, these women let out an "ah!" of relief and satisfaction.

Since it was a special night, Daniel's, which usually closes at three, was going to close at dawn or early morning.

I have never seen so many people together in such a small place. Women arrived alone, in couples, or in groups, they removed their overcoats, they said hello to other women (many seemed to know one another), they began to talk or they went out on the dance floor. I didn't know anyone, and if any woman knew me (quite probable), discretion caused her to refrain from showing it, which put me at ease: I like to observe without being observed.

It was very hot in the bar and the smoke created a kind of evanescent veil that diluted faces and shapes. It seemed to me that all those women were happy, and this comforted me, because I cannot tolerate people who become mournful on New Year's. In order to get a better observation point, I went over toward a corner of the room where people who were not dancing had congregated. The dancing couples (two women's faces, two pairs of breasts, four legs below curves) resembled a merry-go-round of Januses (the mythological Greek god endowed with two heads; but, in this case, there were two female heads).

All of a sudden, into that place full of smoke and moving bodies entered an extravagant couple. They were the most beautiful man and woman I had seen in many years, and their unexpected appearance gave rise to a wave of whisperings. I looked over at Daniela and saw that she received them with a greeting, so I concluded that this wasn't some confused couple who had accidently wandered into a lesbian bar. Their appearance and clothing revealed that they were not from this city, nor, possibly, from the nation. I mean that they could have come directly from a movie still by Visconti or Bertolucci, but never from a film by Buñuel or Almodóvar. They were most surely Italians, with that Renaissance beauty that one only finds in Rome or Milan, or in Genoa or Venice. They were not very young: perhaps they were approaching forty, the age of splendor for a woman. She (I refer to the one dressed as a woman) was as beautiful as Iva Zanicchi, Mina, or Monica Vitti: that sensual and passionate beauty emitted by perfectly classical features, a combination that can be found nowhere else. I couldn't exactly say that she was elegant, despite her sophisticated clothing, because the great Italian beauties (like Silvana Mangano) almost always have a slight touch of coarseness that makes them more earthy, more carnal, more accessible. One night they can be in a theatre box at the Scala in Milan listening to *Un ballo in maschera* and the next day they can be arguing passionately with the common woman selling her wares at the marketplace, with curse words and all.

I thought that many of the young women who were at Daniel's and who reacted with bewilderment before this apparition (these girls, who with great conviction carried off the lesbian model of sexual ambiguity, incertitude, or duplicity) perhaps did not possess the same reference points that I did. They probably would not know who Iva Zanicchi or Mina or Silvana Mangano were. Possibly they were not very sure about Romantic aesthetics, or the game of black and white—like George Sand—or the paleness of Margarita Gautier's lovers. But I knew about this.

I began to stare at the couple, like a spectator in the know: that performance deserved a devoted audience of *connoisseurs*, not beginners. She was dressed in a long black skirt, full and abundant, a white silk blouse with ruffles at the bosom, and very tight black leather boots.

She had very long earrings (matching, in black and white) and, on her arm, a wide gold bracelet from which emerald beads hung like teardrops. She wore a lot of makeup, but in such a peculiar way that paint and skin seemed inseparable. Her body was mature, sensuous: well-curved shoulders, a wide mouth, deep black eyes, nearly opulent breasts, and a full pair of buttocks.

Her escort (I was not willing to undress her to prove that she really had a pair of diminutive breasts, and a vagina hidden between tufts of hair) appeared to be a tall, pale, handsome man, perfectly impassive and distant, but attentive to his lady. He was wearing a fitted suit of black leather, with a bright white shirt discreetly embroidered in linen and closed with gold cuff links. He was slightly taller than she, and his body, admirably narrow, without curves or undulations, had smoothed off those protuberances that always give away a woman. His abundant hair was very nicely cut and he wore it back: its darkness contrasted with the enormous pallor of his face.

They had evidently invested great effort into their roles to obtain such a contrasting pair, so spotlessly shaped, so balanced: they were two excellent actors (or actresses). Nothing escaped from their control, their careful construction of the characters. The only criticism was the excess: they were slightly overacting, too perfect to be real: her red mouth and his pale lips, the black of his suit and her skirt, the white of his shirt and her blouse. It was such a coordinated contrast that, taken together, they formed a perfect unity. (Nature is more baroque: it always has too much or lacks something, as is the case with elephants or giraffes.) They had constructed the ideal couple, simulatively heterosexual.

But something, amid the perfection, denounced the simulacrum. If, however, I did not know that men were refused admittance into Daniel's, I would have believed the spectacle. They had reached the dimension of art: that is, where nature yields to artifice.

I am a writer: I love beauty above all else and I know that it is hardly ever spontaneous, that one must win it and merit it; that is why I was willing to be the audience that the performance needed: a loving audience, comprehending and generous. I become completely humbled before beauty: I revere it, I applaud it, I sing it, I cover it with praises: it is scarce, like the greatest riches.

Although the two women of the couple did not look at the others who were present, poised perhaps in the doorway that led directly to paradise (I am convinced that beauty leads at least to limbo, and that everything else leads to hell), they did not permit themselves a single spontaneous gesture, one that was not studied, a movement of eyebrows or hands that the script had not foreseen; I know, however, that they felt themselves looked at (at least by me), possibly envied, rejected, or loved at the same time.

They did not speak with anyone: positioned in one corner of the room (opposite me), they limited themselves to posing, static and immobile, as if they had already passed into the pages of a book, into a camera obscura, into celluloid; like two statues in a park. Venus and Apollo. They posed in an ostentatious manner, as if among the multitude at Daniel's there were a movie director willing to sign them on, or a Raphael or Leonardo, ready to immortalize them.

Nor did they speak between themselves, although at times they looked at each other in a caressing way that caused me to feel delirious, no matter how studied their gesture (I would never reproach anyone for artificiality: *art* and *artifice* have the same root).

I imagined their nights of love: the fiction that in bed there were a man and a woman; the *representation* of a primitive coitus, impossible, for them, and therefore imaginary. Once again, fantasy triumphs over reality.

Only fools or excessively rational people (sometimes one and the same) would ask themselves why a beautiful woman, in full possession of all her charms, would choose a woman disguised as a man to make love with, when there are so many *real* men roaming free in the world, and very willing. Herein lies the true motive: she does not want real men but rather imaginary ones: women who play at being men, because they are not. Reality lacks fantasy and mystery. She likes representation, simulacrum, fiction. She loves the fascination with the imaginary above the ordinariness of the real. That false man who, despite the perfect disguise, will never be a *real* man, seduces her through the imaginary, and gives her what (s)he does not have, what (s)he is not.[2] The false man offers her the most marvelous and intimate things that one can offer to another: one's dream, one's not-being, one's not-having.

Of course, we could speak about these matters as a perversion. But that is not saying anything: Don Quixote *was not* the mediocre nobleman

Alfonso Quixote [*sic*] but rather what he wanted to be: a knight-errant. *Being* is revealed more in what it desires to be than in what it is. The woman disguised as a man on the night of 31 December 1989 did not wish to be the mediocre woman who she must have been but, instead, the paradigm of the romantic male lover she pretended to be: beautiful, distant, seductive, absolutely in love with one particular woman.

I could imagine with some envy the nights of perverse pleasure enjoyed by that strange couple: the fiction of being *another*, of choosing one's sex like one chooses the color of a dress. The triumph of art over nature, of the imagination over reality.

They posed for one hour, more or less. Each one played her role to perfection, without deviating one millimeter from the script: not one careless gesture, not one hesitation.

I must say that while they remained at Daniel's, all the women there seemed eclipsed, unreal, blurred: such is the power of fiction.

When they had left the bar, I approached Daniela.

"Are they Italian?" I asked, although I was sure of the answer.

"Yes," she answered, with her usual discretion.

"They look like they came out of a movie," I heard someone remark, before the couple exited.

Fantasías eróticas. Colección Biblioteca Erótica. Madrid: Ediciones Temas de Hoy, 1991, pp. 11–18.

NOTES

1. In the original, *local de "ambiente"* (literally, a place with "ambience"). The expression obviously refers to gay and lesbian bars: I use *queer* rather than *gay* since Peri Rossi restricts the latter term to gay men. [Trans.]

2. Since the pronoun is omitted in the original, I use the dual-gendered *(s)he* here in reference to "the false man" to distinguish from the *she*, which refers to the woman playing the role of the woman in the couple. [Trans.]

Cristina Peri Rossi

The Fantasy
of the Passive Object
Inflatable Dolls

Fornicating with a Woman-Container

The North American soldiers who set off to fight in Vietnam filled their knapsacks with condensed milk, chocolate bars, antiparasitic ointments, electronic burners . . . and inflatable dolls. It had to be like this in a throw-away culture. North American industry manufactures a variety of objects intended for one sole purpose, and it also invents desire through those objects. It is true that men have fornicated with everything that has ever come before them: hens, goats, rag dolls, holes in the wall, and so on, but, when owing to extraordinary circumstances of isolation or deprivation they do not find animals or appropriate objects around them, they use simulacra, replicas.

A recent survey, published in a magazine with a high circulation, stated that one out of every thousand Spanish men purchased an inflatable doll in the last three years. A salesman in a sex shop in the Gracia neighborhood of Barcelona is accustomed to selling inflatable dolls to individuals between thirty and forty years of age, generally married men with children. Uninflated, the dolls take up little space and can be skillfully hidden in the trunk of a car, or in a desk compartment or a closet drawer, mixed in among the handkerchiefs and the scarves. These customers of whom we are speaking typically dispatch the family to the beach or the countryside on weekends in order to surrender themselves comfortably to their most secret fantasies with their inflatable dolls in the emptiness of their apartments. An addict confessed to me, "It is much more hygienic than commerce with prostitutes; there is no risk of infection, and, besides,

Translated by Rosemary Geisdorfer Feal

the doll is private property, and no one other than the owner uses it." The same salesman from the Gracia neighborhood told me that a sixty-year-old widowed resident had acquired one a short time earlier. "I told him to use it in moderation," he remarked to me, "but he thrashed around so much with the doll that he suffered a heart attack and had to be hospitalized."

The well-known sexologist and feminist Mary Philips Seattle declared in an interview in 1980, "What can we expect from a generation of males who has practiced sex with inflatable dolls, like big autistic children? While women increasingly demand to be treated as persons in their erotic relationships, that is, as independent beings, with a body, a mind, and desires of their own, men—rejecting this position of equality—continue having relations with inanimate objects."

The surge of inflatable dolls comes about at a time when women's sexual liberation has begun to make headway, which places us squarely before an apparent contradiction: if interpersonal sexual relationships are freer, if women are more willing than ever to explore their sexuality, why do men produce, sell, and consume inflatable dolls? Our initial explanation concerning the Vietnam War and an absence of women is no longer the case: it is the exact opposite.

The feminist demand to be considered as a person, that is, an autonomous being, endowed with her own sexuality, her personal fantasies, her active desires, and her individual personality—a demand increasingly manifested in our cultures—has provoked anxiety, uneasiness, and insecurity in many men, who have had to ask themselves, with great anguish, what do women want? Now there are two people in bed, and not only one desire (the standard formula in conventional relations in the patriarchal world). Male insecurity about these new demands, made in a framework of equality that does not suit him, has triggered a movement to seek refuge in an object: the inflatable doll is his fantasy of a solitary (male) desire, exerted over the appearance of a completely passive woman, that is, without a voice, without independence, without desire.

In the solitude of a room, the male with his inanimate object can recover his dominion over the situation. Here we have the shape of a woman without will, the shape of a woman who gives everything while demanding nothing, who bends, with the docility of rubber, to the desire of the male, and whose satisfaction he does not need to consider for a single minute.

The inflatable doll is an ancient male dream: to fornicate in a completely passive woman-container, the recipient of fantasies that will never exhibit disappointment, or dissatisfaction, or rebellion. True, neither will it show contentment, pleasure, or emotion, but the male who fornicates with a doll certainly does not expect these reactions from his object, and prefers not to think about those matters.

The inflatable doll is an autistic dream of sick and crazy boys, a dream come true because it responds decidedly to a most primitive striving: coitus as power, as domination, as humiliation. In this sense, it is a variant, and only one variant, of sadomasochistic sexual relations characteristic of patriarchal societies. That sadistic tendencies have led to the construction of a woman-object apt for the most absolute submission is a delirium made reality, but the consequences can be quite grave. In the first place, in many cases it prevents the monomaniac from relating on an equal basis with women, who would have a difficult time accepting a role as mere objects, and, in the second place, it widens the gap even further between masculine eroticism and feminine eroticism (always humanized, because it does not separate sexuality from the rest of the person).

How was this perverse dream of the inflatable doll born?

Absolute Submission

The impulse to dominate seems to be characteristic of the human species: it may be observed in babies, when they begin to experiment with the objects that surround them in an attempt to subjugate them to their will. The rattle or spoon that they throw, or the ability to place a pacifier in their mouths and then spit it out, are the first steps in the apprenticeship of control over things. We also have taken control over nature and animals to a certain extent: we ride horses, we train dogs and dolphins, and so forth. But the will to dominate has always been applied to fellow humans as well: slavery, removed from its traditional form, subsists in more elaborate expressions.

The authoritarian supervisor, the despotic boss, the exploitative manager, or the tyrannical husband are models we know only too well. The military, a hierarchical structure par excellence, is an institutionalized example of power relations based on harsh discipline and not on reason. Furthermore, it is not enough to have been a slave in order to rebel against power: slaves have almost always found others to dominate in turn. There are plenty of examples: the hazing of new recruits in barracks, the cruelty of children toward the "different" one (the foreigner, the poor child, the one with mannerisms).

A sexual relationship that is imposed, many times through violence and without the consent of the weaker one—the feminine party or its incarnation—goes beyond physical pleasure: it symbolizes the desire to dominate and to possess (accompanied by the wish to humiliate) that many individuals experience. Power relations have been present throughout the entire history of humanity, and few times has the ideal of harmony and respect succeeded in prevailing. This distribution of power also occurs in the relationship between the two sexes (and even in homosexuality: a significant number of gays have opted for violent sadomasochistic formulas). On the other hand, lesbianism seems exempt from these strivings; even ideologically it loathes an eroticism that splits sexuality from the rest of the personality, whereas the male often carries out his sexual function as a form of narcissism (*I can, I am the master, I dominate*) and of superiority. The inflatable doll is the fantasy of absolute submission: it does not speak, it does not make demands, it does not express itself, and it does not interfere in the desire of the other.

Before turning into an industrially manufactured product, like toothbrushes or television sets, the fantasy of the doll was located in literature, although of course it was much more highly infused with sublimation.

Limiting ourselves to literary antecedents in Spanish, we should cite the short novel by Uruguayan writer Felisberto Hernández, one of the most subtle and delicate authors in Spanish American narrative before the famous Boom. *Las hortensias* (The Hydrangeas), a long story or a short novel, was published despite great economic difficulties in Montevideo (Uruguay) in 1941. It was a lyrical and psychological delirium by a peculiar kind of writer, extravagant, poor, and at the same time highly seductive. The book circulated among friends: it enjoyed a small but avid readership, yet it had an important influence on later literature in Latin America. In a delicate tone, deliberately elliptical yet asphyxiating, the novel recounts the delirium of an apparently happily married man who, with the thought of enlivening the solitary evenings spent by husband and wife, orders a series of life-size dolls, each of which is given its own biography and is dressed up, made up, and prepared specifically to share the couple's leisure. The text, of a most elegant sobriety, avoids sexual allusions and chooses instead to narrate the delirium of the protagonist (who finally falls in love with one of the dolls) and the jealousy of his wife, stripped of her place in the psychic life of her husband by the doll that is her almost perfect replica.

The book, strange and suggestively perverse, was not known in Spain until the year 1974, in which I succeeded in having it published by Lumen, with a short prologue I wrote for that purpose. Shortly afterward, Luis García Berlanga, the Spanish film director impassioned by erotic themes, made the movie *Tamaño natural* (Life-Size) starring Michel Piccoli, which narrates a prosperous dentist's obsession with a doll who gradually displaces his wife.

Even though inflatable dolls form a part of the imagination of many men, few dare to confess their fondness for them. One of these men was Ramón Gómez de la Serna, the Spanish writer. Ramón, original, extravagant, highly inclined to *épater le bourgeois* (the saying that was first made popular by symbolist poets and later by surrealists), kept a movable mannequin in his house that he dressed, combed, and adorned, and with which he enjoyed being photographed at tea time. In his case, and in that of other artists, it is quite possible that the mannequin or semihuman doll has an additional significance: it symbolizes the creator's dream of giving birth to the characters of his imagination, those that he "dresses and undresses" on paper.

Inflatable dolls constitute a blossoming industry in the technified world: in many countries they can be purchased by mail-order, and the customer selects his preferred model from a varied assortment in an illustrated catalogue. In the United States the most prestigious manufacturers produce some dolls with faces of the most famous actresses: Marilyn Monroe, Sophia Loren, Elizabeth Taylor, etc. Another important company, in Sweden, has launched a new model on the market, this one endowed with a kind of rubber skin that, according to the experts, very adequately imitates the texture and temperature of the female epidermis.

As of now the manufacturers of erotic objects have not designed an inflatable male doll with a synthetic penis. This undoubtedly has nothing to do with some unpardonable omission from the market. In the times in which we live, times characterized by a frenzy for objects, it would be difficult to think of an unnoticed omission. There is a much deeper reason here: women are not very good consumers of standardized erotic fantasies, mass-produced in serial fashion. They usually do not accept substitute "objects" for complex interpersonal relationships. An object with those traits (an inflatable doll or a mechanized robot) would incite more laughter than erotic arousal in women, perhaps because the greatest feminine aspiration, even to the present, has been equality in personal relations, not sex as a manifestation of the obscure desire to possess and humiliate.

Fantasías eróticas. Colección Biblioteca Erótica. Madrid: Ediciones Temas de Hoy, 1991, pp. 91–98.

Elena Poniatowska

Mexico, 1933–

Elena Poniatowska is perhaps Mexico's most popular
woman writer, in the dual sense of the term: her books
run to dozens of editions, and she has consistently represented, and spoken on behalf of, the masses, the common folk of Mexico City who live out their lives on
its streets and in its marketplaces and work in its shops
and factories and in the homes of its middle and upper
classes.

Elena Poniatowska earned the right to this popular
voice through a process of cultural adoption. Born in
France in 1933, she came to Mexico with her family
when she was a little girl. Elena's Mexicanness derives
from a childhood growing up with nannies, dark
women with long black plaits and shiny round faces.
These *nanas* and *criadas* taught her to enjoy the cooking
of the many regions of Mexico and to listen to the stories of a mestiza inheritance, born of the traditions,
mysteries, and superstitions of the indigenous peoples
and complicated in the customs of internal migrants;
this continual chain of being that is Mexico is linked at
one end to a far-off village lost in time and at the other
to the pavements and plazas of the largest city on the
continent.

Elena Poniatowska's career as a writer began in a
series of columns on society events and irreverent interviews published in the cultural pages of the *Excélsior*

newspaper. This combination of interview and observation has continued to mark many of her most significant works, including *Hasta no verte Jesús mío* (1969; Until I See You Again, Sweet Jesus), and *La noche de Tlatelolco* (1971; *Massacre in Mexico*), her exposure of the events preceding the 1968 Olympics in Mexico City.

Elena Poniatowska uses a third journalistic technique, or prop, in her creative works—the photograph, the visual artifact that combines both immediacy and history, just as her own words do. Elena Poniatowska's most recent publication, *Tinísima* (1992), a biographical novel of the photographer Tina Modotti, has as one scenario the aesthetic and political significance of photography in Mexico's history. And the essay "El último guajolote," translated here as "The Last Turkey," was one of the texts chosen by the cultural arm of the Ministry for Public Education for a 1982 series entitled *Memory and Forgetfulness: Images of Mexico*. Elena Poniatowska's text adds immediacy and personality to the wonderful photographs of Mexico City's streets and peoples taken from the archives of C. B. Waite and J. Lupercio. Her tone is nostalgic but also critical of the neglect that has caused Mexico City to attract a continuing stream of new inhabitants at the same time as the city itself abuses both its people and its environment. As you read about "the last turkey," you too will wish you had a *real* taco stand at the corner of your street, but you'll probably be glad that you can choose not to live in Mexico City, also.

Among a dozen or so different projects, Elena Poniatowska is currently working on another biographical novel, an oral history of her own family, and has just completed the second volume of her collected interviews over the decades.

IRENE MATTHEWS

The Last Turkey

"What do you want on your sandwich?" I'd ask my little Perico.
I was about to make it with banana, or tamale, or beans, something that would fill him up, put some bulk inside his belly, ver-
micelli or macaroni, but he would say to me, ham, if you please,
ham! And when was I going to make him a sandwich of ham if I
could hardly even pay for the bread?   JESUSA PALANCARES,
Hasta no verte Jesús mío

C *hichicuilotitos vivos*—live sniiiiiipe for saaaaale! Cooked sniiiiiipe
for saaaaale!"
      Live or cooked, Doña Emeteria carried her birds in a basket un-
der a cloth. The live ones hung over her arm so they wouldn't escape, cucuru, cucuru, and the cooked ones had to be protected from the dust,
from people looking, and from people poking at them. "Hey, hey, no
squeezing what you haven't paid for." Emeteria would singsong, "Live
chichi for sale!" and the live ones would mill around in a pile of feathers and brittle bones, and in the other basket lay those that had already
met their fate, beautifully cooked, displaying their tiny breasts and their
golden thighs. The snipe lady came from Texcoco Lake with her water-
birds (snipe live in ponds and have broad feet, leap around all together in
groups and dart their beaks simultaneously into the water as they fish for
pond mosquitoes). Texcoco Lake spread stagnantly right here, just around
the corner from Lecumberri prison. That was where the water collected.
The Peñón—Rocky Hill—was all water and Emeteria, her friend Nemesia, her cousin Finita, slanty-eyed Epigmenia, and other bird sellers who
lived on the edge of the lake spread out their nets to bring their befeath-
ered and defeathered merchandise to the city. But snipe are migratory
birds, and when they began moving on to other lakes, the snipe lady
would fish out of the water the light brown broad-winged fly (completely
different from the real mosquito, the *Anofeles* that unsheathes its sword—
like Holofernes in the Bible—and gives you malaria). The insect that used

Translated by Irene Matthews

to feed her snipe would now be sold around the houses for canaries, mockingbirds, and cardinals—tasting the food of free birds behind their golden bars and digesting it in the sun next to the geraniums.

"Ducks, my dear, warm ducks!"

In the letters she sent back to her own foggy country, England, Lady Fanny Calderón de la Barca sketched the little Indian duck seller, her skirt bound at her waist with a bright colored sash, her pigtails, and her brown shoeless feet.

"Ducks for sale! Duuuuuuuucks for sale."

That cry is as unlikely nowadays as the description of the Viga Canal that Antonio García Cubas offers us in his *Mexico of My Memories*. He describes one by one the network of rivulets that bordered the magnificent beach, the abundant foliage and the waterside walk that stretched through green groves of trees—can you believe it—on the slopes of the "Lost Child," Saint Antonio Abad, and the Mercy Hill. The trees thicketed right up to the feet of the Tacubaya slopes, dotted with simple country cottages where people would come to savor juicy drinks and tasty floury tamales, while the children swung on the swings that hung from the branches of the trees.

All sorts of things came to us from the lake—fronds of greenery and vegetables and soap and yeast. From the ditches filled with stagnant water, Doña Emeteria and her friend Nemesia would peel off a gelatinous layer, cut it into soap-sized blocks, and sell it to their customers for washing floors and particularly greasy clothes. It was natural lye, stronger and more effective than any detergent. They would also hawk limestone from door to door, a natural sodium carbonate that grows around the edges of salt-water lakes and that we all know by the name of Royal and sprinkle into our dough so it'll expand and make our cakes rise nicely, a quality our industrialized delicacies now proclaim for themselves along with those synthetic pancakes that are as "light, light as a feather."

Life came to us from the lake. The peasants would push off their canoes and rafts from its banks and bring in their avocados from Xochimilco, from Mixquic, and from Milpa Alta, their bunches of radishes, their carrots, squash, and pumpkins, and one after another they'd cry: spinach, rosemary, purslane, green beans, string beans, and crisp pork rinds. The herb seller offered their *epazote* and mint, their parsley and their green cilantro, and the father fisherman and his son the little fisherman with their fishes strung on a string sold whitefish or fresh catfish, frogs and mud puppies, and tiny spiny fishes cooked and wrapped in corn leaves or broad banana leaves; there were even some fishermen who came up from Cuernavaca or from Jojutla (along with their companions laden with banana leaves)—their fish packed under green foliage and branches so it wouldn't go rotten.

And if that were not enough, as well as the flowers for sale—tall delphiniums and snapdragons, baby's breath and pinks—the tops of the boats were decorated with flowers: "Catita" in white carnations, "Carmen" with red carnations, "Rosa" with roses (pretty clever!), "Alicia" with cornflowers, and "Mariquita" and "Lupita" with a roof of corn spikes. The gondolas were accompanied by music, just as in Venice, ". . . that beauty spot of yours, sweetheart, next to your lips . . ." and somewhere around sailed the float with the mariachi musicians, the real ones, the ones from Jalisco, from Cocula and from Tecalitlán who've now settled down in Tenampa, or Garibaldi Square " . . . if only every day were Sunday, sweetheart. . . ." Their music had an aquatic tone: the mandolin seemed more like a harp, the guitar made little waves, and the clarinet sounded just like heron on the wing. "The Pelican," "Fishing the Flood," "Tender Greens," "The Two Little Trees," "Blame It on Me," "The King"; we'd listen to this last song as the guitars and violins harmonized and the oarsman slid his vessel over the water crowded with waterlilies. You could even stamp out a wild dance on the wooden floorboards of the gondola while the music of the mariachis standing on the highest point of their vessel mingled with the weeping streams:

> Madam, your little parakeet
> wants to take me down by the river
> and I keep telling him no
> because I'll freeze to death
> pick pick pick parakeet
> pick pick pick at the rose.

Or the one about the dwarves:

> Oh how pretty
> are the dwarves
> when Mexicans
> take them dancing.
> Out comes the pretty one
> and the plain Jane
> out comes the dwarf
> in her ragged skirt.

Make yourself little
make yourself big
now you look just like
a turkey.

But the dwarves
have gotten pretty mad
because they've stripped off
the dwarfwoman's clothes.

Out comes the pretty one . . .

The women selling fresh fruit drinks seemed to emerge from the lake too, clean and graceful as a gannet, sleek under drops of water and with their hair freshly plaited. The "juice lady"—very sweet, according to Antonio García Cubas—would list her beverages: "Chía juice, horchata, lemon, pineapple, or tamarind, which will you have, my dear? Come and refresh yourself." She served them in tall glasses with a ladle made from a small calabash decorated with birds and flowers, and everyone ordered horchata—juice squeezed from rice or corn and flavored with almonds—because it was white and foamy like milk, although nowadays housewives swear that hibiscus juice is a better diuretic. However, what's happened lately is that we no longer hear the noise of the gourd clinking in the water jug but the rough buzz of a blender, because the era of fresh pressed juices has pretty much turned itself over to the reign of the electrical "shakes": strawberry or mamey, alfalfa, guava, or melon and carrot juice whipped up in a "Turmix"—good grief!—with an unholy vaporization of cogs and wheels and screws.

All that water on which Tenochtitlan was founded, the many lakes that surrounded us, the rivers that watered us, were a blessing. The Toluca Valley, where the Lerma River rises, was incredibly rich, Texcoco Lake was an invaluable source of provisions, and while the wise Aztecs built dikes to avoid flooding in the rainy season, in the colonial period Enrico Martínez (who has a street named after him now) began draining the lake and brought us nothing but disasters—we've dried up like herrings, like salted codfish, like mustachioed nuns. And the dust whirling in the dust storms has filled our souls with grit; once upon a time we were volatile and airy, but we never learned how to fly away like the swallows or the snipe that remain only in our memory.

"Won't you buy my live snipe?" Doña Emeteria would sing.

"Chickens for sale!" the chicken seller would cry as his seasick unhappy chickens poked their scrawny chicken necks through the slits in their crate.

"Snipe, live or cooked! Sniiiiipe for saaaale!"

I never saw them myself. I store them in the lithographs of my imagination although it would be better to have them in the lithographs of Linati. The ones I did encounter personally were the Christmas turkeys that, from December first on, trotted the streets of the Colonia del Valle on foot. Shoved around and hustled on by their owner who kept them together on a thin string attached to a stick, they'd cross the street in front of roaring engines and the red bus from Colonia del Valle to Coyoacán. At first there were a lot of them, and they'd shake their crests and their heads quizzically. I felt that they didn't understand and were asking some question I never could find an answer to (well . . . I've never had an answer to anything). Who knows where they were kept at night, but off they'd go at dawn, and from the window you could see their shiny shaggy feather backs and the sudden surprising red of their throats and their voices that came burbling out and hung in the air many hours after they'd gone. By the twenty-fourth there were only a few left waking up suspiciously, two or three, maybe, and the peasant in his cotton trousers tied around his ankles would shake his string over them. "No," the lady was saying to him, "that one's too scraggy, you'd have a hard time finding even a buzzard willing to take a bite out of it. Just think how many miles it's walked since the beginning of the month." The owner hadn't thought about that as he'd pastured it day after day on the asphalt, hot and black as a barbecue pit, and soon the turkey had stopped looking at him so's he wouldn't see the embarrassment in its eyes. All it could do was give out a little painful squawk now and again. In this city there was no one who'd take it in his arms, no one who'd stroke its feathers before slitting its throat, and there it stood like an idiot, wrinkling up, its muscles harder than Charles Atlas'. What was the use of walking so many miles and meeting so many people on the street? Now and then he'd be picked out from among the pile and hefted; and now and then, also, when some dog or another threatened his integrity, the master would tuck him under the warm shadow of his arm for a while, but most of the time was spent walking and walking, and walking and walking, with no way of saying to his owner, "I want to stop right here on this corner for ever and ever."

"Who'll buy my liiiive sniiiipe?"

The occupations of the Mexican people are just like those of the snipe and the turkeys: running round and round the streets, calling their calls on the streets, trotting like a dog on the streets. Trotting and trotting at a never-ending trot, their merchandise on their shoulders, the slings slicing through their foreheads, their huge earthenware jugs on their backs, the tortilla baskets on their rumps, the chickens in their crates, their sombreros strung over their arms—their strong arms—the blocks of ice on their heads, the piles of household furniture on their wheelbarrows, children piggyback on their backs, the common folks of the city trot their little Indian trot, trot trot on, accustomed to absolutely everything because work maketh the man and Juan isn't Juan but the knife grinder and Conchita isn't Conchita but that particular cheese woman with the brazier and the fan on the corner of Bolívar and San Juan de Letrán, the one who fries her tortillas on the edge of the sidewalk, tortillas with pumpkin-flower petals, or potato, or strips of meat, the one who spatters oil on the feet of her greedy customers waiting in a circle. Also in the street, the evangelist props up the eight legs of his table and his chair on the slabs under the Santo Domingo porch. (Sartre and Simone de Beauvoir wrote philosophical essays, too, in the turmoil of the Café "Flore" on little round marble tables scarcely big enough to hold a single coffee cup, but they never made such common spelling mistakes, nor did they resort to the epistolary rhetoric of Latin America.) The vendor of melon seeds arranges her mounds of seeds in the street on a striped cloth and the secondhand bookseller merely slides a newspaper between his incunabula and the asphalt. So the bibliophiles crouch down and Don Joaquín Diez Caneda has to squat on the ground to leaf through the very rare copy of *The Scientific Errors of the Bible*. The herbalists pile up their roots and their dogbane against the evil eye, their little jars of mother of pearl for scabs, their mesquite and "horse's tail" and satinwood, their cures for indigestion and for head colds, boldo fruit and dried sage for outbursts of rage and excess of spleen, orange blossom for weak nerves and a strong heart, cow's tongue, and miraculous creams for corns and bunions. Everything is spread out on the ground, in the dust of the street. The electric-shock man leans against the wall of the street waiting somberly for his next victim and the pot of tamales starts to steam on the sidewalk and a solitary cry rises on the air: "Get your tamales here, sweet tamales, chili tamales and lard tamales." The ice-cream man, who nowadays pushes a little cart painted with a snowy landscape sprinkled with penguins and pine trees, used to walk with his tub on his head, carrying in his hand a basket with little cardboard tubes packed in straw: "Delicious ice cream cones!" he would cry. "Come get lemon ice or milk ice, from the ice-cream man. Lemon and rosewater, from the ice-cream man." Under the sepia tint of a photograph of the ice-cream man, the street-photographer cum press-photographer Waite specified, "Mexican Ice Cream Vendor," which sounds a lot less poetical than the songs or the cries of the vendors who filled the street with magical propositions the whole day long: "I'll swop your glassware and fine china!" "Shoes to mend!" "Drains unblocked!" "Dirt for your flowerpots!" "Seed for your birds!" "Chairs reseated!" "Baskets, fine baskets!" "Baskets and hampers!" "Mats and woven baskets and brooms made of palm!" "Rags and newspapers for sale!" "Tasty nut bars!" "Over here for your *atole* drink!" "Tasty cheese turnovers!" "Thyme, marjoram, indigo!" "Iron and old glass for sale!" and those cries that Antonio García Cubas records for us:

"It's suppertime, sweet cakes and savory fries, come and have supper, children."

The cake seller would chant his cheeky songs to attract his customers:

> What have my trousers done to you
> for you to bad-mouth them like that?
> Don't forget little lady
> that you had them on too.

"Come and get your sweet cakes and savories, children come eat your supper."

> Watch me whistle and you come running
> Watch me send you a sign
> watch how you go for the firewood
> and watch how you go in the woods.

"Come and get your cakes—soft and crisp; all you ragamuffins, come eat your supper."

> The poor man who falls in love
> with a woman who has a master
> is left like the bad thief
> crucified and with no reward.

> The poor man who falls in love
> with a proper young lady
> is like tough meat
> for someone with no teeth.

And this one that sounds like a Renato Leduc:

> A lost soul, totally lost
> who's so lost he gets really lost

If you lose yourself, what do you lose
if what you lose is already lost?

The street signs were also worth collecting, although Antonio García
Cubas made them disappear during his time as governor. He himself
noted them down, however:

DISTRIBUTOR OF STRAW AND ANIMAL FEED
COUNTRY-STYLE CANTEEN

MEXICAN INDEPENDENCE
WHOLESALE AND RETAIL

MEAT DISTRIBUTION
BY PEDRO GONZÁLEZ

THE PROGRESSIVE CANTEEN
WE COOK FOR YOU

MADAME COUSSIN
PARISIAN WHORE

And other exaggerations like "The Reform of Providence." But if García
Cubas censored street signs, he gave wings to the cries of the vendors:
"Tasty almond nougat, by the block or by the chunk, almond nougat!
I've got tallooooooow for you! Puebla soap! Mats fifteen feet wide! Mats
from Puebla!" (very much sought after despite the saying "The man who
talks too much, and the man from Puebla: don't get too close but give it
to them with a stick, 'cos they're nothing but bad, bad luck").
    The modern cries, those of our own era, are also really pretty, like the
one the newsboys cry in the central square, the *Zócalo: Killed his poor little
mother for no reason!* or the one saying *As he puffs away, General X bans the
use of marijuana.*
    Guillermo Prieto, Francisco Sosa, Angel del Campo "Micrós," Gutié-
rrez Nájera portrayed the popular types of Mexico City, collected their
cries, their clothing, and their language, and carefully wrote down their
observations. José Revueltas talks about the research that Enrique Fernández Ledesma did on *The Mexicans Painted by Themselves* for his new edition
in 1935, and the discovery that the "anonymous" authors were none
other than the politicians and historians of a vast culture: Hilarión Frías y

Soto, José María Rivera, Juan de Dios Arias, Ignacio Ramírez, Pantaleón Tovar, and Niceto de Zamacóis. But I've always resorted to Ricardo Cortés Tamayo to know what's going on in my city, what's happening to its youngsters, its dogs and its tramps, its candies and its nougats, the hollering of lottery tickets and its neighborhood festivals. He's the one who tells me about the *tameme*, as the indigenous people called the load carrier, his fiber cinch or sash crossing over his forehead; about the greasy vendors who used to measure out the butter; about the stevedores and their nimble little barrows; about Don Ferruco in the Alameda gardens; the vendors of corrugated fibrous stockings; about the butcher's cat and the butcher himself as he hangs beef quarters and half a cow and even a whole pig from the hooks on the shop ceiling and does home deliveries of ribs and steak and loin, and the cat's pelt and whiskers all stained with blood. Ricardo Cortés Tamayo is so sensitive and attentive that he knows the exact time someone is carried off by the Dance of Death, what went on last night in Garibaldi Square, and why the roast-meat tacos in Santo Domingo taste so good. I consult him eagerly, and I acknowledge him and I envy him: he's the only one who listened one Tuesday the Thirteenth to José Revueltas, hungover and unkempt, haranguing the dogs in the Sunken Park; he's the only one who saw the bread seller surround himself with birds out of sheer delight in their presence: a young man about twenty-five years old, pale and slim, wearing a baker's bonnet on his floury head. Ricardo saw him put down his broad empty bread basket on the rim of the Alameda fountain and then, standing up for what seemed like ages, make a sort of flute with his hands to imitate the trills and warbling of the birds, and lastly throw his hands skywards, fluttering them in the air like wings and calling the birds to him. In a few minutes they would come down from the most distant branches and wheel around his head. "I saw it with these very same eyes that'll one day be buried under the earth." I owe Cortés Tamayo a big debt. I've never seen anything like it. Never, with my stupid luck, have I lived a life like that.

The mailman used to wear a well-brushed uniform and a blue cap, and now he doesn't even warn us with his whistle, he just takes the letters out of his tattered knapsack and stuffs them under the door and flies off on his bicycle. In the old days, the knife grinder used to come down Gabriel Mancera street too, pushing his huge grinding stone on a little cart and damping it down with a can of water—the product of popular genius without any technical scholarship from the government. As he made his wheel whirl, sparks would fly and he'd slice a hair into two in the air, the hair of the city that is really his wife's: he trims her fingernails, he files them to a point, he shines her teeth, he rouges her cheeks, he watches her sleep, and when he sees her getting old and withered, he does her the great favor of sticking her like a slab of butter with a long sharp knife as she sleeps. Then the city softly weeps. But there is no call more terrifying than the wail of the *camotero*, the sweet-potato vendor, which would leave a thunderbolt in the hearts of Mexican children. It sounds like the whistle of the train that slows down time, and the men and women in the fields raise their heads from their hoes and their spades and point out to their children, "Look at the train, the train's going by, there goes the train: one day, you'll take the train."

The train travels loaded, loaded with . . . ? In a ring we'd catch the ball and reply: roasted cornflour, coated chickpeas, sugared peanuts, stuffed tortillas, dried cherries, Puebla candies, sesame seeds, candied pumpkin, seed paste, molasses tarts, coconut patties, candied peel, coconuts that the seller slices open with a smile, roasted corn, glazed fruits, syrupy berries standing in a jar like little golden suns, lemon ice lollies, cinnamon candies, sweeties, jelly beans. (Nowadays we'd only ask for spicy stuff—chilied tamarinds, jicamas, oranges and green mangoes sliced and salted.) But as for me, when I was a little girl nothing impressed me so much as the *mecapalero*—the cincher—or the *tameme*—the cargo-man—the load carrier, ever since I went with my grandmama Lulú Amor to the Central Market to buy a wardrobe with two mirrors (covered over so we wouldn't see our memories) and he carried it home for us (from the center halfway across the city to La Morena on the corner with Gabriel Mancera) loaded onto his shoulders, breaking his back, held on only by the *mecapal*, the fiber sash, bent double, pausing briefly on the street corners to look up and see which way to go, trot, trot, trot. You could say to any carrier, "I want you to take this bed for me to Sun and Moon streets," and off he'd go on a solitary journey with the world on his shoulders. And if he never arrived (because he'd got lost or had toppled over somewhere) you could go like Orpheus to the underworld of the police station and denounce him: "Well, it's like this, officer, you know, carrier number such and such didn't deliver the six chairs and the sideboard and the bleached pine wardrobe he loaded up with in the market at eleven o'clock." All the carriers have a license and at the very first mistake they don't get them renewed. In Jalapa, Juanote, Big John, is a very strong *mecapalero* who loves the concerts by the Jalapa Symphony (the Jalapowski Symphony, they call it, because 80 percent of the musicians are Polish). Juanote wears his badge with his registration number so the authorities know who the carrier is; still, he might well take a notion one day to walk out of the concert hall with the piano on his back and the harp and the cello, to accompany his soul laden with the secrets of an orchestral conductor, overburdened with applause, with encores and amorous violins that sometimes vibrate in sympathy before the bow even attacks them.

The *mecapalero* burrowed into my soul because once, in the afternoon newspaper, the *Diario de la Tarde*, there appeared a photograph of Governor Juan Gil Preciado visiting the disaster areas of Jalisco on the back of an Indian: he went on to cross many other flooded streets by piggyback, on another man. The ring roads around the capital and the subway passages still get flooded nowadays, but in the fifties—during the presidency of Miguel Alemán—in the rainy season Sixteenth of September Street and Venustiano Carranza Street right downtown used to fill with water, and a service of carriers was established to carry out the women clerks of the Bank of London and Mexico on the corner of Bolívar and Sixteenth of September Street. But since the young lady cashiers didn't like to be carried out quite like that, in someone's arms, in the front, cuddled up on someone's chest, snuggled against someone's heart, the carrier had to strap a little chair onto his back, and the princesses were ferried over in that and for the modest sum of two pesos got to the other side. While I was being scandalized that the governor of a state had used another man like a beast of burden, the floods in the center of the city were inspiring the Mexicans to wonderfully devise the means of transforming themselves into Charons and extend their brawny patriotic arms to their cargo, even when the latter would take it into their heads to haggle over the cost: "Oh, listen, make it half a peso, you know I hardly weigh a thing!" The *mecapaleros* rolled up their trousers as high as they could and offered themselves on the corner of Sixteenth of September:

"Carry you across, young man, carry you across?"

And individuals who were in a hurry and didn't want to get wet, without further ado would climb up onto another human being and so avoid having to take off their shoes or roll up their trousers in the middle of the street.

COME ON IN
COME AND DRINK
COME AND PAY
COME AND
GO

That's what's written on the sign the owner of "The Sleepwalker," Distributor of Fine Liquors, hung over his counter, because by disposition of the "authorities" it was forbidden for imbibers to linger in the *pulquerías*, the pulque bars. "Keep Moving!" They had very pretty names: "Semiramis," "Norma," "The Sultana," "The Queen," "The Heroine," "Sancho Panza's Bar," "My Office," "The Pub of the Valiant Moor," "I'll Be Right Back," "Not Even My Mother-in-Law Comes in Here." Edward Weston registered a list of bar names in his Mexican diary while Tina Modotti (who loved the song "I'm Just a Little Bit Drunk") portrayed a woman stretched out on the sidewalk under the warning sign "Entrance prohibited to women and street vendors." Among the names Weston collected are "Hope in the Desert," "Juan Silvetti's Glories," "First Loves," "Death and Resurrection," "Ignorance," and "An Old Love." But none so suggestive as "Recollections of Things to Come." In *Hasta no verte Jesús mío*, Jesusa Palancares talks about the effects of pulque and tells how one day she was walking by the Central Market, and as she went past the door of a pulque bar called "The Impediment" she saw a young girl, very young, very unsteady on her feet, feeding her baby and "speckled with flies, filthy and covered with vomit. She kept on nursing her baby but she was so drunk that she fell on her face, and as she toppled over she threw up all over the baby. I said, 'Is that where I'll end up? No, please God! Do me the favor of getting me off the booze!'"

The pulque bars were painted with draperies, golden ropes, fringes and tassels, fans and landscapes, sunsets, palm trees, and peacocks, and they were christened "The Wandering Jew," or "A Journey" on one side, "To Japan" on the other. Almost all the *pulquerías* stood on a corner, and Japan was supposed to invoke the magic of the Orient, although the mural painting on the wall of the "A Journey to Japan" bar looked more like Versailles, with long striped curtains, garlands, and extravagant dangly bits, or like the tents Arabian sheiks set up in the desert. Even today one bar, "The Great Vat, Supreme Pulques," has murals with sumptuous draperies, and the image of the *pulquería* as an oasis in the desert is still quite current. In the smart part of town, on London Street to be more precise, a luxurious bar with padded seats offers a pulque special with strawberry or celery flavor, and tourists rush in there as if they were at the "Refugee Inn," because it's a novelty to initiate oneself into Mexican cuisine on a tissue-paper tablecloth under a ceiling fringed with perforated paper garlands. Duck stew and *mancha manteles*—spicy cloth-staining sauces—are served in fancy oriental china and pineapple- or cactus-flavored pulque comes in elegant glass liter "screws" under liquor barrels and *naif* paintings that recall the pulque farms on the Apam plains in Hidalgo province.

The streets of Mexico are dotted with *pulquerías*, but you don't notice them because the "authorities" won't allow them to hang eye-catching signs up. They fight against *pulquerías* above all because of social prejudice: because pulque is the drink of the poor people, the lower class (with no offense intended for anyone present here today), and the "authorities" decided in one fell swoop that it was more respectable to drink beer and undertook to place obstacles against the sale and the consumption of pulque at the same time as they encouraged advertising the sale of beer though beer sometimes contains more alcohol than pulque. Antonio García Cubas tells us how pulque and its nauseating stink were transported by donkey or mule in filthy pigskin sacks, and he continues indignantly, "A dirty liquor, in dirty barrels, with dirty carriers, dirty measures, and dirty vats. It's incredible that such a lot of filth should produce such a lot of money." The "authorities" argued that pulque was not prepared hygienically, that the *tlachiqueros*, the peasant farmers, extracted the pap with their mouths (but don't the French squash grapes with their feet?) and that everything that went on inside a *pulquería* was ordinary and vulgar. A series of laws institutionalized the cleanliness they demanded from the very beginning in the beer saloons (though some of them with their unswept sawdust floors are also very dirty); but over pulque weighed the curse of "the liquor with bugs in it" and social condemnation. In "The Spy of the Great World," as one former *pulquería* was called, the barmen waited on you in shirtsleeves and with their "pulque bellies" hanging over their trousers. Pulque is the drink of the penniless, of the shantytowns, of people who live hand-to-mouth. "Kid, you've got a mouth like a load carrier": the carriers drink pulque like all the poor people do.

Frida Kahlo had her pupils paint murals in indigo blue and Mexican pink in "The Little Rose" *pulquería* on a street corner in Coyoacán, but within a year the owner had it painted over in white for fear of some fine or other. If *pulquería* painting has disappeared, then the maguey worms will fade away pretty soon, too. Only in Prendes Restaurant in exchange for 450 pesos will they give you a little handful of crunchy worms that taste like chicken. Or ants' eggs—a delicacy without equal, food of the gods, scrumptious—very much like the red ants that they served on a salver in *Mondo Cane* to a poor little rich girl who looked a lot like Barbara Hutton in *Lutèce*, the most expensive restaurant in New York. How about that?

While maguey worms have wormed their way well out of reach of popular consumption and now are sky-high, and the *pulquerías* are now the poor and shameful relatives of the saloons, some of the latter display couches covered in rich brocade and a young lady who takes your coat at the entrance and another, equally skillful, who sells cigarettes and cigars. In "The Opera" the fantastic velvets and the antique watered silk and the booths give off an impression of Asiatic opulence, and the platformed toilet in the "Ladies' Powder Room" is almost thronelike as it seats you opposite the huge bathroom mirror framed in gold. Antonio García Cubas talks of how the Beautiful Young People or Rich Daddies' Boys would get together to plan their futures in front of the mirrors, old lamps, and modern lighting (sunken spotlights), the bottles strung like jewels along the countertop, around the wood and wire chairs in the *barroom*. These young men were called *pisaverdes, mequetrefes, petimetres, catrines, rotos, currutacos,* and *lagartijos*—dandies and whippersnappers and dudes and swells and cads and sports and fops—and fulfilled the pie maker's song to the last letter:

> If you want to get rich,
> All you little swells,
> Shake off the underdogs,
> And nose after whoever's on top.

A Filipino waiter silent as a pillar of salt would wait on them as quick as a wink, and they never mingled with the "lepers," the pimply horde that stun you with their bellowing, the drunkards who bawl:

> So I'm drunk the people say,
> So I'm drunk on hard liquor
> I fell in love with a real saint, Oh yes!
> And for having an unholy love, Oh no!
> My little saint got damned to hell, Oh yes!
> and I was pretty close myself, Oh no!
> Boy, what a fright I got, Oh yes!
> That's why I'm sitting here
> in my little corner!

Then the fops and the swells and the cads and the sports would go to the bullfight, but I know almost nothing about bullfights and bullfighters except the only thing I remember is this little poem:

> One young woman at the bullfight
> Nearly fainted dead away

> Because when the bull came rushing out
> She thought it was her husband.

Around the streets of the center pullulate the taco crowd, the sandwich mob, the *pozole* people, the soda swillers; on every corner a pot is boiling, a tub of tamales is steaming, on a brazier oil floats in a big frying pan. Inside little popovers are crackling, or enchiladas, or tacos, or crisp tortillas, or meat patties and smoked sausage or spicy slices of *chorizo*. The street is the large intestine of the earth, a bloody tumultuous trench called Manuel Payno, Main Post Office, Tobacconists, Roldán, Justo Sierra, Belisario Domínguez, Luis González Obregón, The Maidens, Santa María La Redonda, The Candelaria of the Ducks, Francisco González Bocanegra, Leandro Valle, Tucuba, Uruguay, and The Republic of Cuba. "Tell me what you eat and I'll tell you who you are." Oh, I only eat pure meringues and sweets and nuns' farts! says fancy Miss Nancy. Oh, well, I eat royal balls, candied yams, and spermy chews (Sonovabitch, what on earth are those?), replies sanctimonious Miss Sugarpie. If we are what we eat, I have to confess with all humility that I lost a boyfriend forever when I took sausage rolls dripping with Mobil Oil one day to the country instead of the dainty little watercress sandwiches that should emerge from the picnic basket along with a checkered cloth and little silver cups, called *gobelets* in French. But for sure, Mexican innards are definitely street-smart, full of potholes and no entrances. Mexican taco eaters stuff themselves on tacos made of *maciza*—the finest pork fillet—and also on tacos made of tongue and belly and ears and snout and blood. (In San Cristóbal, Chiapas, they sell pigs' heads and cows' tails strung on a pole and sally forth into the street shouting "Piggy's Face.") Taco folk. "Tacos, young man, let's go get a taco, I'll spring you a taco." Now you can get tacos made of charbroiled lamb, mushroom tacos, pork slivers in cream, tacos made of chops, made of steak, made of liver, made of pork crispies, made of spiced meats, made of pigskin, oxtail, thin or thick and dripping marrow. In Mexico, the taco stand is a business that can't fail; everyone—bricklayers, paperboys, street sweepers, garbage collectors, violinists, truck drivers, nuns, journalists, secretaries, historians, chorus girls, students, hairdressers, bullfighters, mariachi musicians, florists, astronomers, and Carlos Monsiváis—we all flow with the taco tide, we all eat tacos, we all snatch them up in our hands, we gulp them down at top speed, we lick our fingers because licking your fingers is what tacos are for, with a full belly, happy heart, a buttery belly, well oiled, stuffed with cilantro and parsley, our hearts filled with patriotic fervor, for sweet Mexico I love Mexico if I die far away from you, because Long Live Mexico, Sons of a Taco! Long Live Mexico, Sons of a *garnacha*! Nowadays, right in 1982, in San Diego, California, there's a "Taco Tower," a building with a lot of apartments making up a tower purchased entirely by Mexicans who converted their pesos into dollars and rolled them up into teeny weeny little rolls to bring them into the United States. If they want to go on eating tidbits and tacos they'll have to bring them in again in a basket of pathetic pesos, although if the truth be told their tacos still get ordered (with no offense intended for anyone present here today): lamb by politicians, charbroiled by representatives, ground meat by senators, red sauce by Latin American presidents, green sauce by archbishops, and the whole works by cardinals, each one in a placid casserole disposed to remain a long time on the fire, because they no longer get cooked at boiling point however celebrated they might be. Cuauhtémoc tacos! Cuauhtémoc tacos! Now what might those tacos be made of?

Of toasted trotters, stupid!

Antonio García Cubas tells us of how life in the city used to get going before you'd heard the "dawn toll" in the cathedral "replied to by the resounding bells of the churches of the Grace of God, San Agustín, Santo Domingo, and San Francisco, and already the strident noise of the heavy coaches leaving at four in the morning from Dolores alley, now the First of Independence. One, from the interior, would head for Tepic via Cuautitlán, Tepeji, Soyanaquilpa, Arroyosarco, San Juan del Río, Querétaro, Celaya, Salamanca, Irapuato, Guanajuato, Silao, León, Lagos, San Juan de los Lagos, Pequeros, Tepatitlán, Zapotlanejo, Guadalajara, and Tequila, and the other one for Veracruz, via Río Frío, Puebla, Perote, and Jalapa. The first one's route took seven days, the second three and a half."

It's incredible to read about all that today, especially when García Cubas goes on to talk about the cows that headed for the small squares to be milked in public and how they were the first to break the silence of the night with their mooing. I read this with incredulity because it seems to me as unlikely as the declarations of the Sabines brothers, Jaime the poet and Juan the politician, who in the '70s milked their cows in the stables on the outskirts of the Federal District, the capital city, then went around delivering it: "Miiiiilk!" leaving the bottles on the doorstep accompanied by a poem for single ladies only.

As the nightwatchmen left their street corners and went to bed, the servants ran out to shop for the first supplies of the day for their masters. The bustle increased with the shouts of the street sellers:

"Coal for the master," from the Otomí Indian, black as an African under his layer of soot.

"Butter for a *real* and a half," another Indian chanted nonstop, carrying his merchandise in a crate on his shoulders.

"Kitchen wares and crockery from Cuautitlán, for sale."

"The washerwoman could hardly stretch her arm round the basket she carried filled with bits of laundry to be washed, or else you could see her carrying on her shoulders a half dozen petticoats on her way to return them to the house she worked in." (The washerwoman pummeled the clothes in the wooden trough she'd selected from among the products of the traveling salesman.)

The wood seller would knock from door to door, his firewood piled high on two donkeys sagging under the weight of the load; from one fragrant bundle he'd extract a pine branch, the only thing capable of lighting the blaze. The coal man no longer exists nor the mat seller nor the plump coconut vendor who'd make the coconuts roll as if they were our heads. Nor is there any cane to reseat chairs and there's no more cry of "Cane for your chairs," "Cane for caning," "Chairs to be seated." It's many years now since I last saw a tallyman on my street, or a vendor of feather dusters, brooms, carpet beaters, or kitchen stools. There no longer exist neighborhood clowns nor cobblers seated on their benches studded with shoes. They left, never to return. You used to hear the cry "Exchange your old clothes for taffy," a dark sugary liquid that they bartered for clothes. In fact, it was molasses that the vendor drizzled from her big spoon to see if it was at the right point of thickness and delicacy. That's where we get the saying "the quality of the taffy." Also, all the various crafts associated with *charrería*—festive horsemanship—are disappearing: the trappings for the horses, their harnesses, the irons for the hardware, the fancy riding saddles, the whips, the cinches and the sashes, all the saddlery, the leather of Mexico renowned for its good tanning—very fine finish and easy to work. Very few associations maintain the tradition of fancy horsemanship, because you need a lot of money not only to rear a horse but also to dress it up on holidays and to dress yourself as a *charro*, a Mexican "cowboy." You need a specialized tailor to make the riding gear with its very particular cut and decorated with elaborate details that need hours of handwork. There are sumptuous brilliant ones like Emiliano

Zapata's costume with silver buttons stitched onto the finest black woven cloth. And even more of a disaster is that nowadays in the countryside of Mexico donkeys no longer exist, nobody loves them or wants them. Everyone prefers a car, even though it's falling to pieces, to feeding a donkey.

Though the first thing that happens to the people who come in from the countryside is that they turn themselves into street vendors, there are also some stable trades brought in from the country: a legal office gets itself set up, or on the vacant lot next door a blacksmith shop will appear with its forge and its anvil, and all day long you can hear the hammer ringing on iron—one of the symbols of human strength at its most beautiful. Before we succumbed to industrialization, ours was a society of artisans who made everything we needed. (In Spain, the Law of Trades and Crafts considers the hairdresser to be an artisan just like the potter or the harness maker.) Now, however, the pulque extractors have turned themselves into laborers in Sahagún City and smelt railroad wagons and assemble automobile parts. In the capital, many artisans have tried to preserve the status of their crafts guilds through their special saints: the carpenters, for example, still dedicate their feast day to Saint Joseph with a procession through the central streets of the city. The candy makers used to make their sweets at home, using the old recipes with pine nuts and scorched milk, vanilla and cinnamon, and would go out into the streets to sell them along with savory pies, stuffed tortillas, refried beans—real home cooking. In them there was an eagerness to preserve the small-town way of life, calm and busy, but big cities usually abuse people and turn them into mincemeat. Lady Calderón de la Barca, who as far as we can tell didn't know that everything has a use including even things that are useless, remarks with horror on a street where half-breeds piled up on top of each other, the poorest of the poor, almost naked, lying in the doorways and living off the garbage from the markets. They also appear in lithographs, tattered and discombobulated, and the photo title calls them "the lepers." The citizens, the decent folks, were afraid of them, as if they might be attacked. They were the Untouchables, the homeless, the orphans, the rancorous, the good-for-nothings. Listen, friend, it's pretty bad when you don't know who your father or your mother is, when you don't know anything about anything. And they also live pell-mell, all stirred up like turkeys with no idea of where to flap or turn. So there in the street "the lepers" lived, all of them nowhere, rolled up into a ball, with no tomorrow, only tonight. They looked like chunks of black shredded from a dark starless night. They lived in blackness, they descended breathless into the blackness and fell asleep with no idea what day it was; in fact, they never knew what day it was, the only thing that kept them company was the noise of the city, the immense tumult that comes from humankind.

Without its popular customs, its vendors and its tamale stands, the city would have no reason to exist. Of course, there are also the massive stone palaces in the center, the Angel of Independence, Reforma Boulevard, Madero that exits into the Zócalo and takes our breath away because suddenly we find ourselves facing the most beautiful square in the world, Santo Domingo looking like a white dove fallen from the heavens, the cathedral, the blue tiles of the House of the Blue Tiles, the church of the Saint of the True Cross and the church of San Antonio sitting face to face ready to take a train ride, Alvaro Obregón Avenue with the lights lit in its reflecting lamps, Chapultepec, its lake and its castle, Coyoacán, San Angel, Chimalistac, the Square of the Little Shell. But without its popular types, without the Vaselined hairdos sleeked inside the necks of black undershirts, without the balloon man (the one in Coyoacán always takes his daughter along with him, a little girl with luminous dark eyes who runs up to you with a balloon, her hair floating in the air), without the cotton-candy seller, without the peanut vendor and the rag-and-bone man, where would we be? Just to hear them announce their presence in the street, just their familiar cries calm us down like the "there, there, there, it's better now" of the mother who picks up her child for a cuddle; only the assurance that "they're there" gives our life the savor of a neighborhood, of warm tortillas, of life really lived. What would we do without them? Really, it would lower the quality of the taffy.

It's the knife grinder, the sweet-potato seller, the street sweeper, the mailman, the little servant girl damping down the sidewalk who hold the life of the city in their arms, who cradle it, who rock it, who give it its reason to be. A whole craft tradition supports the man who sells straw hats woven in a warm cave in Becal, Campeche, wetting the straw so it can be folded. That's where they make flexible bags and knapsacks and the so-called "Panama hats." We Mexicans are high-hatted people: it's the sombrero that crowns our ideas, that dresses them up, that tops them off; we walk under our hats as though under a roof protecting us from the sun. The revolutionaries had a sombrero and a rifle—they could walk around headless but not hatless, they could walk around with as much sense of direction as people playing blindman's buff, bumping heads against each other, all over the place, urging each other along with their hats, singing under their hats with their sonorous drawstrings, galloping under their hats, their hats mercifully closing their eyes at the moment of truth.

A whole artisanal tradition also swells behind the ironing and starching of the collar of white shirts, and you have to know how to give the exquisite final touch to tamales, to glazing sweet breakfast buns, to treacling sugar, to candying fruits. Everything has its special trick, its secret. It's not a question of "well do me another one, then." The pie stuffed to bursting with the exact amount of sausage and potato demands great care and good sense just like the warm sandwich that emerges from the toasting iron and is sliced neatly in two with one chop and decrumbed at each edge for the sandwich maker to pile on, like a magician, on one side beans with a little wooden stick then on the other side thick cream, then spoonfuls of avocado like green butter, generous chunks of loin, or slices of ham, or shiny sausage, onion, chopped lettuce, *chipotle* sauce, fresh soft cheese, finished off with chips, and chili to each customer's taste. The steaming engine turning heavily with its furnace sputtering with baked sweet potato and plantains disintegrating, melting into caramel, is a veritable feat of household technology, and its engravings and its stoker's whistle should be preserved in the Sound Museum of Mexico or at the very least in the General Archive of the Nation. The baker who carries his enormous basket on his head full of sweet breads and manages to traverse the furious tidal wave of the city can only be compared with Charles Lindbergh on his interoceanic flight. And the cylinder that the barrel-organ man adjusts on a long pole in the doorway of the Brazil Cafe is quite beautiful with its sculptured edges and its decorative scrolls and the red cloth of its horn; and the music roll is beautiful, too—turning in the inside and brought in from Germany to play "Alexandra" and "Green Club."

If the tortillas come out round and slim and have just the right proportions of corn and lime water, and if the sweet buns are delicate and light as broad wafers of sunshine, if our clothes are exquisitely starched and pressed, if woven straw hats fit even the huge head of a Yucatecan, it's because underneath all our inheritance lies indigenous tradition: the tradition of the good potter, of the painter who achieves a perfect finish, of the little Aztec girl whose hands were punctured with a maguey spine or who was punished weeping in front of a smouldering chili to teach her to be "a good little worker." The Nahuatl father's advice to his little girl, little pet, little dove, tender and plump, has a lot to do with the sewing that's well done, with rivets in the right places, with the cradle bound onto a single pole so it'll hold tight, the day employed in tasks fulfilled with love, and the order that proclaims there's a right place for every thing and a right time for every deed.

It's the common folk who've understood that nothing lasts forever, that everything comes to an end, that time will carry everything off. That's why nobody wants to collect things. A street vendor from whom a customer wanted to buy all her merchandise refused: "And what'll I do, then?"

> What has my heart done to you
> for you to treat it so badly?
> If you must wound it little by little,
> better kill it once and for all.

> Neither with you nor without you
> can my suffering be resolved:
> with you because you're killing me,
> and without you because I'm dying.

At times the street musician would play this song: the little Indian with his daughter, with his hat of woven reeds, with his knapsack. Clutching his instrument in one of the many popular squares, he tucks it under his chin and solemnly intones the rasping notes that pave over our hearts, his vinelike fingers (street violinists are nearly always old) pressing on the catgut and causing it to whine. It pierces the air with a pathetic, painful sound.

That we all have a violin inside us can only be proved when a broken string bursts occasionally into pure grief; the sound in the street that can suddenly clip the wings of the morning, that can make our eyes sting, that reminds us of that little song we heard so many years ago, almost like the air in the sonata by Vinteuil that Proust froze for ever in his *Remembrance of Things Past*. How pitiless the street violinist is, with his miserable trousers and his triumphal bow on his strings! My heart turns over and I leave off writing, run down into the street, his music is more resilient, more stubborn than all the mules on the earth, more unpredictable.

> Oh, this old and broken violin!

sang León Felipe.

> How badly it plays!
> With this very same broken violin
> I'm going to play for myself
> a few days from now "The Swallows"
> that very pretty song that Mexicans always sing
> to those who're going away.

I would love someone to play "The Swallows" to me in a haberdashery. I would open old drawers and take out the reels of thread, the bias binding, the elastic, the mother of pearl buttons, the thimbles, pins, safety pins, spools; I would measure out the lace trimming, "top quality and pretty and cheap"; I'd chat with the man selling tallow and wax candles, and with the water carrier who'd tell me how his back can't take it anymore because when he didn't find water at the Waterfall Fountain he had to go all the way over to Tlaxpana to fill his big earthen jug. And then I'd sit down and listen to the little bell of the cash register, to its sharp clunk as it closes. And at night I'd roll down the grill and close it with a lock and go home to my house in whose window alongside the sign saying "Communism, yes; Christianity, no" I'd have placed an advertisement in big printed letters: "Buttonholes made here" or "Buttons covered" or "Clothes for Baby Jesus," the occupation of old maids who preferred to sit at the window by day and dress the Little Saint of Atocha with all his tippets and trinkets than to sit at the window by night and undress some old drunk who did nothing but tipple and tinker.

But since God doesn't fulfill occasional whims, nor straighten up hunchbacks, nor give wings to poisonous scorpions, it's unlikely I'll ever achieve my desire to be a clerk in a haberdashery store. The only thing I ask him, and this shouldn't be too difficult to grant, is that he permit me to accompany the last turkey (Emperor Maximilian, poor little thing, called them *terquailles* because he pronounced everything in French) and let me walk with it around these God-given streets, the streets of my city, till my knees stiffen up and my eyes mist over and I trudge on like Sergeant Pedraza in an improbable marathon, my ears full of the calls and the cries, the offers and the ballads, of Mexico, Mexico, ra ra ra. . . . (Oh yes, and in my belly a little *maciza* taco!)

From *Memoria y olvido: Imágenes de México*. Mexico City: Cultura/SEP, 1982.

List of Contributors

MARJORIE AGOSIN is a poet and literary critic. Her work has focused on issues dealing with gender and human rights. Among her recent publications are *Circles of Madness: Mothers of the Plaza de Mayo* (1992) and *Las mujeres y la literatura fantástica en el cono sur* (1993). She is an associate professor of Spanish at Wellesley College.

MELVIN S. ARRINGTON, JR., is associate professor of modern languages at the University of Mississippi, where he has served on the faculty since 1982. He teaches a wide range of courses in Spanish and Portuguese and participates in the university's Latin American Studies Program. His publications deal primarily with twentieth-century Latin American literature, in particular the Spanish American short story.

MARY G. BERG, a writer and translator who lives in Cambridge, Massachusetts, teaches Spanish and Latin American literature and has long been interested in women writers. Her recent articles include studies of works by Juana Manuela Gorriti, Clorinda Matto, Marta Brunet, Isabel Allende, Elisa Mújica, Sofía Ospina, Cristina Peri Rossi, and Angeles Mastretta. She is currently writing critical biographies of Clorinda Matto and Juana Manuela Gorriti. Her daughter ELENA C. BERG collaborated on the translation of the Matto de Turner essays.

SANDRA M. BOSCHETTO-SANDOVAL is associate professor of Spanish at Michigan Technological University. She is coeditor (with Marcia P. McGowan) of the critical anthology *Claribel Alegría and Central*

American Literature: Critical Essays (1993). Her articles on Hispanic literature have appeared in various critical anthologies and journals, and her research interests include Latin American women writers, literary and cultural theory, and intercultural communication. She is presently at work on a book-length study of the life and work of Amanda Labarca Hubertson.

ROSEMARY GEISDORFER FEAL is associate professor of Spanish at the University of Rochester, where she also teaches courses in women's studies, African and African American studies, and comparative literature. She is the author of *Novel Lives: The Fictional Autobiographies of Guillermo Cabrera Infante and Mario Vargas Llosa*, as well as articles on Luisa Valenzuela, Rigoberta Menchú, José Donoso, Miguel Barnet, Mireya Robles, and on issues such as feminist interventions in Afro-Hispanism, the relationship between the visual arts and literature, and psychoanalytic incursions into modes of representation.

JANET N. GOLD holds a doctorate from the University of Massachusetts at Amherst and teaches Latin American literature at Louisiana State University. She has published numerous articles on Latin American women writers. Her interests include women's biography and autobiography and Central American literature.

PAUL GOLDBERG received his B.A. in Hispanic studies from Connecticut College in 1994. He has lived and studied in Ecuador and is currently continuing his studies on a graduate level at the University of New Mexico.

ELIZABETH D. HODGES graduated in 1993 from Connecticut College with a major in Hispanic studies and is now living in Alexandria, Virginia. She has previously cotranslated a short story by Chilean author Luz Orfanoz.

BETH E. JÖRGENSEN, Ph.D. University of Wisconsin–Madison, teaches Spanish American literature at the University of Rochester. Her research interests include Latin American women writers, contemporary fiction, testimonial literature and feminist theory. She is the author of *Engaging Dialogues: The Writing of Elena Poniatowska* (1994).

GWEN KIRKPATRICK is associate professor in the Department of Spanish and Portuguese at the University of California at Berkeley. She is the author of *The Dissonant Legacy of Modernismo* (1989) and coauthor, with the UC-Stanford Seminar on Feminism and Culture in Latin America, of *Women, Culture and Politics in Latin America* (1990).

JILL S. KUHNHEIM is assistant professor in the Department of Spanish and Portuguese at the University of Wisconsin–Madison. Specializing in Spanish American literature, she has published papers on the work of Rosario Castellanos, Gabriela Mistral, Olga Orozco, and Alejandra Pizarnik. She is presently working on a book about Orozco and post-1940s Argentine poetry.

CAROL MAIER is professor of Spanish at Kent State University, where she is affiliated with the Institute for Applied Linguistics. Her recent projects include translations of Octavio Armand's *Refractions* and Rosa Chacel's *Memoirs of Leticia Valle*. Two other publications due to appear soon are *Between Languages and Cultures: Translation and Cross-Cultural Texts* (coedited with Anuradha Dingwaney) and *Ramón María del Valle-Inclán: Essays on Gender* (coedited with Roberta L. Salper).

CLAIRE EMILIE MARTIN is associate professor in the Foreign Languages and Literatures Department at California State University, Long Beach. She has published articles on Marta Lynch, Isabel Allende, Teresa de la Parra, Marta Brunet, and the Countess of Merlin. Her revised dissertation, "Alejo Carpentier y las crónicas de Indias: Orígenes de una escritura americana," will be published by Ediciones del Norte. She is currently working on a volume on nineteenth-century women writers.

FRANCINE ROSE MASIELLO is professor of Spanish American literature and chair of the Department of Comparative Literature at the University of California at Berkeley. Her most recent books are *Between Civilization and Barbarism: Women, Nation, and Literary Culture in Modern Argentina* (1992) and, coauthored with members of the Seminar on Feminism and Culture in Latin America, *Women, Culture and Politics in Latin America* (1990).

IRENE MATTHEWS, assistant professor of comparative literature at Northern Arizona University, Flagstaff, wrote her dissertation on

"Women Writing and War," a socio-literary examination of women writers of the U.S. Civil War, the Mexican Revolution, and the recent crises in Argentina, Guatemala, and Brazil. Her recent projects include a translation of *The Women of Tijucopapo* by Marilene Felinto of Brazil.

DORIS MEYER is Roman S. and Tatiana Weller Professor of Hispanic Studies at Connecticut College, and the editor of *Reinterpreting the Spanish American Essay: Women Writers of the 19th and 20th Centuries* (University of Texas Press, 1995). She has published other books in the field of Latin American literature, including *Victoria Ocampo: Against the Wind and the Tide* (1979; 2nd ed., 1990), *Contemporary Women Authors of Latin America* (1983, 2 vols., coedited with Margarite Fernández Olmos), and *Lives on the Line: The Testimony of Contemporary Latin American Authors* (1988), as well as many articles and translations. Her areas of specialization are contemporary Latin American women's writing and Hispanic journalism in the territorial Southwest.

MARTHA LAFOLLETTE MILLER is professor of Spanish at the University of North Carolina at Charlotte, where she specializes in twentieth-century Spanish poetry. She has published studies on peninsular authors such as Rosalía de Castro, Jorge Guillén, Luis Cernuda, and Leopoldo Alas, as well as on several Latin American authors. She is currently completing a study of the poetry of Angel González.

ARDIS L. NELSON is professor and chair of the Department of Foreign Languages at East Tennessee State University, where she teaches Spanish American literature. She is the author of *Cabrera Infante in the Menippean Tradition* and a variety of articles, and coauthor of a bibliography on Central American film.

MARY LOUISE PRATT is Nina C. Crocker Faculty Scholar at Stanford University, where she teaches in the departments of Spanish and Portuguese and Comparative Literature. She has published extensively in the areas of linguistics and literature, and discourse and ideology. A founding member of the UC–Stanford Seminar on Feminism and Culture in Latin America, she coauthored its book, *Women, Culture and Politics in Latin America* (1990), and coedited a special issue of *Nuevo Texto Crítico* on Latin American women writers (1989). Her most recent book is *Imperial Eyes: Travel Writing and Transculturation* (1992).

JOY RENJILIAN-BURGY is a faculty member of the Spanish Department of Wellesley College, where she has taught Caribbean literature and culture and Hispanic literature of the United States as well as Spanish language courses and methodology seminars. She is the director of the Mellon Minority Undergraduate Fellowship Program and coeditor of *Album* (1993), an anthology of short stories in Spanish. She has also translated literary works by Amalia Rendic, Nancy Morejón, and Elena Poniatowska.

RICHARD ROSA is writing his doctoral dissertation on Eugenio María de Hostos' *La peregrinación de Boyoán* at Harvard University in the Department of Romance Languages and Literatures.

NINA M. SCOTT is professor of Spanish American literature at the University of Massachusetts at Amherst, specializing in women writers, particularly Sor Juana Inés de la Cruz and Gertrudis Gómez de Avellaneda. Coeditor of *Breaking Boundaries: Latina Writing and Critical Readings* (1989) and *Coded Encounters: Writing, Gender and Ethnicity in Colonial Latin America* (1993), she has also translated Avellaneda's *Sab* and her *Autobiography* (1993) and is now compiling a bilingual anthology of early Spanish American women writers.

KIM STARR-REID is in the doctoral program in comparative literature at the University of California at Berkeley. Her interests include the relations of Latin and Romance literatures, translation, and subjectivity.

PATRICIA OWEN STEINER is a graduate of Smith College and describes herself as a "late, late bloomer." Works she has translated include *The Banners of the Champions*, an anthology of medieval Andalusian poetry (with Arabist James A. Bellamy), and *Don Segundo Sombra*, by Ricardo Güiraldes. She is now preparing a book about Victoria Ocampo, focusing on women.

Contents of Volume One, *Reinterpreting the Spanish American Essay: Women Writers of the 19th and 20th Centuries*